## Studies in Liturgical Musicology
### Edited by Dr. Robin A. Leaver

# A THEOLOGY OF MUSIC FOR WORSHIP DERIVED FROM THE BOOK OF REVELATION

by

## THOMAS ALLEN SEEL

Studies in Liturgical Musicology, No. 3

The Scarecrow Press, Inc.
Metuchen, N.J., & London
1995

British Library Cataloguing-in-Publication Data available

**Library of Congress Cataloging-in-Publication Data**

Seel, Thomas Allen, 1954-
  A theology of music for worship derived from the Book of
Revelation / by Thomas Allen Seel
    p.    cm.    --(Studies in liturgical musicology ; no. 3)
  Revision of the author's thesis (D.M.A., Southern Baptist
Theological Seminary).
  Includes bibliographical references and index.
  ISBN  0-8108-2989-4 (acid-free paper)
  1. Music in churches--Biblical teaching. 2. Music in the Bible.
3.  Church music--To 500. 4. Bible. N.T. Revelation--Criticism.
interpretation, etc.    I. Title.    II. Series
ML3001.S394    1995
264'.001--dc20                                          94-48093

To Diane,
whose deep spirituality and unfailing character
are an inspiration to me;
and to my boys,
Matthew and Joshua,
may their unbridled joy continue to grow
throughout their lives.

# Contents

# Editor's Foreword

IN the Book of Revelation there are many passages that imply a liturgical form of worship in which music was a fundamental part. The nature and extent of this liturgical music forms the substance of this study. In the process of evaluating the linguistic and historical background, the author reveals something of the multicultural context in which these musical terms and performance practices developed—an amalgam of Jewish traditions and contemporary practices of the Graeco-Roman world, as modified by the Christological experience and eschatological hope for the early church.

But this book is more than a study of biblical theology set within the historical framework of the first few centuries of the Christian era. In the final chapter Thomas Seel makes the following observation: "...contemporary Christianity is historically tied to its past and eschatologically pulled into its future" (see page 136). Accordingly, having established the framework of a theology of music in worship from evidence found within the Book of Revelation, the author examines some of the implications of this theology for music in the worship of contemporary churches.

The book originated as a DMA-Church Music dissertation at The Southern Baptist Theological Seminary, Louisville, Kentucky, and has been significantly revised for publication. Its respectful biblicism reflects the evangelical perspectives of the author and of the seminary for which the dissertation was written. Nevertheless, the author's findings challenge many of the current presuppositions and practices of evangelical Christianity. There is a widespread short-sighted view that music in worship is simply entertainment or propoganda that is useful for an anthropocentric here-and-now. By contrast, the Book of Revelation presents a more far-sighted view of music in worship in which a theocentric future is anticipated.

Thomas Allen Seel is an experienced church musician. He is

currently an assistant vice-president and investment officer of the
Presbyterian Church (U.S.A.) Foundation, and minister of music of
Fern Creek United Methodist Church, Louisville, Kentucky.

Robin A. Leaver
Series Editor

Westminster Choir College of Rider University
and Drew University

# Preface

CHURCH musicians and worship leaders have been frustrated for 2,000 years because the New Testament has so few specific guidelines regarding the use of music for worship. Consequently, the normative standards for the use of music in the church have been reasoned out through the centuries based on general theological considerations. The purpose of this study is to show that the New Testament, particularly the largely ignored Book of Revelation, does have practical, "down-to-earth" and specific things to say regarding the use of music for worship in the life of the contemporary church.

The theology of music for worship which this books attempts is by no means complete; it is offered as a beginning. If this work catalytically can prompt a helpful discussion to ensue, it will have served its purpose. It is my hope that more and more church professionals and laypersons will continue to grow in their understanding of what the scriptures have to say concerning worship and music in worship through the remaining days this side of eternity.

The glimpse into eschatological worship has implications for the contemporary church professional and layperson. Based on the work of Bowman, Fiorenza, and more recently Blevins, this study assumes the dramatic approach to the interpretation of the Book of Revelation. This study assumes that it is no accident that the writer of the Apocalypse chose to portray his eschatological glimpse in terms of the best music traditions that he knew in his past and present time.

Eight Greek words for worship occur in the New Testament, yet the writer of the Apocalypse uses only προσκυνέο (*proskuneo*) to describe the worship of the end-times. Προσκυνέο (*Proskuneo*) has Jewish patriarchal, tabernacle, temple and synagogue and early pagan origins which differ greatly from its usage in the first century C.E. An understanding of worship in the Revelation influences both the type of music as well as the performance practice which is implied in the text.

The study analyzes the forms of music, performing groups and the performance practice within the Book of Revelation. Each of these aspects is traced historically through the early pagan, Jewish, Greek, Roman and early church periods. This historical perspective provides the groundwork from which a decalogue of theological guideposts is developed. These points of a theology of music for worship are historically, biblically and eschatologically supported and made relevant to the contemporary Church. This Christian theology considers briefly the entire biblical account from Genesis to Revelation, focussing on the last book of the Bible.

This attempt at a theology of music came into being out of my concern that few books prior have sought to create a set of rules to help church professionals increase their understanding of music based on the large amount of musical material in the Book of Revelation. So many before have considered this glimpse of the future as unattainable today and have dismissed it as enviable. While I agree that perfection this side of eternity is impossible, how dare we not try. **All** scripture was given for "...teaching, rebuking, correction and training in righteousness" (II Timothy 3:16), not just those parts which appear to be easier to comprehend and understand.

Balancing life has to be a growing experience where the only constant is God. My inspiration and drive comes from seeking to please my Lord and Master, doing it "...heartily unto the Lord, not unto men" (Colossians 3:23). One must be consumed with his/her knowing God and willfully fashioning his/her life-style after Christ's excellent example on a moment-by-moment basis daily; poring over scripture and the Christian traditions and applying insights thereby gained into daily living is my willful aim as I seek to fulfill the Great Commission in my life.

Special appreciation is extended to the talented Mary Lynn Green whose computer skills were patiently applied to the writing of this text and to the Presbyterian Church (U.S.A.) Foundation for the use of their software and computers. To my wife Diane and boys, Matthew and Joshua, I give my thanks for allowing me time away from home to work on this manuscript.

Thomas Allen Seel<br>Louisville, Kentucky

# Abbreviations

ASJ      Henry Barclay Swete. *The Apocalypse of St. John.* London: Macmillan and Company, 1909.

ATM     Alfred Pike. *A Theology of Music.* Toledo, OH: The Gregorian Institute of America, 1953.

BI       Anthony Baines. *Brass Instruments: Their History and Development.* London: Faber and Faber, 1976.

DD      Robin A. Leaver and James H. Litton, eds. *Duty and Delight: Routley Remembered.* Carol Stream, IL: Hope Publishing Company, 1985.

DH      John Julian. *A Dictionary of Hymnology.* London: John Murray, 1907.

DOX    Geoffrey Wainwright. *Doxology: The Praise of God in Worship, Doctrine and Life.* New York, NY: Oxford University Press, 1980.

ECB    James Strong. *The Exhaustive Concordance of the Bible.* New York, NY: Abingdon Press, 1890.

EIHM  Johann Ernst Altenburg. *Essay on an Introduction to the Heroic and Musical Trumpeters' and Kettledrummers' Art.* Trans. by Edward H. Tarr. Nashville, TN: The Brass Press, 1974.

GEL    Henry George Liddell and Robert Scott. *A Greek-English Lexicon.* Ed. by Sir Henry Stuart Jones. Oxford: Clarendon Press, 1948.

GELNT   William F. Arndt and F. Wilbur Gingrich. *A Greek-English Lexicon of the New Testament and Other Early Christian Literature*. Ed. by Walter Bauer. Fifth edition. Chicago, IL: University of Chicago, 1958.

GGNT    A. T. Robertson. *A Grammar of the Greek New Testament in the Light of Historical Research*. New York, NY: Hodder and Stoughton, 1914.

HMI     Curt Sachs. *A History of Musical Instruments*. New York, NY: W. W. Norton and Company, Inc., 1940.

IB      George A. Buttrick, ed. *The Interpreter's Bible*. Nashville, TN: Abingdon Press, 1982.

JLD     A. Z. Idelsohn. *Jewish Liturgy and Its Development*. New York, NY: Holt, Rinehart and Winston, 1967.

MAI     Alfred Sendrey. *Music in Ancient Israel*. New York, NY: Philosophical Library, 1969.

MHBT    Don L. Smithers. *The Music and History of the Baroque Trumpet*. Carbondale, IL: Southern Illinois University Press, 1988.

MSR     Alfred Sendrey. *Music in the Social and Religious Life of Antiquity*. Cranbury, NJ: Associated University Presses, Inc., 1974.

NED     Merrill Unger and W. White, Jr., eds. *Nelson's Expository Dictionary of the Old Testament*. Nashville, TN: Thomas Nelson Publishers, 1984.

NGD     Stanley Sadie, ed. *The New Grove Dictionary of Music and Musicians*. London: Macmillan Publishers, Ltd., 1980.

NGDMI   Curt Sachs, ed. *The New Grove Dictionary of Musical Instruments*. London: Macmillan Press, Ltd., 1984.

OTP  James Hamilton Charlesworth, ed. *The Old Testament Pseudepigrapha and the New Testament*. Garden City, NY: Doubleday and Company, Inc., 1983.

PIW  Sigmund Mowinckel. *The Psalms in Israel's Worship*. Trans. by D. R. Ap-Thomas. Oxford: B. Blackwell, 1962.

RD  James L. Blevins. *Revelation as Drama*. Nashville, TN: Broadman Press, 1984.

SIA  R. H. Charles. *Studies in the Apocalypse*. Edinburgh: T. & T. Clark, 1915.

TDNT  Gerhard Friedrich, ed. *Theological Dictionary of the New Testament*. Trans. by G. W. Bromiley. Grand Rapids, MI: William B. Eerdmans Publishing Company, 1968.

THM  J. Murray Barbour. *Trumpets, Horns and Music*. East Lansing, MI: Michigan State University Press, 1964.

TSB  Eric Werner. *The Sacred Bridge: The Interdependence of Liturgy and Music in Synagogue and Church During the First Millenium*. London: Dennis Dobson, 1959.

VED  W. F. Vines. *Vine's Expository Dictionary of Old and New Testament Words*. Ed. by F. F. Bruce. Old Tappan, NJ: Fleming H. Revell, 1981.

VGNT  James Hope Moulton and George Milligan. *The Vocabulary of the Greek New Testament*. Grand Rapids, MI: William B. Eerdmans Publishing Company, 1982.

WSE  John E. Burkhart. *Worship: A Searching Examination of the Liturgical Experience*. Philadelphia, PA: Westminster Press, 1982.

# 1

# Introduction

MUSIC abounds in the Revelation. When the writer of the Apocalypse chose the nomenclature which could best describe the visions he received, he chose to portray a certain type of music in worship. It can be no accident that he chose to couch the music of his visions in traditional Jewish, Greek, Roman and early Church, as well as pagan terms. This study will seek to develop a theology of music in worship as discerned in the Book of Revelation.

Key terms which will be used in this study are defined in the following manner.

## Music

A common definition of music is "the science or art of incorporating pleasing, expressive, or intelligible combinations of vocal or instrumental tones into a composition having a definite structure of continuity."[1] Dr. Hilda Schuster, an expert on the views of Emile Jacques-Dalcroze, defines music as an activity which consists of three primary elements: time, space, and energy.[2] Epperson equates the term "music" with "musical symbol." He claims that a definition for a musical symbol less general than "an intelligible structure of sound, apprehended through actual hearing in its own modality of virtual time and motion" would entail "qualifications appropriate only to specific

---

[1]Philip Babcock Gove, ed., *Webster's Third New International Dictionary* (Springfield, MA: G. and C. Merriam Company, 1976), 1490.

[2]This writer studied for a summer at the Dalcroze School of Music, New York City, in 1973. Dr. Hilda Schuster, president, used this definition repeatedly.

1

examples."[3] In summary, music can be defined as an "aural art" which gains meaning through acculturation.

## Theology

Revelation, as a source of theology, is "God's act of disclosing himself by his 'Word' and actions through time."[4] Faith is the human acceptance of this revelation.[5] Scripture is the written record of God's revelation of himself, and the Articles of Faith which Christians espouse are creedal declarations which preserve our witness of and to God.[6] Then, theology springs as an "overspill of divine faith into all levels of human reasonableness:...and search[es] for reasons why, whence, how, and what it is all about." Theology embodies all that makes the theologian someone other than God, the angels, and the beasts.[7] Although the term "theology" appears nowhere in scripture, it has been said that it is the church thinking "aloud."[8] The purpose of theology is to study the tenets of one's belief by means of "reason enlightened by faith" in order to promote a deeper understanding of it.[9] The broad categories of theology consist of (1) biblical theology which uses the Bible as its only source, and (2) systematic theology. While it uses the Bible as its primary source, systematic theology can use other sources as well.[10] Systematic theology attempts

methodically and in the light of faith...to organize all divinely revealed truths and their explanations according to some form of regular, intrinsic, and rational plan, connection, and/or interdependence. It is based on the comprehensive exhibition of

---

[3]Gordon Epperson, *The Musical Symbol: A Study of the Philosophic Theory of Music* (Ames, IA: Iowa State University Press, 1967), 292.

[4]Paul Kevin Meagher, ed., *Encyclopedic Dictionary of Religion* (Washington, DC: Corpus Publications, 1979), Vol. O-Z, 3498.

[5]Ibid.

[6]Ibid.

[7]Ibid.

[8]F. L. Cross, ed., *The Oxford Dictionary of the Christian Church* (London: Oxford University Press, 1983), 1363.

[9]Ibid.

[10]Paul S. Karleen, *The Handbook to Bible Study* (New York, NY: Oxford University Press, 1987), 363.

essential principles, or dogmatic, historico-salvation, moral, and/or existential facts and attempts to form one organized and intelligible whole.[11]

Systematic theology leads to a synthesis. In synthesizing, systematic theology's task is to locate the "nexus" between the mysteries of faith and to establish harmony between faith and reason by "illuminating the unity among the ontological, logical, and semantic orders."[12] Theology is that "ultimate speech about the nature and the works of God which is mankind's response, however, halting, to God's revelation."[13]

## Theology of Music
A philosophy of music within the context of the Book of Revelation becomes by its nature a theological endeavor. The church musician needs to have a value system that is based upon Christian theology.[14] Yet, nowhere within scripture is a specific theology of music to be located. Still, "music is the accompanying counterpoint to the Divine message and in the mighty acts of God music is never very far away."[15] Music is evident from Genesis to the Revelation—from creation to the Song of Moses, to the angel's proclamation of the Messiah's birth, to the end of time. Music is therefore "bound up with theology and theology with music."[16] A reciprocal relationship exists between theology and music. When the two become separated, music in worship becomes (1) entertainment, (2) music to set the mood, and/or (3) an "aural lubricant" which serves as a transition between other parts of the service. Without music, theology likewise suffers. It can become "dry, soulless, and brittle."[17] A theology of music begins with the notion that worship is an attitude of the inner self. Everything else,

---

[11]Paul Kevin Meagher, ed., *Encyclopedic Dictionary*, Vol. O-Z, 3498.

[12]Ibid., Vol. O-Z, 3442-3443.

[13]Erik Routley, *Church Music and Theology* (Philadelphia, PA: Muhlenberg Press, 1959), 13.

[14]Calvin M. Johansson, "Some Theological Considerations Foundational to a Philosophy of Church Music." D.M.A. dissertation (Fort Worth, TX: Southwestern Baptist Theological Seminary, 1974), 34.

[15]Robin A. Leaver, "The Theological Character of Music in Worship," DD, 48.

[16]Ibid., 48-51.

[17]Ibid.

including music, is an outward display of this inner self. Thus, music provides worship with both expression and experience.[18]

**Worship: Προσκυνέο (Proskuneo)**
Eight Greek words for worship occur in the New Testament. The exclusive Greek word for worship which the writer of the Apocalypse employs in his visions is προσκυνέο *(proskuneo—*see Revelation 4:10). In patriarchal times, this term implied the literal prostration of oneself before a person of dignity, a person of royalty, a god, or Yahweh. By the time of Christ, however, it will be shown that this word for worship implied only a mental or spiritual prostration to a god or God.[19] The early church of the first century did not view the work of worship, liturgy ("the work of the people"), as a secular cultic practice. The early Christian community viewed liturgical worship as the realization and participation in the "Kingdom of God"[20] which was at hand.

While this study is limited to the development of a theology of music in worship in the Book of Revelation, the rest of the Bible and other sources are incorporated. In order to do this, it seeks to discover the origins of the music which the writer of the Apocalypse employed. The study seeks to categorize the various types of music found in the Book of Revelation, but it is not an in-depth study of them. The study analyzes various song traditions including the ode, hymn and psalm which were used in early worship. This study is not a full exegesis of the Revelation. Not all levels of musical structure are analyzed, but only those contributing to an overall theology of music. In order to arrive at a theology of music, a brief overview of the concept of worship in the Book of Revelation is discussed. The study centers on the biblical writer's reason for using the music he employed. This study entails a consideration of the origins of the music and the performance practices which he implied, based on his music sources.

---

[18]LeRoy Evert Wright, "The Place of Music in Worship," Ph.D. dissertation (Evanston, IL: Northwestern University, 1949), 329.
[19]WSE, 104.
[20]Leaver, "The Theological Character of Music in Worship," DD, 39.

Although John Wick Bowman supposes that the Book of Revelation utilizes the combined formal structure of letter and drama,[21] this study assumes the dramatic approach to the interpretation of the book as set forth most recently by James Blevins in *Revelation as Drama*.[22] It is Blevins' contention that the writer of the Apocalypse could not express the visions which he received from the Holy Spirit in prose. Rather, he chose a medium which requires the utilization of all the senses, i.e., Greek tragic drama. Blevins, Bowman, Fiorenza,[23] and others divide the Apocalypse into a multi-act drama.

Some biblical scholars dispute the Apocalypse's authorship. Culpepper[24] holds the position that the Book of Revelation is the result of a collection of assorted writings assembled by a "Johannine School," an informal group who followed the writings of the Apostle John. Others believe that authorship is uncertain and cannot be pinpointed precisely. Ford[25] conjectures that the writer could be John the Baptist or John the Apostle. But regardless of any particular author, the writer would have to exhibit the following characteristics: (1) one who understood the prophetic tradition of Israel, (2) one who believed in the "imminence of the Kingdom," and (3) one who was able to speak the language of the prophets.

Kümmel[26] shows that Dionysius of Alexandria (bishop ca. 247-265 C.E.) believed that the Apostle John could not have written the Book of Revelation and the other books (the gospel and the epistles) based on the linguistic and stylistic differences between them. By holding this position, Dionysius hoped ultimately to have the Book of Revelation excluded from the canon.

---

[21]John Wick Bowman, *The First Christian Drama* (Philadelphia, PA:  The Westminster Press, 1955), 11.

[22]RD, 26.

[23]Elisabeth S. Fiorenza, *Invitation to the Book of Revelation* (Garden City, NJ:  Image Books, 1981).

[24]R. Alan Culpepper, *The Johannine School: An Evaluation of the Johannine-School Hypothesis Based on an Investigation of the Nature of Ancient Schools* (Ann Arbor, MI: University Microfilms International, 1985).

[25]J. Massyngberde Ford, ed., *Revelation, The Anchor Bible* (Garden City, NY: Doubleday and Co., 1975).

[26]Werner Georg Kümmel, *The New Testament: The History of the Investigation of Its Problems* (Nashville, TN:  Abingdon Press, 1972), 15.

However, both Buttrick[27] and Guthrie support the view that the Apostle John was the author of the Apocalypse. Guthrie[28] shows that the following writers from the second and third centuries C.E. assumed that the Apostle John was the author of the Book of Revelation: Justin, Irenaeus, Clement, Origen, Tertullian, and Hippolytus.

This study assumes that the Apostle John, inspired by the Holy Spirit, received the vision of the Revelation while a prisoner on the Island of Patmos in C.E. 95. The Apostle John was born and reared a Jew, but became "Christianized" by his close association with Jesus Christ. Following Pentecost, John traveled extensively throughout the world of his day and ultimately settled down in and around the area of Asia Minor known as Ephesus. As a result of his multicultural background, incorporating primarily Jewish, Christian, and Greek life-styles, it is not unlikely that these elements heavily influenced his writing of the Book of Revelation.

By studying the origins of the music of the Revelation, it is posited that the writer of the Apocalypse combined some original first-century "Christian" elements within a greater context of borrowings from other cultures of his time. These other cultures are primarily Jewish and Greek. Music in the Book of Revelation is the result of this blending of cultures, which resulted in the creation of a "new" theology of music. This theology of music also includes elements of the Seer's eschatological vision.

The purpose of this study is to develop a theology of music in worship in the Book of Revelation so that the contemporary church professional can glean greater spiritual understanding and appreciation of music in worship in the first century. Many church professionals today look back as far as the early church for instruction in the practice of music in worship. Few consciously consider that Jewish music traditions, principally derived from patriarchal, tabernacle, temple, and synagogue times, carry any musical weight. Nor do many contemporary church professionals consider that music from other cultures, whether Roman, Greek, or other pagan, could influence the music which is performed on a week-to-week basis in this century. But if the writer of the Apocalypse chose to couch his visions in Jewish and

---

[27]IB.

[28]Donald Guthrie, *New Testament Introduction* (Downers Grove, IL: Intervarsity Press, 1970).

other traditional music of his time, then why should today's church professional continue to ignore them? The development of a theology of music in worship through the Book of Revelation will provide a tool which can be used as a possible aid in grasping a hitherto mysterious and hard-to-interpret mass of apocalyptic material.

An attitude of complacency from the leaders in the churches exists today regarding well-balanced worship and music in worship. Many Christian circles have reduced the act of worship to a matter of academic, mentally-disciplined rhetoric; and the laity have become passive. Music serves largely to pacify and break the tedium of an otherwise too-routine monologue. It becomes the worship leader's role to entertain the laity in an easily understood, largely non-liturgic and non-threatening manner.

Often, today's congregation is a generation of "takers." Sitting on the sidelines, contemporary Christian consumers want easy answers. They want to feel good and to "have it their way." They represent "easy consumerism." In his day, Kierkegaard[29] experienced much the same problem. He criticized his church by observing that its ministers and musicians were the actors, the congregation was the audience, and God was the absentee playwright. But corporate worship is more than a period of entertainment with a reasoned, comprehensible lecture at the close. Kierkegaard spoke of worship as drama.[30] He described a model worship service consisting of the congregation as actors, the ministers and choir as leaders, and God as the audience. Not often enough in contemporary American Christian corporate worship does the congregation depart the worship service drained of all of its corporate and individual energy because it "gave" so much in the service. Perhaps every congregation should desire actively to "give and take" in this manner during every act of corporate worship.

Worship is a two-fold process. It is both "theocentric" and "anthropological";[31] it is God-centered, but God-centered from mankind's point of view. This process should "...awaken the (whole) person to the capacity of God."[32] Raymond Bailey calls on the

---

[29]Soren Kierkegaard, *Purity of Heart Is to Will One Thing* (New York: Harper Brothers, 1938), 164.

[30]Ibid.

[31]Leaver, "The Theological Character of Music in Worship," DD, 40.

[32]Ibid.

Christian community of the twentieth century to allow worship to touch our whole being—our "head, hand, heart, and imagination."[33] Perhaps this can best be realized through the holistic process called drama.

The scriptures have much more to teach us concerning the act of worship than we have been willing to accept in the past. Although effective worship can and does occur in both "low" and "high" liturgical traditions in different locations every week, perhaps what scripture still has to teach us could somehow connect the diverse traditions together by appealing to the whole person and the whole community of believers. Perhaps if we perceived well-balanced worship as drama we would be better able to experience the Spirit's fullness within the community of the Church at large and within God's temple—the whole person.

As important as music is to any worship service, and as important as it is that the church professional be skilled in the practical skills of his or her endeavor so that he or she can produce the aesthetic and pragmatic objectives which the local church and his or her conscience demands, it is critical that he or she and the congregation understand that music is a means to a greater spiritual end. To that end, this church professional is obligated to continue his quest by searching the scriptures for greater insights.

Every church professional should develop a philosophy or theology of music and worship. This provides him or her a value system with definable boundaries.[34] Many wish to espouse "this or that" philosophy or theology; some even claim to be guided by none. But just as a "nonconformist has to conform to his or her nonconformity," the church professional who chooses to adopt no theology has indeed made his or her choice.

The historical background of this study is rooted in the field of comparative liturgies which is two to three centuries old. Werner's study[35] is the first comprehensive volume on the topic.

---

[33]Raymond Bailey, "From Theory to Practice in Worship," *Review and Expositor*, 80(83):33.

[34]Calvin M. Johansson, *Music and Ministry* (Peabody, MA: Hendrickson Publishers, Inc., 1986), 3-7.

[35]TSB, 577.

A brief survey of the general use of music in early pagan, Jewish, Greek, Roman and the early church follows (see Appendix A for a timetable of these cultures).

## Early Pagan

Sumerian and Assyrian hymns and secular songs contain similar first lines of many poems and songs of various types. These various types of poems and songs consist of royal psalms, festival songs and lamentations, poems of "victory and heroic acts," and also love songs.[36] A wide variety of liturgical music exists because of the major role which cultic and religious ceremonies played in the lives of the Sumerian people. The largest temples had schools of music associated with them. The liturgists (*kalu*) and psalmists (*naru*) led the temple services by administering the daily sacred ceremonies to which they also provided vocal background. These sacred singers were members of their own guild and consisted of male and female singers. They were led in performance by a "special officer," while another leader was responsible for rehearsing them.[37]

Sumerian temples employed all types of instruments, although the psalmists used principally stringed instrumental accompaniment only. The harp (*al* or *zag-sal*) and the seven-stringed lyre (*shebitu*) were favored. In sacred music, the Sumerians preferred the *balaggu*, the flute and the drum. The most often cited wind instruments were the

> "covered" pipe (*kanzabu*), the single-pipe, an oboe-type (*malilu*), [and] the double-pipe (*shem*)..., sometimes combined with the timbrel (*me-ze*).[38]

Among instruments extant from this period are harps, lutes and double oboes. Written records do not exist, but other evidence indicates that these same instruments were used widely in Babylonia as well.[39]

---

[36]MAI, 35-36.
[37]Ibid., 37.
[38]Ibid.
[39]Homer Ulrich and Paul A. Pisk, *A History of Music and Musical Style* (New York, NY: Harcourt, Brace and World, Inc., 1963), 10.

According to Galpin, lyrics in Sumerian song "were put to music in a free recitative style."[40] Word accent determined the rhythm of the melodic line. These accents were given instrumental emphasis by accompanying harps and drumbeats. However, Sachs rejects Galpin's theory as "untenable." Sachs indicates that

> there are no signs for single notes. They indicate intervals, ascending or descending... The vocal notations used in connection with religious texts indicate stereotyped groups of notes. They provide evidence of that particular ornamental style that we roughly call "Oriental."[41]

Sumerian music is believed to have provided much of the impetus to the development of early Jewish music even though the Sumerian empire predated the Jewish culture in time. The Sumerian culture is dated from the third millennium B.C.E. (ca. 3000-2300 B.C.E.) when "organized temple music with singers and players existed."[42] Ulrich and Pisk attribute the great number of similarities between the two cultures' music to a common musical ethos which they shared. Each contained similar uses of emotion even though time separated them so widely. The Sumerian music of the third millenium B.C.E. is often religious in character. It also possessed a "vigorous" folk tradition.[43]

The music which survives from the Egyptian era is very scant. Little more than pictorial representation survives. Interestingly, most of what is known of Egyptian music comes from foreign sources. While Babylonian and Assyrian monuments reveal instruments from all nations, the types of Egyptian instruments were more diverse and richer sounding than those of other cultures during their time. The harp *(ben* or *bin)* was the most prominent instrument used, followed by the lyre.[44]

---

[40]Francis William Galpin, *The Music of the Sumerians and Their Immediate Successors the Babylonians and Assyrians* (Cambridge: Cambridge University Press, 1967), 62.

[41]Curt Sachs, "The Mystery of the Babylonian Notation," in *Musical Quarterly* 27(1941),1:68.

[42]Ulrich, *A History of Music*, 10.

[43]MAI, 35.

[44]Ibid., 39.

Sacred Egyptian music was dominated by the soft and mellow timbre produced by stringed instruments. Sendrey conjectures that this was the character of the music in order to match the *"claire-obscure"*[45] of the temple halls. This type of music could provide the type of tonal background necessary for their mystic ceremonies.[46]

Music of the Babylonian cult was performed by the priest (*kalu*), the *zammaru* (singer) and for lamentations, the *lallaru* (singer of wailing). The most important Babylonian and Assyrian evidence which survives today portrays the victorious return of their conquering kings after battle. Musicians and singers are praising the king while the king reviews his prisoners. Other bas-reliefs show palm trees being felled in a war-torn city while the musicians are performing their ritual dances. They accompany themselves on drums and cymbals. Also pictured are women clapping their hands as they sing and dance.[47]

Babylonian music is not very different from that of the Egyptians. The principal instruments from the two cultures are the horizontal and vertical angular harps, different types of lyres, the double-oboe, drums, cymbals and other percussion instruments. The ten-stringed instruments and flutes were commonly reserved for love songs. Similar to the music tradition of Sumeria, the Babylonians trained their young priests in special schools that were attached to the largest temples.[48]

The Phoenician religion was based on the cult of Ishtar. It praised the cruel service of Moloch who demanded appeasement via human sacrifice.[49] Plutarch recorded that these sacrifices were accompanied by flutes and drums "so that the cries of the wailing should not reach the ears of the people."[50] The *kedeshot* ("dedicated ones") were responsible for the music and singing in the morning and evening sacrificial rites. They also raised money practicing religious prostitution which they presented to their goddess as offerings.[51]

Aristides Quintilianus (ca. 1-2 century B.C.E.?) wrote of Phoenician music in *De Musica* that

---

[45]Ibid., 40.
[46]Ibid.
[47]Ibid., 44.
[48]Ibid., 45-46.
[49]Ibid., 54.
[50]Ibid.
[51]Ibid.

In the realm of (musical) education there are two degenerate trends: one is the entire lack [of] (*amousia*), and the other the wrong practice of art (*kakomousia*).[52]

This view of Phoenician music is perhaps too narrow. Aristides is perhaps speaking of only one special aspect of the music. Unfortunately, he does not address the other musical practices of the Phoenicians.

Early Phoenician music possibly was descended from the classical Egyptian tradition which was "solemn, sedate"[53] and full of dignity. Likewise, the Assyrians and Lydians had music of nobler character, apart from the music of their respective orgiastic rites.[54]  The basic trend in Assyrian music was toward "refinement" during the period of the great kings, just as it was in the "golden" age of the Egyptians.[55]

**Jewish**
Generally speaking, Jewish music is a utilitarian art form.  From its beginnings, the Jewish culture demanded that its music exhibit a "heteronomous artistic phenomenon"[56] which subsequently developed into a music with a "strong spiritual and ethical significance."[57]

More so than in other languages, the Hebrew language is designed to express the human vocal sound in a roughly physical manner.  But the Jewish tradition borrowed heavily from the Greek in order to express instrumental musical terms.  This can be shown by comparing Greek and Hebrew transliterated terminology for similar instruments:

| English | Greek | Hebrew |
|---|---|---|
| lyre | *kithara* | *qathros* |
| strings | *nema* | *ninim* |
| stringed instrument | *psalterim* | *psanterin* |
| consonance, ensemble | *symphonia* | *sumponia*[58] |

---

[52]Ibid.
[53]Ibid.
[54]Ibid.
[55]Ibid., 45.
[56]Ibid., 32.
[57]Ibid.
[58]TSB, 334.

The first attempt to catalog Jewish song was begun by Idelsohn in the first part of the twentieth century. In the liturgies of both the Babylonian and Yemenite Hebrews, he found song tune patterns very close to the chants used by the Catholic Church many centuries later. Because the Babylonian and Yemenite Hebrews were separated physically from their Palestinian counterparts and separated from the Catholic tradition in time, Werner contends that the existence of these tunes in later Catholic traditions must be attributed to the passing of the tunes by the Jewish-Christians communities of the first century. One "can rely on the analyses and the resulting conclusions" derived when "at least one of the Jewish or Christian sources is based...upon a well-authenticated [oral] tradition."[59] This oral tradition was fostered and nurtured in the early church by Jewish cantors who migrated to the church.[60] Many of Werner's specific conclusions are now called into question, though there is clearly a general affinity between the liturgical music of Judaism and early Christianity.[61]

The pervasive use of Greek music in the Jewish culture caused many Jewish leaders to consider it detrimental to Israel's faith. In fact, after the destruction of the temple in the sixth century B.C.E., instrumental music was forbidden in Jewish practice, except for restricted use as expressions of mourning for the destruction of the temple. It was shunned by the Jewish leaders because of the syncretistic manner in which it had been used. Vocal music was exempt from this exclusion as long as it maintained a purely spiritual function.[62]

Early Judaism (from the third century B.C.E. to the end of A.D. second century) believed in a cosmic theology. Above the earth were the heavens. The heavens were not silent but always full of activity. Pseudepigraphal literature of the day (see the *Ascension of Isaiah* and the *Testament of Adam*) portrayed the heavens as full of singing angels. The harmony of the heavens was occasionally interrupted while sinners were being punished.[63]

---

[59]Ibid., xviii.

[60]Ibid., xiii.

[61]See James McKinnon, ed., *Music in Early Christian Literature* (Cambridge: Cambridge University Press, 1987), and J. Smith, "The Ancient Synagogue, the Early Church and Singing," *Music and Letters*, 65 (1984):1-16.

[62]Ibid., 335.

[63]James Hamilton Charlesworth, *The Old Testament Pseudepigrapha and the New Testament* (Cambridge: Cambridge University Press, 1985), 59-65.

## Greek

The surviving corpus of Greek melody consists of fewer than 600 measures. The main features of the monophonic music are described in the writings of Aristoxenus (fourth century B.C.E.),[64] and in the *Harmonics* of Claudius Ptolemy (from the second century B.C.E.). The primary type of music in Greek life was choral music. It was used in the cult worship of the gods, at marriages, at funerals, and to celebrate famous men or athletes. The choirs consisted of unskilled musicians who had received rudimentary music instruction as part of their general education.[65]

Pythagoras viewed music as "a microcosm" of sound and rhythm within the greater mathematical laws which affected the whole of creation. These different sounds developed into modes with their own unique character (ethos).[66] The two primary divisions of the doctrine of ethos consist of music which could create calmness and be uplifting, or create excitement and be enthusiastic. The former became characteristic of those who worshiped Apollo and is spoken of in connection with classical style. The Apollonian school strove for clarity and moderation in their music. The latter became characteristic of those who worshiped and followed Dionysus. This is often referred to as romantic style. Characteristic of the Dionysian school was the perpetual drive towards the fantastic and orgiastic.[67]

Plato wrote in his *Republic* that "music can affect not only the emotions temporarily but also can permanently affect one's character."[68] In his *Laws*, he rejects music styles that are "plaintive" (as portrayed in the Mixolydian and Syntonalydian modes) and "effeminate"[69] (as portrayed in the Ionian and Lydian modes) in favor of the Dorian and

---

[64]See Appendix B for a summary of the dates of the Greek philosophers and others mentioned in this study.

[65]R. P. Winnington-Ingram, "Greece, Ancient," NGD, 7:659-660.

[66]Warren D. Anderson, *Ethos and Education in Greek Music* (Cambridge, MA: Harvard University Press, 1966), 52-53.

[67]Donald Jay Grout and Claude V. Palisca, Jr., *A History of Western Music,* second edition (New York, NY: W. W. Norton and Company, 1973), 7-10. This citation is not in later editions.

[68]Denis Arnold, ed., *The New Oxford Companion to Music* (New York, NY: Oxford University Press, 1984), 67. See also Isobel Henderson, "Ancient Greek Music," in *New Oxford History of Music,* ed. by Egon Wellesz (London: Oxford University Press, 1957), I:336-339.

[69]Ibid.

Phrygian modes, which he believed portrayed "courage" and "sobriety,"[70] respectively.

On the contrary, Aristotle wrote in his *Politics* that "carefully selected music" can help one attain "virtue." Aristotle tended to be less "puritanical" than Plato because he allowed for music of relaxation and he claimed that rhythms and melodies "represent[ed] moral qualities" which could directly influence and "affect" the soul.[71] Both Aristotle and Plato's highest ideal was to preserve the "purity" of their music.[72] Music, for the Greek mind, was aesthetically representative of the qualities of "beautiful" and good." Καλοκαγαθια (*Kalokagathia*) —καλός *(kalos)* meaning "beautiful" and αγαθος *(agathos)* meaning "good"—was the union of beauty and virtue.[73] Plato wrote that music leads the arts in importance. In *Timaeus*, Plato said

> the philosopher sees an analogy between the movements of the soul and the musical progressions; therefore the aim of music cannot be mere amusement but a harmonic education and perfection of the soul and the quieting of passions. The primary role of music was a pedagogical one, which implied the strengthening up of one's morals and character.[74]

Music was also used:[75]

(1) as accompaniment to sacrificial worship;
(2) to provide ἀποτροπαικ *(apotropaic)* protection from evil gods;[76]

---

[70]Ibid.

[71]Ibid.

[72]Manly P. Hall, *The Therapeutic Value of Music* (Los Angeles, CA: The Philosophical Research Society, Inc., 1955), 33.

[73]Paul Henry Lang, *Music in Western Civilization* (New York, NY: W. W. Norton and Company, Inc., 1941), 1.

[74]Ibid., 13.

[75]TSB, 322.

[76]The ἀποτροπαιχ *(apotropaic)* function of music can be illustrated by: (1) the *sistra* of the Egyptians which were used to drive away the evil Typhon; (2) the bells of the Phrygians which were used to chase away evil shadows and dreams; and (3) *Paamonium* on the dress of the Jewish High Priest which were worn when he entered the Holy of Holies (see HMI).

(3) as an ἐπικλεσε (*epiclese*);[77]
(4) as a καθαρσις (*katharsis*) before and initiation into the mysteries;[78]
(5) at funerals;[79]
(6) during the performance of magic; and
(7) as an accompaniment to sorcery.

## Roman

Roman music was influenced early by the Etruscans. Later, as the Roman Empire grew, it was influenced by the Greeks and "assimilated, modified and extended the music of the nations they conquered,"[80] including the Orient. After the second century B.C.E., they overtook the Macedonians, Syrians and the Egyptians.[81] However, the Roman culture never achieved as high a cultural independence in its music as did the Greeks. This is due largely to the fact that the doctrine of ethos never appeared in Roman music.[82] The high point for Greco-Roman music existed during the reigns of Augustus (27 B.C.E.-C.E. 14) and under the subsequent dynasties of Julius and Claudius (C.E. 14-68), the Flavians (C.E. 69-96) and the Antonines (C.E. 96-192). During this period

> professional virtuosi, mainly of Greek origin, sang and played instruments; outstanding Egyptian and Syrian *pantomimi* performed in public; Greek and Roman musicians and actors

---

[77]A person in a posture of prayer commonly used music to invoke the gods to lend aid and assistance (ἐπικλεσις—*epiclesis*). In the Rhea Kybele cult (a popular religion in Asia Minor), cymbals and bells were used. It has been speculated by H. Gressman in *Musik und Musikinstrumente im Alten Testament* (Gieszen: J. Ricker'sche Verlagsbuchhandlung, 1903) that the *shofar* and trumpet served the same function in the Old Testament period.

[78]The utilization of music for a cathartic purpose is a primary characteristic of Pythagoreanism. Catharsis is the "purification or purgation of the emotions primarily through the arts that brings about spiritual renewal or a release from tension" (Henry Bosley Woolf, ed., *Webster's New Collegiate Dictionary* (Springfield, MA: G. and C. Merriam and Company, 1976), 345.

[79]Flutes and cymbals were used at funerals in all the religious cults of Asia Minor and Palestine.

[80]Guenter Fleischhauer, "Rome," NGD, 16:146.

[81]Ibid.

[82]Ulrich, *A History of Music*, 10.

were active in organized bodies at Rome and elsewhere; dancers and musicians were imported as slaves from all parts of the empire; musical instruments and musical scholarship were developed; and the participation of music lovers in public events increased.

At the same time philosophers and historians, including Seneca, Quintilian, Plutarch, Juvenal and Tacitus, attacked the demoralizing and effeminate effects of theatrical music, and the 'decline' of music in the service of luxury, on national, social, musical and moral grounds. Many actors, dancers and musicians continued, nevertheless, to enjoy public favour, despite their low legal and social position.[83]

The ritual music of the Romans was influenced by the mystery religions of Cybele (the *magna mater* in Phrygia), Dionysus (Bacchus in Greece) and Isis (in Egypt). The cult of Cybele, introduced in Rome in 204 B.C.E., held a several-days-long festival with scenic games (*ludi Megalenses*). This festival was held annually

to commemorate the dedication of her temple on the Aventine. Priests carried the cult-idol of the goddess in triumphal procession to the music of the bronze *cymbala*, frame drums or *tambours* (tympana), *cornua* (horns) and 'Phrygian *auloi*' or 'Berecyntian *tibiae*' whose deeper-sounding left pipe had an upturned horn-shaped bell.[84]

These same instruments were used at the orgiastic dances of the priests in the temples. The purpose of this music was partly practical. The loud beating of the drums and cymbals muffled the cries of those being violated![85]

When Rome conquered Egypt in 30 B.C.E., the cult of Isis spread through the empire. The traditional and characteristic instrument of the Isis cult was the *sistrum*—a bright-sounding metal rattle, used to dispel the influence of evil spirits. Other instruments used by the cult were Egyptian vertical long flutes and angle harps. As in the Cybelian and

---

[83]Fleischhauer, "Rome," NGD, 16:146.
[84]Ibid., 16:148.
[85]Ibid.

Dionysian cults, instrumentalists and hymn singers were employed by the temple priests.[86]

## Early Church

"Early church" refers to the Christian Church of the first century up through the writing of the Apocalypse. The early church did not have to travel outside of Palestine in order to be significantly influenced by Greek, Roman, and other pagan ideas. The terminologies of the mystery religions were well known, although the influence of these mystery religions should not be overestimated. For the most part, the mystery religions did not succeed in Palestine because of their "offensive idolatrous base." Hengel[87] theorizes that the mystery religions were thwarted from too much influence over the early church because "the solution of humanity's predicaments and the explanation of human existence" had already been "attractively elaborated"[88] via the crucifixion and resurrection of Christ.

The principal references to music in the New Testament are found in Colossians 3:16 and Ephesians 5:19 and "certain heraldic references in the singing of the heavenly hosts in the Book of Revelation."[89] Vocal forms are referred to and consist of:

(1) psalms—"scriptural praises set to music";
(2) hymns—"nonscriptural spontaneous songs of praise" to God; and
(3) spiritual songs—"ecstatic utterances of joy."[90]

The Pharisees' views on music during the time of the Apostle Paul's writings were the strictest in relation to both synagogue and temple worship. The Pharisees "antimusical" views consisted of:

(1) an opposition to the more liberal attitudes of the Sadducees;

---

[86]Ibid.

[87]Martin Hengel, *Judaism and Hellenism: Studies in their Encounter in Palestine During the Early Hellenistic Period*, trans. by J. Bowden (Philadelphia, PA: SCM Press, 1974), 1:202.

[88]OTP, 81-82.

[89]Routley, *Church Music and Theology*, 23.

[90]David P. Appleby, *History of Church Music* (Chicago, IL: Moody Press, 1965), 20.

(2) an opposition to the use of instruments, because of the "clarinet [*sic*], cymbals, gong and drum's association with the mystery cults of Asia Minor"; and

(3) the general overall historic association of instruments with pagan cults.[91]

Perhaps the Apostle Paul portrayed a new appreciation for the use of music in the early church since he was found to be singing in the Philippian jail with Silas. He also encouraged the Corinthians "to sing with understanding," and he exhorted the Colossians to "sing with grace."[92]

The early church adopted attitudes towards Hellenistic music similar to their contemporary Jewish counterparts. While both utilized instrumental music, both were reluctant to use instrumental accompaniment in their respective religious services. The early church fathers from the second century C.E. considered vocal music more pleasing to God than instrumental music.[93]

Because the early church's vernacular contained Greek and Latin phrases, the infiltration of these pagan fragments into their liturgy was more likely. Consequently, the early church Fathers sought to limit the texts of their songs to biblical passages, primarily from the Psalter.[94] Eventually, the early church gave up on their exclusion of "pagan influences" as exemplified in their acceptance of the Κύριε Ελεισον (*Kyrie Eleison*—"Lord have mercy"). The origins of this first song of the Ordinary of the Mass stem from an *Helios-Mithra* hymn.[95]

Music was used not only in the various religious cults of the time, but also in the symposia, the theater, in concerts, in recitals and in the secular processions and parades. Between all of these religious and pagan practices of music, the early church existed. It is interesting to note that while the early church basically forsook instrumental music

---

[91]Ibid., 19-20.
[92]Ibid.
[93]TSB, 335-336.
[94]Ibid., 336.
[95]Ibid.

in favor of pure vocal music, the Book of Revelation portrays the elders, prostrate before the lamb, playing a new song on their harps.[96]

Present-century concepts of the aesthetic and the moral are not at all comparable to Jewish and early church ideas. While "beauty" may not be mentioned in the I Kings 5-8 description of the Temple, it is heavily implied—accurate stonework, carved cedar wood, the overlaying of gold, the depiction of lilies, pomegranites, etc. But in Old Testament literature, for example, the idea that music was beautiful was unknown. While music had a decided place in the Temple ritual and served as a spontaneous expression of a person or a group, it was nowhere aesthetically intended to be beautiful as a lower human virtue. Rather, music served in the role of a higher virtue under the locus of worship.[97]

**In the Book of Revelation**
Characteristic of the music and worship of Revelation is that it is lacking entirely of any introspection on the part of the participants, and it focuses exclusively on the characteristics and acts of God.[98]

In his first-century study of hymns, Michael Harris[99] indicates that contemporary authors are reluctant to show a direct relationship between hymns and liturgic practice of the first century. David Carnegie[100] argues that the hymns of Revelation are specifically original creations of the writer of the Apocalypse, not borrowed or assimilated from the surrounding cultures.

However, the fact remains that the author of the Book of Revelation did use specific types of music and implied specific modes of musical performance which this author will show contain multicultured roots. According to Werner

all Christian liturgies of the Churches which originated during the first millenium have evolved around the same nuclei. Yet

---

[96]Ibid., 344.

[97]James McKinnon, *Music in Early Christian Literature*, 5.

[98]Donald Guthrie, *The Relevance of John's Apocalypse* (Grand Rapids, MI: William B. Eerdmans Publishing Company, 1987), 85-89.

[99]Michael Anthony Harris, "The Literary Function of Hymns in the Apocalypse of John" (Ph.D. dissertation, The Southern Baptist Theological Seminary, 1988), 3.

[100]David R. Carnegie, "Worthy Is the Lamb: The Hymns in Revelation," *Christ the Lord: Studies in Christology Presented to Donald Guthrie*, ed. by H. H. Rowdon (Leicester: Intervarsity Press, 1982), 246-247.

the differing languages, regional customs, and the specific folklores have wrought vast cleavages between them, both in form and content.[101]

According to Werner, the starting place of early Christian liturgy was neither the scriptures nor the Jewish temple, but rather, the synagogue,[102] The early Christian community borrowed its substance and other musical practice from the synagogue and borrowed various musical forms, such as the canticle, response and refrain from the Jewish temple.

More recent scholarship demonstrates there was no musical borrowing of synagogal tradition in the early church before the destruction of the Temple in C.E. 70; or at best several synagogal traditions coexisted. Mowinckel states that "services in the synagogue in ancient times had no singing";[103] musical texts were recited, not sung. McKinnon further states that Temple psalmody was not used in the synagogue tradition: "recitation of scripture in the ancient Synagogue was not a dry reading in the modern sense, but rather some sort of elemental declamation or cantillation."[104]

The singing of psalms occurred domestically and in the Temple. Two types of singing occurred in two Jewish sects, the Essenes and Therapeutae. The first consisted of the president's solo singing before a meal accompanied by choral responses. The second occurred as all those present formed an antiphonal "single choir" during the vigil. Smith conjectures that the early church may have borrowed singing and fellowship at meals from private Jewish religious gatherings.[105] Two examples are the Last Supper which ended with a hymn (Matthew 26:30 and Mark 14:26) and the account of Pentecost as concluded in Acts 4:25 with the singing of psalms and hymns.

---

[101]TSB, xvi.

[102]Ibid., 19.

[103]PIW, I:4.

[104]James McKinnon, "The Exclusion of Musical Instruments from the Ancient Synagogue," *Proceedings of the Royal Musical Association*, cvi(1979-1980):85. See also McKinnon's, "On the Question of Psalmody in the Ancient Synagogue," Iain Fenlon ed., *Early Music History*, 6(1986):159-191.

[105]J. Smith, "The Ancient Synagogue, the Early Church and Singing," *Music and Letters*, 65(1984):6,11,16.

Smith claims that "no relevant notational remains or technical descriptions of Christian song sufficient to provide specific information about the style of the singing during the first or even second century" exists. Smith further argues that songs in the Book of Revelation, as well as in "other hymnic passages in the New Testament, are unreliable as evidence about the nature of early Christian singing and therefore also about whether early Christians sang Jewish material."[106] Regardless, this study will clearly show that the writer of the Apocalypse used the breadth of his multicultured life experiences to portray the fulness of the vision he received from the Godhead.

The early Christian community absorbed and modified many regional and pre-Christian traditions as they primitively sought to develop an organized liturgy. Cullman suggests that the entire Book of Revelation is couched in and full of allusions to the liturgical usages common to the early worshiping community of the first century. The Seer (Revelation 1:1) sees his visions on the Lord's Day. This is the time when the Christian community traditionally gathered.[107] The Seer sees the entire drama of the last days in "the context of the early Christian service of worship."[108] The use of the church's oldest songs, coupled with Pliny's mention of antiphonal singing by the early church, suggests that "liturgically ordered singing"[109] was already prevalent and practiced by the church as early as the late first century.[110]

In spite of the fact that the writer of the Apocalypse wrote what he saw, "this fact does not preclude the possibility of his visions incorporating established patterns of worship in the church,"[111] just as freely as he had incorporated many passages from the Old Testament.[112]

Little work, beyond some text-related hymnological studies (see Bibliography), has been done primarily dealing with the music of the

---

[106]J. A. Smith, "First-Century Christian Singing and Its Relationship to Contemporary Jewish Religious Song," *Music and Letters*, 75(1994):2, 13.

[107]Oscar Cullman, *Early Christian Worship* (Philadelphia, PA: Westminster Press, 1953), 7.

[108]Ibid.

[109]Ibid.

[110]Ibid.

[111]Robert E. Coleman, *Songs of Heaven* (Old Tappan, NJ: Fleming H. Revell Company, 1975), 17-18.

[112]Ibid.

Revelation. Klaus-Peter Joerns[113] has identified 30 hymns[114] within the text of Revelation, but he focuses the bulk of his attention on the hymn texts of Chapters 4 and 5. Other authors have identified a different number of hymn texts in the Book. Cullman has identified six hymns (5:9; 5:12; 5:13; 12:10-12; 19:1-2; and 19:6),[115] while Harris has most recently enumerated seven (4:8-11; 5:9; 7:10; 11:17-18; 12:10-11; 15:3; and 15:4b).[116] Harris' study of the hymns is typical of that of the other authors. He approaches the hymns from a purely literary viewpoint. His study primarily uses narrative criticism to argue for the hymnic unit divisions within the text.[117] Church and Mulry identify eleven hymns in the Revelation (Revelation 1:5-8; 4:11; 5:9-11; 5:12-13; 11:17-18; 12:10-12; 15:3-4; 18:22-23; 19:1-9; 22:16-17; and 22:20).[118] While hymnological studies in the Book of Revelation are valid, they only peripherally touch on the topic at hand. They address neither the nature of the music itself nor its performance practice.

During the first century, both hymnody and psalmody were widely practiced within the Greek world. According to Didymus (ca. second half of the first century B.C.E.), it was common for "the man of practical life [to] prefer psalmody; [and for] the man of theoretical life [to] prefer hymns."[119] That is, psalms should be sung by the common man everyday, whereas hymns held a place of higher esteem. They were used by others in a more discriminating manner.[120] Where and when did musical concepts, forms and aesthetic values emerge and develop to produce a synthesis between the Temple and other Jewish practice and early church traditions of music? The same question could be asked regarding the relationship between the music of the early church, the Greeks, and the other cultures of the first century. If it

---

[113]Klaus-Peter Joerns, *Das Hymnische Evangelium: Untersuchungen zu Aufbau, Funktion und Herkunft der hymnischen Stücke in der Johannesoffenbarung* (Goettingen: G. Mohn, 1971).

[114]For a summary listing of hymn texts by various authors see Appendix C.

[115]Cullman, *Early Christian Worship*, 8.

[116]Harris, "Hymns in the Apocalypse," 305.

[117]Ibid., 3-7.

[118]F. Forrester Church and Terrance J. Mulry, *Earliest Christian Hymns* (New York: Macmillan Publishers Company, 1988), x.

[119]TSB, 319.

[120]Ibid., 319.

were possible to conclusively answer this type of question, we could gain a much deeper insight into the history of religious music.

In this century, there has been an increased desire to educate ministers and the laity concerning the act which Christians call worship. Segler defines worship as "man's loving response in personal faith to God's revelation of himself in Jesus Christ."[121] A trinitarian formula for worship might augment the preceding definition with ". . . through the Holy Spirit." While this definition might satisfy the reasoned, rational mind of a technological, scientific-age person, perhaps contemporary Christianity has failed to comprehend the full spectrum of what the act of worship, using music, embraces.

The thesis of this study is that there is a discernable theology of music which the writer of the Revelation assumed. The Book of Revelation does not consist of a collection of unrelated visions and music. Rather, the music provides the basis of a well-conceived theology of music in worship. The thesis of this study breaks new ground and has not been addressed directly in any other study to date.

A theology of music in worship in the Book of Revelation has not been dealt with as a topic, except for peripheral glances in a few articles, such as R. Bauckham's "The Worship of Jesus in Apocalyptic Christianity."[122] By dividing the Book of Revelation into seven acts and suggesting that the book be acted out as a performable drama, James Blevins has shown that the music serves both pragmatic and aesthetic roles.[123] Classical musical works, such as *Messiah* by Handel, draw heavily on the hymn texts of the Book of Revelation. All of these works pertain directly or indirectly to music, yet none hypothesize a theology of music related to the Book of Revelation.

While Benson discusses the New Testament backgrounds of music in a general overview, he fails to mention any of the music of the Revelation.[124] Neither do other authors. Perhaps most authorities think of the music in Revelation as future oriented and not suitable for contemporary practice.

---

[121]Franklin M. Segler, *Christian Worship: Its Theology and Practice* (Nashville, TN: Broadman Press, 1967), 12.

[122]R. Bauckham, "The Worship of Jesus in Apocalyptic Christianity", *New Testament Studies*, 27 (3, 1981), 322-341.

[123]RD, 3-24.

[124]Louis F. Benson, *The Hymnody of the Christian Church* (New York: George H. Doran Company, 1927), 25-53, 233-236.

Several authors have written histories of worship, philosophies of music and/or worship, or theologies of music and/or worship in the twentieth century. Representative histories of early Christian worship include Martin's *Worship in the Early Church*[125] and Webber's *Worship: Old and New.*[126] Martin brings to light New Testament teachings concerning early Christian principles of worship and discusses at length the practice of corporate worship, but he makes no attempt to apply the principles to the worship of today. While Webber discusses Jewish and early Christian worship practices, he ignores Greek and pagan worship practices altogether.

In *Jubilate II! Church Music in Worship and Renewal,*[127] Hustad seeks to develop a practical working philosophy for twentieth-century American church musicians from the perspectives of ethnomusicology. He judges music in worship by whether or not it fulfills its best function as a means to a greater spiritual end. Franklin Segler[128] indicates that "all churches are mutually indebted to many historic treasures to which no one denomination or tradition can lay exclusive claim." Segler concerns himself with the meaning of worship, the means of expressing worship, and the planning and conducting of worship in today's church.

Perhaps the bedrock of theological writing on worship and music in worship in the twentieth century has been accomplished by Underhill. Her aim was "to explore those primary realities of man's relation to God which our devotional action is intended to express."[129] She dealt with worship at its very core, as response to the Godhead. She does not specifically bring up the shortcomings of all the different worship traditions within Christianity. Rather, she believes that although the various traditions contain negative traits worthy of ridicule, all pale in comparison to what she calls "the positive element" of each: "man's

[125]Ralph P. Martin, *Worship in the Early Church* (Grand Rapids, MI: William B. Eerdmans Publishing Company, 1964).

[126]Robert E. Webber, *Worship: Old and New* (Grand Rapids, MI: Zondervan Publishing House, 1982).

[127]Donald P. Hustad, *Jubilate II! Church Music in Worship and Renewal* (Carol Stream, IL: Hope Publishing Co., 1993).

[128]Cited in footnote 121 above.

[129]Evelyn Underhill, *Worship* (New York, NY: Harper and Row, Inc., 1936), vii.

upward and outward movement of adoration, self-oblation and dependence..."[130]

Several theological works on music and worship have appeared within the last fifteen years. Burkhart[131] seeks to sketch a theology of worship by incorporating evidence from the anthropological, biblical, historical, and theological disciplines as well as from a compendium of liturgical experiences. Martin,[132] following up on the basis which he laid in *Worship in the Early Church*,[133] constructs a model or philosophy of Christian worship that is both theologically and pastorally helpful. He touches on the components of both the traditional and contemporary worship service.

Johansson[134] provides one of the freshest and most insightful theologies of music to date. He considers that "no single doctrine or theological topic is intended to stand alone." He juxtaposes opposite ends of the music-practice spectrum in a counterpoint which results in a well-balanced look at the development of a theology of music.

Paul Hoon states that "a viable liturgical theology" must be tested against "the empirical life of the Church" where the central issues are the "gathered congregation" and the need for "a pastoral liturgy."[135] In his Christologically-conceived theology of worship, Hoon analyzes many aspects of the Church's life in worship.

The pinnacle of contemporary writing in the area of worship has been compiled in Wainwright's[136] systematic theology of worship. It is written from a liturgical perspective and proceeds to show "a liturgical way of doing theology." He claims that

a historical community, in this case the Christian Church, can transmit a vision of reality which helps decisively in the interpretation of life and the world.[137]

---

[130]Ibid., viii.

[131]Cited in footnote 19 above.

[132]Ralph P. Martin, *The Worship of God* (Grand Rapids, MI: William B. Eerdmans Publishing Company, 1982).

[133]Cited in footnote 125 above.

[134]Cited in footnote 34 above.

[135]Paul W. Hoon, *The Integrity of Worship* (Nashville, TN: Abingdon Press, 1971).

[136]DOX.

[137]Ibid., 1-2.

Donald Pass uses several key scripture passages, most notably Genesis 1:3, Acts 2:46-47, Colossians 3:16 and Ephesians 5:18-20, to formulate a "theological theory of church music." Pass shows that music has played a vital role in each of the historical "orders" of God's dealings with humankind: creation, preservation, and redemption. His intention is to show how the whole of scripture can speak directly to the contemporary church musician.[138]

Idelsohn has been able to illustrate the similarities between isolated Jewish groups with various Gregorian chants. Following on Idelsohn's idea, Douglas shows that the relationship between these two traditions' musical types are:

(1) chanting;

(2) the use of inflected monotone in scripture readings;

(3) congregational refrains in the singing of the psalms;

(4) "festal jubilations" of the alleluia type;

(5) the use of prose rhythm;

(6) some "practically identical" melodies; and

(7) a general similarity of style which has noble dignity. This characteristic is quite unlike the secular music of its day.[139]

While Idelsohn is able to relate the similarities between the Jewish tradition and Christianity from the Patristic Age,[140] no one has attempted to do the same with the music of the first century. Appleby contends that the types of music in worship were not seriously debated before the fourth century C.E. Consequently, endless speculation has occurred in the centuries that followed concerning music of the Church in the pre-fourth century C.E. period. Although the New Testament has little to say concerning particular stylistic characteristics of music, Appleby cites several examples which indicate that Jesus "had little quarrel" with the forms and types of music and worship which he

---

[138]Donald B. Pass, *Music and the Church* (Nashville, TN: Broadman Press, 1989), 7-8, 23, 36-38, and 88-91.

[139]Charles Winfred Douglas, *Church Music in History and Practice*, revised edition (New York, NY: Charles Scribner's Sons, 1962), 18-19.

[140]JLD.

observed in the Temple.[141] His objection arose with the attitude which produced it.

These works represent the literature related to the topic at hand. They provide the guidelines from which this writer will attempt to develop a theology of music in worship in the Book of Revelation. This study analyzes the Book of Revelation and identifies all musical references to worship. Once identified, this study then categorizes each musical reference according to its specific or blended origins. By studying the music and practice of the various origins, this writer will show that these various elements meld into a unified whole which subsequently is summarized in a theology of music within the context of the Book of Revelation. By studying the role which the writer of the Revelation ascribes to music in worship, it is shown that the music and performance practice implied in the Apocalypse have origins both from other times and cultures as well as from within the early church.

The primary methodological tool implemented in this study has been philosophical/theological research. This procedure has consisted of three steps:

(1) to identify musical occurrences in worship within the Apocalypse;

(2) to analyze them in an attempt to codify not only their nature or type but also to show their origins; and

(3) to interpret them in order to formulate a theology of music which can assist the church musician in the present century.[142]

In pursuing this methodology, a historical study through the earlier and contemporary cultures has endeavored to find borrowings from them.

The Revised Standard Version of the Bible[143] has been used in studying the text of the Revelation. In order to discover the philosophical tenets of Jewish, Greek, and other pagan music, this writer has utilized both primary and secondary sources. The primary

---

[141]Appleby, *History of Church Music*, 18.

[142]Roger P. Phelps, *A Guide to Research in Music Education* (Metuchen, NJ: The Scarecrow Press, Inc., 1986), Third Edition, 103.

[143]Herbert G. May and Bruce M. Metzger, eds., *The New Oxford Annotated Bible with the Apocrypha*, Revised Standard Version (New York, NY: Oxford University Press, 1977).

Greek sources consist of selected writings.[144] The primary Jewish music sources consist of selected sections of the Old Testament, the Torah, Old Testament Pseudepigrapha, including Apocalyptic writings, and the Apocrypha, as well as various authors of the first century such as Josephus.[145]

Sources for the study of first-century Christian music have included the New Testament and writings of Patristic authors, as well as secondary authors.[146] After this introductory chapter, Chapter 2 focuses on the exclusive Greek word used for worship in the Book of Revelation. Προσκυνέο (*Proskuneo*) has Jewish patriarchal and other-culture origins which differ greatly from its usage in the first century after Christ's birth. An understanding of worship in the Revelation has influenced both the type of music as well as the performance practice which is implied in the text.

Chapter 3 focuses on the music inherent in the text. The types of music found in the Book of Revelation are discussed. Examples of these include accompanied and unaccompanied odes and songs. The background of the types of music found in the text have been analyzed according to their respective early pagan, Jewish, Greek, Roman and early church origins. Chapter 4 seeks to discover the various musical ensembles which are evident in the text. Chapter 5 studies the types of sounds which were made in producing the music for worship based on a study of Greek verbs found in the text. It also discloses the manner in which those sounds were made.

Chapter 6 summarizes and lists the characteristics of the various elements of music for worship found in the Book of Revelation. This summary and subsequent dialog comprises a theology of music for worship derived from the Book of Revelation. Chapter 7 then shows how this theology of music might be woven into the fabric of contemporary Christian music and worship practice. The musical references in the Book of Revelation have been dealt with in a topical manner. The culminating theology of music consists of a list of the key characteristics of the music of the Revelation. This list constitutes a synthesis of the music and music practices in the Book of Revelation. From it, the contemporary church professional may be able to

---

[144]See Bibliographic entries under Early Pagan, Greek and Roman Music.
[145]See Bibliographic entries under Jewish Music Sources.
[146]See Bibliographic entries under Church Music and Drama.

understand better the methodology of music and worship practice in the Apocalypse and thereby find a way in which he or she can incorporate it into his or her present-day worship services.

# 2

# The Origin and Usage of Προσκυνέο

EIGHT Greek words occur in the New Testament which imply the process of worship. Of these, the most common forms are σέβομαι (*sebomai*—"to revere"), λειτουργία (*leitourgia*—"liturgy"), and λατρεία (*latreia*—"worship").[1] All eight words speak of a human response to the Lord and Maker of all creation. Inclusive in this list is προσκυνέο (*proskuneo*—verb: "worshiping"). It is the only word for worship used in the Book of Revelation.[2]

**Definitions**
The Greek word προσκυνέο (*proskuneo*) appears 58 times in the New Testament, with 23 of those occurrences in the Book of Revelation. Προσκυνέο (*Proskuneo*) is a compound of two roots: προς (*pros*) meaning "towards" and κυνέο (*kuneo*) meaning "to kiss."[3]

Κυνέο (*Kuneo*) is analogous to the Latin *os*, as in "osculate," or *ora*, as in "oral," "orate," and "adoration."[4] In combination, προς (*pros*) and κυνέο (*kuneo*) mean "to do obeisance to" and "to worship."[5] A note to Matthew 2:2 in the Revised Standard Version of

---

[1]Ralph P. Martin, *The Worship of God* (Grand Rapids, MI: William B. Eerdmans Publishing Company, 1982), 11.
[2]ECB, 1190.
[3]NED, 1247.
[4]WSE, 103.
[5]VGNT, 549.

31

the *Passages*, *IV*, says that the word denotes an "act of reverence, whether paid to man [*sic*] (Matthew 18:26) or to God (Matthew 4:10)."[6]

## Style of Writing and Syntax in Revelation
Professor Moulton says of the Hebraic style of Revelation

> that even the Greek of the Apocalypse itself does not seem to owe any of its blunders to Hebraism. The author's uncertain use of cases is obvious to the most casual reader... We find him perpetually indifferent to concord. But the less educated papyri give us plentiful parallels from a field whose Semitism cannot be suspected. Apart from places where he may be definitely translating a Semitic document, there is no reason to believe that his grammar would have been materially different had he been a native of Oxyrhynchus, assuming the extent of Greek education the same...[7]

Charles agrees and further states that he believes that the language of Revelation differs from that of the Septuagint and other versions of the Old Testament—from the Greek of the Apocrypha and the Pseudepigrapha to that of the papyri. Although the language of the Revelation is basically consistent with the standard Greek of its day, it nevertheless possesses a unique character. The most notable difference is the high number of solecisms[8] which occur in the Revelation text. Charles supposes the reasons for this could be that the writer purposefully "set at defiance" the grammarian and the ordinary rules of syntax. Because the writer was successful in this, Charles does not believe that the writer did it intentionally. Or, the writer of the Revelation wrote in Greek, but likely thought in Hebrew. Charles contends that the writer probably never mastered the Greek language idiomatically. Still, despite the numerous solecistic irregularities of its form and syntax, in the process of translation these difficulties

---

[6]NED, 1247.
[7]SIA, 79-80.
[8]An inconsistency in grammatical usage.

disappear leaving "its essential greatness alike in thought and expression."[9]

The writer uses προσκονενε (*proskonene*—present infinitive: "to worship") with the dative case and implies only the worship of God. When the accusative form is used in the text, it is rendered "homage" or a lesser form of worship is implied. Such a usage is consistent with Septuagint language, although Abbott showed that the Synoptics reserve the accusative case for the worship "due to God or God's Son."[10] In the Samaritan *Dialogue* and in the Temptation Narratives, the Synoptics employ "a deliberate differentiation of the two Greek constructions" (προσκυνενε [*proskunene*] is translated as the "worship of" in the accusative case and "prostration to" in the dative case). The Synoptic writers "appear to use προσκυνέο (*proskuneo*) with the accusative [case] as meaning that such worship should be paid to God alone."[11] In Ptolemic inscriptions it is used with the accusative case only and means "to do obeisance to" a god.[12]

Robertson indicates that προσκυνέο (*proskuneo*) can be used freely in both the accusative and the dative cases. He proposes no excuses for the syncretism of the cases as do Charles and Moulton. Robertson points out that προσκυνέο (*proskuneo*) occurs approximately 60 times in the New Testament with 30 instances in the dative case and 14 in the accusative case.[13]

In summary, the five positions mentioned of the use of προσκυνέο (*proskuneo*) in the Book of Revelation are: (1) Septuagint usage of προσκυνέο (*proskuneo*) in the dative case was reserved for the worship only of God or gods, while the verb in the accusative case was used "to pay homage" to a person; (2) Charles excuses the writer for his inconsistencies of syntax due to his supposed Hebraic background; (3) Moulton believes that the casual use of προσκυνέο (*proskuneo*) is either the prostrating of oneself before kings or queens, other superiors, or the gods and images of the people. Its use in either the dative or accusative cases was typical of the

---

[9]SIA, 81.

[10]R. H. Charles, *A Critical and Exegetical Commentary on the Revelation of St. John* (Edinburgh: T. & T. Clark, 1920), cxli.

[11]Ibid.

[12]VGNT, 549.

[13]GGNT, 476.

cross-cultural syntax of the first century Greek and Jewish worlds; (4) Abbott contends that the Synoptics reversed the Septuagint's usage; and (5) Robertson argues that προσκυνέο (*proskuneo*) was used indiscriminately in either case to render obeisance to a god or a person. It will be shown that Septuagint usage was normative for the writer of the Apocalypse.

## Origins of Its Usage
Origins of προσκυνέο (*proskuneo*) follow.

## Early Pagan
The earliest use of the root προς (*pros*) comes from the Oriental fashion of the physical κυνέο (*kuneo*) act of either throwing a kiss to the recipient or kissing his or her feet, his or her garment, or kissing the ground. The Persians performed this act to honor their deified kings or queens, and the Greeks performed this act before a god or deified image only.[14] The gesture of throwing a kiss is represented in Sumerian and Babylonian monuments which have been uncovered from ancient times.[15] Later, προσκυνέο (*proskuneo*) would come to signify merely a greeting of welcome and respect to a person, as well as an act of adoration and obeisance to a god.[16]

## Jewish
In the Septuagint, προσκυνέο (*proskuneo*) is the only translation of the Hebrew word *shetachavah* and the Aramaic words *sagad* and *segid*. All translate "to bow." Other Jewish uses imply a translation of "to the earth" or "to do obeisance." Most often the verb is used in respect to the worship of Yahweh or other gods, with the remaining percentage of the time owing to other people whom the chosen people honored or who appeared as the elect of Yahweh. By way of explanation, Greeven points out that what is appropriate for Yahweh is also appropriate for his chosen people. Even the most casual Hebraic use of προσκινεσις (*proskynesis*) to a person recognized "that the one thus honored is God's instrument."[17] Illustrative of this are the following

---

[14]GELNT, 716.
[15]GEL, 1518.
[16]Ibid.
[17]Heinrich Greeven, "Προσκυνεο (*Proskuneo*)," TDNT, 6:761.

examples: Moses before Jethro (Exodus 18:7); David three times before Jonathan (I Samuel 20:41); David before Solomon's ministers (I Kings 1:47); and Solomon before Bathsheba (I Kings 2:19). Other examples of προσκινεσις (*proskynesis*) before superiors follow: Jacob before Esau (Genesis 33:3-7); Jacob's sons before Joseph (Genesis 37:9; 42:6; 43:26, 28); the Egyptians falling down at Moses' feet to petition pardon (Exodus 11:8); David before Saul (I Samuel 24:9); Bathsheba and Nathan before David (I Kings 1:16, 23, and 31); and Ruth before Boaz (Ruth 2:10).[18]

Gestures of deference were common in the ancient world. "Bowing, kneeling, throwing a kiss, kissing someone's feet or the hem of someone's garment, biting the dust, or prostration" represented the recognition of the power of someone or something over another. The act of bowing or prostration expressed not merely a physical attitude but also a mental attitude of submission.[19]

The Hebraic *shetachavah* ("bowing down") and the Greek προσκυνέο (*proskuneo*) are linguistic equivalents. According to George E. Mendenhall:

> The symbolic action denoted by the Old Testament Hebrew term *shetachavah* (Greek equivalent—προσκυνέο [*proskuneo*]) consists of kneeling before the god or person having power, and then leaning forward until the face rests on the ground, or sometimes becoming completely prostrate. Sometimes the act is completed and acknowledged by the god's or king's placing his foot on the head or neck of the worshiper..."[20]

It is interesting to note that the Islamic term *mosque* is derived from the Arabic *masjid*, which means the "place of prostration."[21]

Wainwright appears to have a broader view of *shahah* (the root of *shetachavah*). He believes it covers both the Oriental idea of homage to one's superiors and the attitude of reverence towards a deity, in this

---

[18]Ibid., 6:760-761.

[19]WSE, 102.

[20]George E. Mendenhall, "Biblical Faith and Cultic Evolution," *The Lutheran Quarterly* (1953), 5:240.

[21]WSE, 103.

case, Yahweh. He points out that in New Testament times Jesus embodied both points of view within his resurrected body.[22]

Rabbinic Judaism utilized προσκινεσις (*proskynesis*) as an attitude of prayer. Though the standard of prayer in public is upright, when one prays in private it becomes one of physical prostration. Rabbinic Jews expand on this idea to include prostration before a rabbi, with the thought that those who study the teaching of the Torah have a particularly privileged relationship with Yahweh.[23]

Josephus generally followed the Septuagint in connoting προσκυνέο (*proskuneo*) to mean the worship of persons, gods or God. However, to differentiate between Jewish and non-Jewish worship, Josephus preferred to ascribe προσκυνέο (*proskuneo*) to the non-Jewish practice and to implement *serene, threskefene* and *timan* for Jewish worship. Also, while Josephus readily ascribed προσκυνέο (*proskuneo*) to Jewish kings and prophets, he restricted the honor he paid to other people of his day to one of mental acknowledgment only, without the physical gesture of prostrating himself before them.[24]

Philo disdained the worship of wealth and material power in the work of his day. He had no misgivings in ascribing obeisance to men or women, as the ten brothers to Joseph, etc., but he preferred to use προσκυνέο (*proskuneo*) only when relating to the veneration of holy things like the Temple, the Day of Atonement, and Holy Scripture. But in worshiping these material images, Philo recognized the potential idolatry in these, and he "censures men [sic] who have idolatrously yielded to the pomp and arrogance of city life."[25]

By the first century, Jewish thought, as per Josephus and Philo, ascribed προσκυνέο (*proskuneo*) only to a god or deified image alone. Προσκυνέο (*Proskuneo*) to persons was no longer practiced. This, προσκυνέο (*proskuneo*) had been transformed to a higher, more specifically spiritual dimension.

**Greek**
Originally, the word meant "nothing more than the Greek term for a phenomenon of Oriental life." Προσκυνέο (*Proskuneo*) was an act

[22]DOX, 47.
[23]Greeven, "Προσκυνέο (*Proskuneo*), TDNT, 6:763.
[24]Ibid., 6:762.
[25]Ibid., 6:763.

of "casting oneself to the ground." General consensus indicates that it originated in the Tragedians, with Persian origins presupposed. But those against this position argue that the Greeks would not have employed a term from another culture to express as high and noble a thought of their own worship, because the Greeks "rejected and regarded" this form of worship as "undignified." Secondly, there is no conclusive evidence to satisfy the debate of whether the "blown kiss to one of higher rank" is an original part of the gesture of προσκυνέο (*proskuneo*).[26]

The "adoration of chthonic deities"[27] provides an early source of the derivation of προσκυνέο (*proskuneo*): "the man [*sic*] who wants to honour an earth deity by kissing must stoop to do" it.[28] An example of the origins of προσκυνέο (*proskuneo*) can be found in Greek drama: Odysseus and Agamemnon prostrated themselves and kissed the earth after successful seaship landings.[29]

During the Tragedian period, the early usage of the physical act of prostration and kissing the earth was transformed directly to a mental or spiritually inward attitude. This is supported with documentation that shows that προσκυνέο (*proskuneo*) was used to express respect for the bow (archery) of Heracles (Hercules). Further evidence comes from the following examples: (1) an Aesulapius aretalogy[30] of the second century begins with an exact description of the process of healing; (2) a female slave from the second century in a letter to her master who became ill on a journey; and (3) from a son asking his father to correspond with him.[31]

**Early Church**

In the New Testament, προσκυνέο (*proskuneo*) occurs 58 times, with 23 occurrences in Revelation. The general tendency in New Testament thought is to deify the object of προσκυνέο (*proskuneo*). To utilize the verb with action towards something or someone not divine would

---

[26]Ibid., 6:759.

[27]The Greek gods that predate the Olympians.

[28]This pagan practice was probably the origin of the liturgical practice in Christianity of the "altar kiss," according to Franz Joseph Dölger in "Zu den Zeremonien der Messliturgie, II: der Altarkuss," *Antiqua Christiana*, (1930), 217-221.

[29]Greeven, "Προσκυνέο (*Proskuneo*)," TDNT, 6:759.

[30]The worship or praise of the gods of Aesulapius.

[31]Greeven, "Ποσκυνέο (*Proskuneo*)," TDNT, 6:759-760.

be "to devalue" the meaning. The word is found often in the Gospels, Acts, and Revelation, but generally is absent from the Epistles with the exception of Old Testament references in Hebrews 1:6, 11:16 and I Corinthians 14:25. The Corinthian passage is the only instance illustrating προσκινεσις (proskynesis) in the primitive Christian community. But Greeven argues that Paul's usage here is for the "unconditional subjection which the ἄπιστοσε [apistose— "unbeliever"] confesses."[32] By doing this, the Apostle Paul borrows the Old Testament usage of προσκυνέο (proskuneo).

While other New Testament passages, which refer to "kneeling for prayer (Acts 9:40, 20:36) and "raising the hands in prayer" (I Timothy 2:8), might appear by their physical action to imply προσκυνέο (proskuneo), it is interesting to note that the Greek word προσκυνέο (proskuneo) is not used. Its omission is consistent with New Testament usage. In the Gospels, Acts, and especially Revelation, προσκυνέο (proskuneo) is used only in the presence of the exalted Jesus.[33] New Testament authors are consistently careful to distinguish between the ministry of the man Jesus on the one hand and the resurrected Lord on the other. With the resurrected Christ, his lordship is recognizably manifested by the use of προσκυνέο (proskuneo) when he is addressed.[34]

A listing of the New Testament passages which incorporate προσκυνέο (proskuneo) supports the claim that the object, whether in the accusative of the dative cases, is generally always a divinity or a deified image:

(1)  God the Almighty
        Matthew 4:10
        Luke 4:7; 24:52
        John 4:20 (twice), 21, 22, 23, 24
        Acts 8:27; 24:11
        I Corinthians 14:25
        Hebrews 11:21
        Revelation 4:10; 5:14; 7:11; 11:1, 16; 14:7; 15:4; 19:4, 10; 22:8, 9

[32]Ibid., 6:763-765.
[33]Ibid., 6:765.
[34]DOX, 47.

(2) Jesus Christ
   Matthew 2:2, 8, 11; 8:2; 9:18; 14:33; 15:25; 20:20;
   28:9, 17
   Mark 5:6; 15:19
   John 9:38
   Hebrews 1:6
(3) A man (person)
   Matthew 18:26
   Acts 10:25
(4) The dragon
   Revelation 13:4
(5) The beast
   Revelation 13:4, 8, 12; 14:9, 11; 19:20; 20:4
(6) The image of the beast
   Revelation 13:15; 14:11; 16:2
(7) To demons
   Revelation 9:20
(8) To idols
   John 12:20
   Acts 7:43
(9) Satan
   Matthew 4:9
   Luke 4:8[35]

Other instances of προσκυνέο (*proskuneo*) appearing in the Greek world of the first century find the object to be in the idol-worshiping of polytheism and, particularly common, in the worship of angels.[36]

As the angel rebukes the writer of the Revelation in chapters 19 and 22, so Peter turns away the προσκινεσις (*proskynesis*) which Cornelius attempts to give him when he says in Acts 10:25 "I am too a man." When Jesus is met by the Samaritan woman in John 4:20-24, προσκυνέο (*proskuneo*) seems to take on a new meaning. It is implied in a wholly figurative sense because Jesus speaks of the act "in spirit and in truth." The previously restricted προσκυνέο (*proskuneo*), which is physically bound in place and gesture, is lifted to a new dimension—the realm of "spirit and truth." Jesus is perhaps

[35]NED, 1247.
[36]GELNT, 716.

ushering in the concept that there is no longer to be an exclusive place
of worship, though prayer, an element of worship, can still occur at
prescribed places and with "specific gestures."[37]

Reicke observes that "nowhere in the New Testament does
προσκυνέο (proskuneo) mean technical worship performed by
Christians on this earth." Reicke argues that because προσκυνέο
(proskuneo) involves physical directionality, those who had prostrated
themselves to Jesus during his lifetime suddenly had no place toward
which to turn after his final ascent to heaven.[38]

In the New Testament, there appeared to be a move from the idea
of God as a "conquering hero" (as he was perceived in the Old
Testament) to that of a "generous host" (through Jesus' atoning work).
In the ancient world, human worth was dependent upon the number of
slaves or subjects one had; thus, more slaves implied greater worth.
By the first century, the image of God appeared to have shifted and the
model was no longer "master/slave," but rather, "host/guest." The
good host was now measured in terms of his love for his guests. When
Christians gathered in the New Testament period, their characteristic
gesture towards Christ was not προσκινεσις (proskynesis).
Burkhart argues that προσκινεσις (proskynesis) is abandoned by
God, because God no longer seeks the abasement which
προσκινεσις (proskynesis) implied. It is Burkhart's contention that
the "salute" for New Testament Christians was the greeting shared
among the community of believers. The act of προσκινεσις
(proskynesis) was transformed from one of vertical obeisance to a
horizontal "holy kiss."[39] Προσκινεσις (proskynesis) was
transformed into ψιλέμα (philema), that is, abasement was replaced
by companionship. In his treatise on prayer, Tertullian spoke of the
"holy kiss." This "kiss of peace" (osculum pacis) was, according to
Tertullian, the "sealing of prayer" (signaculum orationis) for "what
prayer is complete without the bond of a holy kiss?"[40]

---

[37]Greeven, "Προσκυνέο (Proskuneo)," TDNT, 6:764.
[38]WSE, 104.
[39]Ibid.
[40]By the Seventh Ecumenical Council at Nicaea (787 C.E.) a differentiation between
τιμετικε προσινεσις (timelike proskenesis—physical prostration) and
αλετινε λατρεία (aletine latreia—true "spiritual" obeisance) will be made.
The former may be offered to icons and only the latter can be paid to the θεια
ψυσις (theia fusis—natural deity, "God"). See Greeven, "Προσκυνέο

Supported by Jewish thought of the first century, New Testament usage of προσκυνέο (*proskuneo*) witnessed two transformations: (1) προσκυνέο's (*proskuneo*) object was delimited to include only gods or deified images, and (2) the physical act, which earlier only "casually" implied spiritual assent, predominantly assumed an internally spiritual context. The act of physical prostration became obsolete for the writers of the Gospels and Acts.

**In the Book of Revelation**

All Apocalyptic literature contains a considerable amount of contemporary liturgical fragments, but none nearly so much as the Revelation. Underhill observes that in Revelation there is an example of the worship services of the Christian churches of Asia Minor in the late first century.[41] There existed a developed form of worship performed by the "whole company of the faithful" (generally congregational), and it was centered around and upon the altar of the Lamb. All of the participants were doing something. The "sensible accompaniments of an ordered cultus" (song, music, incense, ritual movements and prostration) were evident and "taken for granted." Thus, liturgical worship was a true part of primitive Christianity, at least ideally, "though we may suppose that the circumstances of the early church seldom allowed that ideal to find adequate expression."[42] Where else could the writer of the Apocalypse have obtained the liturgy that he used? And what would have appealed to his readers more than being told that the elements of their own familiar worship were used in heaven?[43]

Greeven's observation that the object of προσκυνέο (*proskuneo*) in Revelation is generally a deity, whether good or evil, can be witnessed in the following categorization:

| Addressed to: | Text: |
| --- | --- |
| God Almighty | 4:10 |
| The Lamb | 5:14 |
| God Almighty | 7:11 |

---

(*Proskuneo*)," TDNT, 6:765.
   [41]Evelyn Underhill, *Worship* (New York, NY: Harper and Row, 1936), 231.
   [42]Ibid., 55-91.
   [43]IB, 12:410.

| God—Temple | 11:1 |
| God Almighty | 11:16 |
| God the Creator | 14:7 |
| Lord God | 15:4 |
| God Almighty | 19:4 |
| Angel | 19:10 |
| Angel | 22:8 |
| God | 22:9 |
| Demons | 9:20 |
| Beast—Image | 14:9 |
| Beast—Image | 14:11 |
| Beast—Image | 16:2 |
| Beast—Image | 19:20 |
| Beast—Image | 20:4 |

*Revelation 4:10.* Before John's eyes the worship of heaven consisted of "constantly repeated προσκυνέο (*proskuneo*—see also Revelation 5:14; 7:11; 11:16; and 19:4).[44] Beasley-Murray contends, however, that it is more consistent with the idiomatic language to interpret "whenever" as a simple "when." This implies not an unbroken process of προσκυνέο (*proskuneo*), but rather, notable occasions when God "'comes' and manifests his sovereignty in judgement and redemption."[45]

Until this point in the Book of Revelation the elders have been silent observers. But now they "fall upon their knees and prostrate themselves on the floor of heaven" in "readiness" (preparation) to offer praises and their crowns of victory at the foot of the throne. Swete implies that this act of offering crowns is done either to pay homage to an overlord or to seek mercy from a conqueror. In Jabbuk 1:55, the Pharaoh and Kings of the Feast took off their crowns in the presence of Moses and Aaron. This was consistent with Old Testament usage. The crowns of the elders in Revelation are not σιασεματα (*siasemata*), but στεψανόι (*stefanoi*—"wreaths, crowns, rewards"), and thereby are symbols of victory and eternal life.[46] This supports the

---

[44]Greeven, "Προσκυνέο (*Proskuneo*)," TDNT, 6:764.

[45]G. R. Beasley-Murray, *New Century Bible: The Book of Revelation* (London: Marshall, Morgan & Scott, 1974), 118-119.

[46]ASJ, 74.

argument that Burkhart advances. Προσκυνέο (*Proskuneo*) is no longer concerned with the physical act of adoration or submission. For the writers of the New Testament, particularly the Apostle of the Apocalypse, προσκυνέο (*proskuneo*) had become embued with a higher spiritual notion which theses crowns of "victory" and "eternal life" connote. Προσκυνέο (*Proskuneo*) is the exclusive word used for "worship" in the Revelation. Other words which imply προσκυνέο (*proskuneo*) are "to bow down" and "to fall down." The former does not occur in Revelation, but the latter occurs once. In this verse the "four elders 'fall down' before him who is seated on the throne and worship him who lives for ever and ever;..." Because προσκυνέο (*proskuneo*) has been divorced from the physical act of "falling down," the writer specifically couples this action with the spiritualized προσκυνέο (*proskuneo*). The writer is fusing the spiritual act with the physical one.

*Revelation 9:20.* Both in the Old and New Testaments, heathen worship is regarded as paid to demons. New Testament thought rigorously maintained this old Hebrew protest against idol-worship. And though Paul proclaimed that "an idol is nothing in the world" (I Corinthians 8:4) and has no spiritual meaning, it was, however, a visible symbol of men's and women's revolt against God. The writer of the Apocalypse used Old Testament terminology here to exhibit his scorn for this demonic worship.[47]

*Revelation 11:16.* The angels, as they did in Revelation 11:1, and the elders, as creatures, share common προσκινεσις (*proskynesis*) before the throne.[48]

*Revelation 14:7.* God is established as the ultimate Creator, and as a result, all peoples of the earth are called to bow down and worship him.[49]

*Revelation 14:9.* Worship of the beast is always idolatry (see also Revelation 14:11; 19:20; and 20:4), whereas, worship of God is always selfless. The beast continually encourages self-indulgence, not so much for the reason that one should prostrate him or herself before Satan, but rather, to reject God. To worship Satan, self, or any other object or person is to reject God.

---

[47]Ibid., 125.
[48]Ibid., 142.
[49]James L. Blevins, *Revelation* (Atlanta, GA: John Knox Press, 1984), 68.

Both those who fear God and those who worship the dragon and the beast are called προσκυνουντες (*proskunountes* participle, third declension). At the end of the existence on this earth, however, "not only will [all] nations come and worship before God (Revelation 15:4), but those who serve Satan...will also come and worship before the angel of that [God's] church" (Revelation 3:9).[50]

*Revelation 15:4.* This passage looks forward to the time in which all nations will willingly προσκυνέο (*proskuneo*) in submission to God in the kingdom of Christ.[51]

*Revelation 16:2.* Those who choose to worship Caesar will bring upon themselves the ulcerous sores of their punishment.[52]

*Revelation 19:4.* All the peoples literally "...fell down on their faces."[53]

*Revelation 19:10.* The practice of προσκινεσις (*proskynesis*) can be seen from the "repeated rejection of this gesture by the interpreting angel" (see also Revelation 22:8). Why did John prostrate himself before the angel? Was John overcome with the majesty of the angel or did John misinterpret the angel's form as being the resurrected Christ? Swete says that John "can [could] scarcely mistake an angel for Christ or for God." In either case, John's error was soon corrected. Because angel-worship lingered long in Asia Minor, John's inclusion of this "reprimand" could say much to his audience. The obvious conclusion from the passage is that it is wrong to offer religious homage to an angel.[54]

*Revelation 22:8.* So "astounded by his [the] whole vision," the writer "not improbably entertained some suspicion that it was the Redeemer himself who had manifested himself to him."[55] Primasius agrees and maintains that the writer believed himself to be worshiping Christ even though the angel speaks in the "person of Christ."[56]

The angel rejects John's προσκινεσις (*proskynesis*) again. Swete says "still less can it be maintained that it is Christ who refuses

---

[50]Greeven, "Προσκυνέο (*Proskuneo*)," TDNT, 6:764-765.

[51]Beasley-Murray, *New Century Bible*, 236.

[52]Blevins, *Revelation*, 76.

[53]Fred. C. Conybeare, *The Armenian Version of the Revelation, Apocalypse of John* (Amsterdam: Philo Press, 1907), 49.

[54]ASJ, 248.

[55]Ibid., 458.

[56]Ibid., 304.

the worship." Swete concludes again, as he did in the previous passage, that the writer is discouraging angel-worship by the example of his own lapse.[57] It is implied that the writer should προσκυνέο (*proskuneo*) only to the ultimate deity, the Godhead. This remains consistent with the views previously concluded in the discussion of προσκυνέο (*proskuneo*) in the New Testament.

## Summary

The form of worship which προσκυνέο (*proskuneo*) implies has been traced from its earliest beginnings up through its usage in the early Christian church. Προσκυνέο (*Proskuneo*) is a compound of the two roots: προσ (*pros*) meaning "towards," and κυνέο (*kuneo*) meaning "to kiss." When united, the roots imply the honor, respect, and obeisance which an inferior demonstrates to a superior. The inconsistent use of syntax which προσκυνέο (*proskuneo*) experiences in the Apocalypse does not present a problem of consequence to Robertson, although Charles disagrees.

Early use of the word in the Semitic and non-Semitic world required a physical prostration before the one to whom προσκυνέο (*proskuneo*) was addressed. The object could be equally a god, king, or another person. But by the first century C.E., a transformation of the word seemed to occur. Prominent Jewish evidence, primarily from Josephus and Philo, tells of an initial discrimination in the use of προσκυνέο (*proskuneo*). Both scholars demonstrate a narrower application of the word which allows it to be enacted in front of either a deity, deified image, or kingly personage. No longer is προσκινεσις (*proskynesis*) implemented as "casually" as it had been before. It can no longer be directed to a "mere" person. New Testament thought acquiesces. Thus, the object of προσκυνέο (*proskuneo*) becomes a more specific personage. Both Apostles Peter and John illustrate this new use of προσκυνέο (*proskuneo*). For them this form of worship is worthy of only the ultimate and highest deity, the Godhead.

Another metamorphosis transpired in New Testament times: the purely physical προσκινεσις (*proskynesis*), which included prostration, acquired a thoroughly more prominent spiritual dimension.

---

[57]Ibid.

Jesus' ministry and resurrection together provide the transition from the physical (Jesus the Incarnate) προσκυνέο (*proskuneo*) to the spiritual (the resurrected Lord) use of the word. The Gospel writers and Paul illustrate this well as Burkhart points out. But Burkhart fails to recognize that the writer of the Apocalypse fuses the physical and spiritual continuum of προσκυνέο (*proskuneo*) together in his vision. For the writer of the Apocalypse, the highest form of spiritual worship includes physical activity.

## Conclusions

Although the writer of Revelation arguably may not have been a keen student of Greek syntax, he did, however, specifically employ προσκυνέο (*proskuneo*) to display the type or worship activity which he witnessed in his vision. Was the writer aware that the idiomatic usage of προσκυνέο (*proskuneo*) in the New Testament times excluded the physical act of prostration in favor of the spiritual, mentalized act of adoration and obeisance? It seems so, or why would the writer have included "falling down" with προσκυνέο (*proskuneo*) in Revelation 4:10?

What form of worship will be practiced in heaven through all eternity? Does John provide a hint as to what it will consist of? Some contend that John's visions are limited to what he had actually witnessed in the churches of his day; when he wrote his vision down he was idealizing contemporary worship practice of the first century. Perhaps the writer was attempting to revitalize the spiritual lives of the Christians in the churches of Asia Minor. However, one could contend that what John described was not limited to a summary of the best of worship practice of his day. Possibly what he transcribed was his "glimpse" into eternal heaven via the Holy Spirit. If so, then maybe his "glimpse" was merely coincidentally similar to the idealized practice of his day. In either case, it is clear that the writer's visions do require a balance between the physical and spiritual acts of worship. Inclusive in these finite and infinite realms are embodied the emotional, mental and social worshiper of God. To forego one for another is not complete worship.

The type of worship activity expressed in Revelation calls for a balance between physical, mental, social, emotional and spiritual worship. We are exhorted to examine our intellectual spiritualism and discern whether there is room for other expressions of worship activity.

The appeal of worship to our whole being seems to be desired by the writer of the Apocalypse. There needs to be more balance in the use of our minds, hearts, hands, and imaginations.

Music falls within the context of worship in the Book of Revelation. But this music no longer fills a functional void as it did in the early pagan, Jewish, Greek and Roman cultures preceding the early church. Functionalism gives way to music for worship which possesses a largely doxological character. Music and worship possess an "intrinsic spiritual quality."[58] While music can be regarded as a practical art, worship is an end in itself. But both seek a common end. They both seek "the experience of worship itself."[59] It is only in this environment that every worshiper truly will be able to focus solely on the Godhead.

---

[58]LeRoy Evert Wright, "The Place of Music in Worship," Ph.D. dissertation, Northwestern University, Evanston, IL, 1949, 329-343.

[59]Ibid., 342-343.

# 3

# Music Forms

WITHIN the Book of Revelation exist both direct and indirect references to music. In most cases these references are obvious, but in some instances they are not. This study seeks to determine differentiations of both music forms, performing groups (Chapter 4) and musical practice (Chapters 5) within the text of the Revelation. A sequential listing of all music and musical practices found in the Book of Revelation can be found in the Appendix. In the Book of Revelation two forms of music occur—the ode and the trumpet call.

## Ωδή *(Oda—"Ode")*

The exclusive Greek word used to imply "song" in the Book of Revelation is ώδή *(oda—*"ode"). Throughout ancient times, it was generally defined as "a fresh song of praise." Odes[1] were newly composed songs to commemorate special occasions. Generally synonymous with the terms ώδή *(oda)* and song in the time preceding the early church are hymns and psalms. A song is "a piece of music for voice or voices, whether accompanied or unaccompanied, or the act of singing."[2]

---

[1]ASJ, 80.
[2]Geoffrey Chew, "Song," NGD, 17:510.

**Early Pagan**
In early pagan times, an ode was a poem which was sung, usually to honor a special event or as part of a play. It was the generic term for song and could be performed either solo or chorally.[3]

Both solo singers and choral groups, accompanied by a variety of instruments, performed in the "private settings of the homes of nobility" as well as in sacred and secular courts. Extant evidence, however, cannot show whether vocal music predominated as a main cultural force in early pagan times, as it did in later Jewish times.[4]

**Jewish**
Jewish religious song consists primarily of psalms from the Temple tradition and hymns from domestic worship. Early instances of singing occurred around the golden calf (see Exodus 32:18-19). Later, instances of singing took place at secular occasions. When King Saul returned victorious following a battle with the Philistines, he found the Israelites singing and dancing (see I Samuel 18:6-7). By the time of King David, the music that was used in religious Temple observances had become codified.[5]

Jewish songs consist of religious songs of praise (doxological) or repentance, psalms, hymns, elegies, educational songs, plus all types of secular songs including cradle songs and children's songs. All of the foregoing types of songs are mentioned in the Old Testament.[6]

Traditional Jewish song can best be represented by the Book of Psalms. This collection of psalms implied various styles of performance based on their respective textual structures. These appear in later Christian practice (beginning from the second century A.D.) via the church's use of direct, responsorial and antiphonal psalmody and litanies with refrains.[7] But they also appear in the Book of Revelation.

The psalms can be classified into two categories:

(1) "I" and "we" royal psalms which contain a corporate personality; and

---

[3]Michael Tilmouth, "Ὠδή (Oda—'Ode')," NGD, 13:497.
[4]MAI, 40.
[5]Ibid., 167.
[6]Ibid., 169.
[7]Chew, "Song," NGD, 17:1512.

(2) Hymns of Praise. At the heart of the hymns of praise is the idea that the congregation, while singing them, is in the presence of the Almighty. Characteristic of hymns of praise are:
   (a) the exhortation to sing praise to God;
   (b) the exhorters are mentioned;
   (c) the laudatory attributes of God are mentioned; and
   (d) reference is made to Yahweh's special deeds in history.[8]

Traditional Jewish and Christian interpretation held that the psalms had "a more private, individual origin" and, consequently, had no place in public worship. Mowinckel says that scholars, such at Wette, Wellhausen and Briggs, believe that the psalms originated from individual life experiences. However, Smend[9] found a "poetical personification" of the corporate Jewish body in the "I" psalms. He called his theory the "collective I" psalm. Through the "form-historical" (*formgeschichtliche*) and "type-critical" (*gattungsgeschichtliche*) methods, Hermann Gunkel was able to prove that much of the psalm poetry of the Jewish tradition could be found in the public religious rites of the people, not in their individual experiences. Various types of psalms were composed which recalled the acts of Yahweh as He dealt with the Jewish body as a whole.[10]

Psalm singing provided the bridge to higher aesthetic artforms for the Israelites. According to Riehm

Psalm-singing was the starting point for the higher development of Jewish music. Like poetry, tonal art, too, was governed by

---

[8]DH, 7.

[9]Julius Smend, *Vorträge und Aufsätze zur Liturgik hymnologie und kirchenmusik*, trans. by Sigmund Mowinckel (Guetersloh: C. Bertelsmann, 1925).

[10]PIW, 12-13. See also Walter Brueggermann, *The Message of the Psalms: A Theological Commentary* (Minneapolis, MN: Augsburg Old Testament Studies, 1984); Brueggermann, *Abiding Astonishment: Psalms, Modernity and the Making of History* (Westminster: John Knox Press, 1991); Patrick D. Miller, Jr., *Interpreting the Psalms* (Minneapolis, MN: Augsburg Press, 1986); Clinton J. McCann, *A Theological Introduction to the Book of Psalms: The Psalms as Torah* (Nashville, TN: Abingdon Press, 1993); Claus Westermann, *The Living Psalms*, trans. by J. R. Porter (Grand Rapids, MI: William B. Eerdmans Publishing Company, 1989); and Westermann, *The Psalms: Structure, Content and Message*, trans. by Ralph D. Gehrke (Minneapolis, MN: Augsburg Fortress, 1980).

the supreme influence of religion; therefore, singing and playing have had primarily a serene, solemn, but by no means dull or gloomy character.[11]

The primitive Psalter became the "liturgical hymnal of Israel." In early Temple practice, psalms were performed by the Levitical singers as soloists and grouped in choirs. As time transpired, Sendrey speculates silent worshipers desired to participate more actively in order to satisfy a longing. Initially, the participation by the laity consisted of single word acclamations. In time, the acclamations became refrains. This process could illustrate the beginning of active lay participation in liturgical singing. From this practice developed the antiphonal and responsorial styles. This is speculative as there are signs that psalmody was congregational from its origins in both tabernacle and Temple worship.

The Psalter contains the following hymns: Psalms 8, 19, 29, 33, 46, 47, 48, 76, 104, 135, 136, and 145-150. Other hymns in the Old Testament are found in Amos 4:22, 13; 5:8; and 9:5. Two main types of hymns exist in Jewish tradition:

(1) a general type of hymn which singles out Yahweh's lasting qualities and glorious deeds (see Psalm 136); and

(2) a specific type of hymn which directs its attention to a particular feature of Yahweh or one of his acts (see Psalms 46, 48, 76 and 114).[12]

Occasionally, hymns end with a short wish or prayer for the "future prosperity of the congregation" (see Psalms 29:11; 104:3; and 135:19). This prayer or wish was usually general in nature. Hymns were recited and accompanied by stringed instruments, cymbals and the flute (see Psalms 150). Hymns were also accompanied by cultic dance.[13]

The hymns of Israel "clearly show its [their] place of origin to the holy place." The hymn belonged in the cultic festival where the people congregated and witnessed Yahweh's presence and repeated his mighty

---

[11]Eduard Carl August Riehm, *Handwoerterbuch das biblischen Altertums*, trans. by Alfred Sendry (Bielefeld and Leipzig, 1893-1894), 1029.

[12]PIW, 81-85.

[13]Ibid., 89.

acts. Hymns were later used in the daily rites of the "great temples" (see Psalm 89:17; I Chronicles 9:33; and Sirach 47:8). They also played a major role in the daily morning sacrifices, in Temple processions and around the altar (Psalms 24 and 118). Within Jewish corporate religious practice, the hymn always had a "prominent place." The Book of Psalms is often referred to as "hymns of praise."[14]

A constantly recurring theme in the "hymns of praise" is creation, where Yahweh demonstrated his "omnipotence, wisdom and loving kindness." Yahweh is revealed in nature throughout the psalms. He is shown in storms, thunder and lightning, fire and earthquakes. Yahweh is represented in nature to show his "awful majesty, his merciful care and his flaming wrath when he comes to judge his enemies." Yahweh's mighty voice continues to be able to "ring out...thunder."[15]

Sacred singing poured over into more private settings. It became common to sing at the Passover celebration in the home. The use of the *Hallel* (Psalms 113-118) in this setting is an example of the domestic use of psalms.[16]

The Song of Moses (see Revelation 15:3-4) was regularly sung at each Sabbath evening's worship in the synagogue as a remembrance of the time when Yahweh had delivered his people from the land of Egypt (see Exodus 15:2-18).[17] This social event caused the people to burst into antiphonal and responsorial song, and it also resulted in Miriam's leading the women in dancing.[18] Because this particular song originated uniquely in the Jewish faith, it had no connections whatsoever with pagan ritual, other than the fact that both sacred and secular incidents of a significant nature in the life of any corporate body of people were often commemorated or memorialized in song.

The "talent for improvisation of [or by a] Jewish singer" was continually mentioned or alluded to in the Old Testament. Specific reference to "the prophesying of the prophets with a psaltery and a harp" (I Samuel 10:5, 19:20; and II Kings 3:15) were probably

---

[14]Ibid., 89-90.

[15]Ibid., 101.

[16]MAI, 172-174.

[17]Robert E. Coleman, *Songs of Heaven* (Old Tappan, NJ:  Fleming H. Revell Company, 1975), 176.

[18]MAI, 72, 167.

instances of improvised music. However, the practice of free improvisation in the doxological sense in subsequent Christian liturgy has no support. This is due to the fact that the music of the Temple came about on a "rigorously traditional basis." No portion of the sacred ceremonies was left to chance. They were programmed meticulously in every detail. The freedom to improvise simply did not exist in the Temple tradition.[19]

The psalms and hymns of the Jewish traditions in the period 100 B.C.E. to C.E. 200 which directly influenced the early church are the *Psalms of Solomon*, *Qumran Hoduyoth*, the *Hellenistic Synagogal Prayers* and the *Odes of Solomon*. Although the canonical Old Testament in Hebrew (the Masoretic Bible) is composed of 150 psalms, modern scholarship has uncovered five more psalms of David and a part of a sixth (Psalm 151B). Four of them (Psalms 151A, 151B, 154 and 155) are present in the Qumran Scrolls and date from the first half of the first century C.E. Because five more psalms of David are contained within the Qumran Psalter, it is conjectured that the entire Psalter was basically set by the second century B.C.E.[20]

The *Psalms of Solomon* number 18 and are the response of the Jewish people to the capture of Jerusalem in the first century B.C.E. by the Romans. Modern scholarship asserts that the odes of Solomon represent very early Christian hymns. Although the character and tone of them appears Jewish, it is evident that their content is inherently Christian. They exhibit the Christian characteristics of a "joyous tone of thanksgiving for the Advent of the Messiah who had been promised" (see 7:1-6 and 41:3-7) and "for the present experience of eternal life and love from and for the Beloved" Savior (see 3:1-9; 11:1-24; 23:1-3; 26:1-7; and 40:1-6). The *Odes of Solomon* date from the late first to the early second century C.E.[21]

*Pseudo-Philo* 32:1 demonstrates a Jewish faith familiar with hymnody: "Then Deborah and Barak the son of Abino and all the people together sang a hymn to the Lord on that day, saying..." In *Testament of Job* 14:1-5, hymns are accompanied by a lyre.

---

[19] Ibid, 150-151.
[20] OTP, 2:607-609. Old Testament pseudepigraphal passages are taken from this two-volume compilation.
[21] Ibid., 2:639, 725.

And I used to have six psalms and a ten-stringed lyre. I would
rouse myself daily after the feeding of the widows, take the lyre
and play for them. And they would chant hymns. And with the
psaltery I would remind them of God so that they might glorify
the Lord. If my maidservants ever began murmuring, I would
take up the psaltery and strum as payment in return. And thus
I would make them stop murmuring in contempt (see a parallel
reference in Job 21:12).

Other examples of hymns in Old Testament Pseudepigrapha are found
in *Joseph and Aseneth* 14:8; 16:20-22; 18:9; and 21:10-21.

### Greek
In Greek aesthetic philosophy, music occurred at "the height of the
intensity of feeling and excitement" when the spoken word could
proceed no further. Music alone was able "to express the emotions
when the deeply stirred soul of man [*sic*] can [could] utter only
inarticulate cries."[22]

Although Greek sources weigh more heavily toward instrumental
music than vocal, it cannot be assumed that instrumental music stood
apart from vocal music. In fact, while vocal music was the constant or
the given in Greek society, instrumental music provided the variable
element. While chanted or sung words provided the liturgy,
instrumental accompaniment provided the ταλεα (*talea*--"color").[23]

Basically, all of the extant ancient songs are of Greek origin and
come from the Hellenistic period. Although the quantity is small,
"certain limited conclusions" can be drawn from the literary and art
sources from the period. From these sources it is possible to ascertain
the types of songs which were performed and to speculate about the
method of accompaniment. The chief type of song employed in Greece
before 700 B.C.E. was the oral bardic tradition of epic song. Other
simpler functional songs were used which were "presumably
unrehearsed and often sung by a leader with choral refrains." These
types of songs can be found in Greek, Roman and Old Testament
Jewish literature. These songs were basically secular in character and

[22]Paul Henry Lang, *Music in Western Civilization* (New York, NY: W. W. Norton
and Company, Inc., 1941), 12.
      [23]TSB, 331.

consisted of work songs, lullabies, victory songs, songs for weddings and funerals, and songs of a mocking and/or satirical nature. These kinds of songs were later absorbed into the art music of Greece.[24]

Beginning in the seventh century B.C.E., accompanied song was lyric, either for solo or choral groups, and accompanied by either the lyre or the *aulos*. Solo lyric song or monody could relate to the modern strophic song which represents the "personal feelings of the composer in a series of shortish stanzas identical in metre [*sic*]."[25]

Choral lyric song was characteristically religious in nature and included dancing. It expressed the feelings of a community or city-state. It consisted of elaborate patterns (*systemata*) "of strophe, antistrophe and epode, and the component parts were much longer than the stanzas of choral [*sic*] lyric [song],"[26] Both solo lyric song and choral lyric song were the main original elements in Greek drama from the fifth century B.C.E.

The Greek ode is a generic term for song. Choral odes became very important in early Greek drama. Odes were classified by the Greeks according to their respective function rather than their structure: Paean; Epinikian; Threnody; Dithyramb; Hyporchema; Encomuim; and Parthenian. Paean and Hyporcheman odes were used at festivals to honor the Greek god Apollo or a city. Encomuim odes were sung to honor a guest at a banquet. Parthenian odes served as processional hymns, and Epinikian odes were performed to celebrate either war or Olympian victories.[27]

By the late fifth century B.C.E., a "new music" tolerated "unprecedented modal and rhythmic variety." It also allowed for instrumental interludes and melismatically set texts (pathogenic). Prior to this time the music always served the text (logogenic). Evidence indicates that this "new music," however, was not "universally adopted."[28]

The song up to the fifth century B.C.E. exerted the most influence on music of subsequent centuries. The music of the Hellenistic period was considered too decadent. From the Hellenistic period the song of

[24]Chew, "Song," NGD, 17:511.
[25]Ibid.
[26]Ibid.
[27]Tilmouth, "Ode," NGD, 13:497.
[28]Chew, "Song," NGD, 17:511-512.

the Greek theater spread to Rome and elsewhere, and song composition reached a high point in the *cantica* of the comedies of Plautus.[29]

## Roman

The Roman religion believed that music had magical qualities. Companies (*sodalitates*) of priests known as the *salii* flourished in the Era of the Kings (ca. 750-510 B.C.E.). By Imperial times (the Early Republic 509-265 B.C.E.), this group consisted of 12 members of nobility. A lead singer (*vates*) and a lead dancer (*praesul*) performed archaic militaristic dances and responsorial *carmina* (songs) in honor of the Roman gods Mars and Quirinus. Numerous folksongs and work songs were used in common everyday situations. They included table songs, songs of mourning, lullabies, nursery rhymes, soldier's victory songs, birthday and wedding songs, songs of love and joy, and songs of satire. From the middle of the third century B.C.E., Roman theatrical music was influenced heavily and increasingly by the Greek theater.[30]

## Early Church

An important event in the gathering together of the early church was corporate singing. Pliny was asked by Emperor Trajan in the early second century if he knew of "any possible crimes" which the Christians might be guilty of. Pliny wrote

> The sum total of their guilt or error amounted to no more than this, they had met regularly before dawn on a fixed day to chant verses alternately among themselves in honor of Christ as if to a god, and also to bind themselves by oath, not for any criminal purpose, but to abstain from theft, robbery and adultery, to commit no breach of trust and not to deny a deposit when called upon to restore it. After this ceremony it had been their custom to disperse and reassemble later to take food of an ordinary harmless kind.[31]

---

[29]Ibid.

[30]Guenter Fleischhauer, "Rome," NGD, 16:147.

[31]F. Forrester Church and Terrance J. Mulry, *Earliest Christian Hymns* (New York, NY: Macmillan Publishing Company, 1988), ix.

Ephesians 5:19 provides evidence that perhaps the early church differentiated between various types of song: psalms, hymns and spiritual songs. The early church borrowed the psalms from the Jewish tradition. They used hymns of the Jewish and Greek cultures. And perhaps the spiritual songs were original musical compositions composed within the early church. They were the "new songs" which spoke of the "new" work which Christ had accomplished at the cross and resurrection. But Martin says of both the Ephesians 4:19-20 and Colossians 3:16 passages that it is

> hard to draw any hard-and-fast distinction between these terms; and modern scholars are agreed that the various terms are used loosely to cover the various forms of musical composition. 'Psalm' may refer to Christian odes patterned in the Old Testament Psalter. 'Hymns' would be longer compositions and there is evidence that some actual specimens of these hymns may be found in the New Testament itself. 'Spiritual songs' refer to snatches of spontaneous praise which the inspiring Spirit placed on the lips of the enraptured worshipper, as I Corinthians 14:15 implies. These 'inspired odes' would no doubt be of little value, and their contents would be quickly forgotten.[32]

The "psalms, hymns and spiritual songs" mentioned in Ephesians 5:19 and Colossians 3:16 "were probably unaccompanied," for

> the poor and frequently clandestine Christian assemblies can hardly have boasted instruments. If stringed music (*phallein*) is referred to, it is 'in the heart only.'[33]

As a Greek word, "hymn" needed neither to be religious nor sung by a corporate body. It was nothing more than a

> song of a serious kind making use of poetry and music in a way which tends to exalt the mind of the singer and listener towards

---

[32]Ralph P. Martin, *Worship in the Early Church* (Grand Rapids, MI: William B. Eerdman's Publishing Company, 1964), 47.

[33]C. F. D. Moule, *Worship in the New Testament* (Richmond, VA: John Knox Press, 1961), 65.

lofty subjects—whatever subject may be recognized by that particular community as lofty.[34]

In the early church the hymn was not always a congregational song.[35]
Hymns are "a kind of song; but they differ from a professional song, or an art-song, in being songs for unmusical people to sing together."[36]  Routley defines hymn tunes for the early church as "the folksongs of the Christian faith."[37]  Because hymns are "communal" songs, they are much like folksongs.  People care little who composed folksongs; consequently, people have little critical concern about them.  As a result, people have little appreciation for folksongs in comparison to the appreciation which a professional musician would exhibit toward them.[38]

Early church hymns "appear to have been sung from a very early date"[39] in the first century.  Textual evidence points directly to Jesus' singing of a hymn at the supper in the upper room (see Matthew 26:30).  Jesus' utilization of a hymn (probably the Jewish *Hallel*) in this setting leads one to believe that this was not a new practice for Jesus and the disciples.

Within a generation after Pentecost, Christians were singing hymns regularly.  Before this time they had primarily sung psalms.  When the writer wrote the Apocalypse, he chose to "punctuate the narrative with snatches of ceremonious poetry (see Revelation 5:13).[40]  Routley contends that the writer "may" have quoted what was familiar to his audience (the Christians in Asia Minor), but even if he did not, the writer was quoting what he knew they would perceive as being a familiar style.[41]  The most hymnic sections in the New Testament are

[34]Erik Routley, *Christian Hymns Observed* (Princeton, NJ: Prestige Publications, Inc., 1982), 5.
[35]Ibid.
[36]Ibid., 1.
[37]Ibid., 4.  See also Lionel Adey, *Hymns and the Christian "Myth,"* (Vancouver: University of British Columbia Press, 1986); Adey, *Class and Idol in the English Hymn* (Vancouver: University of British Columbia Press, 1986); and F. Forrester Church and Terrance J. Mulry, *Earliest Christian Hymns* (New York, NY: Macmillan Publishers Company, 1988).
[38]Ibid., 1.
[39]Chew, "Song," NGD, 17:512.
[40]Routley, *Christian Hymns Observed*, 5-7.
[41]Ibid., 7.

Ephesians 4:14; I Timothy 3:16; Philippians 2:6-11; Colossians 1:15-20; Hebrews 1:3;[42] and Ephesians 5:14 (an ancient baptismal hymn).[43] According to St. Augustine

> hymns are praises to God with song. Hymns are songs containing praises to God. If it is praise, and not to God, it is not a hymn; if it is praise, and to God, but it is not sung, it is not a hymn. It is essential therefore that, if it is a hymn, it have these three qualities: praise, and to God, and song.[44]

According to McKinnon, however, Augustine refers to "a category of psalm not a non-biblical hymn"[45] with the above definition. Similarly, Augustine further states

> Would you know what a hymn is? It is song with praise to God. If you praise God, and do not sing, you speak no hymn; if you sing, but you do not praise God, you speak no hymn; if you praise something which does not pertain to the praise of God, even if you are singing praises you speak no hymn. A hymn therefore has those three qualities: song, and praise, and to God.[46]

Historically, however, these definitions come too late. Originally, in early pagan and Jewish times a hymn was simply a song of praise. The Hebrew pattern of hymnody consisted of (1) the thesis which recognized the Creator God; (2) the antithesis which focused on mankind's dilemma; and (3) the synthesis which spoke of man's righted relationship with Yahweh. This pattern was used early in the psalms and was consequently employed in the early church where it

---

[42]Martin, *Worship in the Early Church*, 47.

[43]Moule, *Worship in the New Testament,* 58.

[44]Augustine, *Enarrationes in Psalmis* (Psalm 72:1), as quoted in R. C. Trench, *Synonymns of the New Testament* (Grand Rapids, MI: W. B. Eerdmans Publishing Company, 1958), 298.

[45]James McKinnon, *Music in Early Christian Literature* (Cambridge: Cambridge University Press, 1987), 158.

[46]Trench, *Synonyms*, 298.

incorporated the crucifixion and resurrection of Christ.[47] Werner states that

> the few hymnic passages of the New Testament were considered canticles in the early church...[and] are generally recognized to be, in spirit as well as in form, a direct continuation of Old Testament poetry or apocryphal verses, such a Ecclesiastes 51. At which point then, is it proper to speak of hymnody? Later fragments such as the communion hymn of the *Didache* or the poetic part of the *Epistle to Diogentus* can here be mentioned only in passing, since they were, in all probability, not rendered musically.[48]

The Apostle Paul distinguished between canonical poems and free hymns (see the Prayer of Jesus in the apocryphal Acts of John).[49] Several authors, such as Joerns[50] and Harris,[51] have indicated that as many as 30 hymns occur within the confines of the Revelation. Apparently, these authors have assumed a very liberal definition of the term hymn, perhaps as "...original, spontaneous outbursts of religious emotion."[52]

We may assume that the early church sang songs at their services. Some were newly improvised solos (see I Corinthians 14:26), while others had refrains on which others could join in singing. Consequently, the early church reflected the *Imago Dei* ideal by composing songs for use in worship. Berkouwer describes the narrow *Imago Dei* as "the image of God in man as it is restored in Christ."[53] Routley theorizes that extended congregational works did not exist in

---

[47]Carl F. Price, "Hymn Patterns," reprinted for the "Hymn Society of America" from *Religion in Life* (New York, NY: Abingdon-Cokesbury Press), Summer 1947, 6.

[48]TSB, 207.

[49]Ibid., 208.

[50]Klaus-Peter Joerns, *Das Hymnische Evangelium Untersuchungen zu Aufbau, Funktion und Herkunft der hymnischen Stücke in der Johannesoffenbarung* (Goettingen: G. Mohn, 1971).

[51]Michael Anthony Harris, "The Literary Function of Hymns in the Apocalypse of John" (Ph.D. dissertation, The Southern Baptist Theological Seminary, 1988).

[52]Ibid., 250.

[53]G.C. Berkouwer, *Man: The Image of God* (Grand Rapids, MI: William B. Eerdmans Publishing Company, 1962), 99.

the early church because they would not have easily been memorized. They would have had to have been written down, and no extant manuscripts have been unearthed.[54] But this begs the question that in non-literate societies, the capacity to memorize extended accounts was prodigious.

**In the Book of Revelation**
The exclusive word used specifically in the original Greek text of the Revelation is ῷδή (*oda*). This study has already related the manner in which the ῷδή (*oda*) has come down through the divergent music cultures studied, that is, the psalms of the early Babylonians could have been passed along to the Jewish faithful. From there they were passed into the early church. The songs of early tradition became odes in the Greek culture. The odes of Revelation have been interpreted in modern times as hymns. Because the writer of the Apocalypse does not distinguish between ode, song, hymn and psalm as music forms in the text, it could be assumed that differentiation was unnecessary. For the writer of the Apocalypse, perhaps the terms ode, song, hymn and psalm were synonymous. Smith agrees.[55] In order to differentiate the possible vagaries of distinction, an in-depth textual study would need to be done—as Harris, Carnegie[56] and others have attempted. Such a study is outside the scope of the present research.

Mowry focuses on the "four utterances of hymnic character" in Revelation 4 and 5. Mowry contends that three of these four passages rely on Old Testament texts and are consequently "linked" with Jewish worship services of the first century C.E. They are:

(1) Revelation 4:8 sung by the four beasts. The Old Testament parallel is Isaiah 6:3;
(2) Revelation 4:11 sung by the 24 elders. Its Old Testament reference is found in Psalms 19:1;

---

[54]Routley, *Christian Hymns Observed*, 7.

[55]J. A. Smith, "First-Century Christian Singing and Its Relationship to Contemporary Jewish Religious Songs," *Music and Letters*, 75(1994):9-10.

[56]David R. Carnegie, "Worthy Is the Lamb: The Hymns in Revelation," *Christ the Lord: Studies in Christology Presented to Donald Guthrie*, edited by H. H. Rowdon (Leicester: Intervarsity Press, 1982).

(3) Revelation 5:9-10 and 12 which is performed antiphonally between the four creatures and the 24 elders. Because it is a "new" song, no earlier scripture passage is alluded to; and

(4) Revelation 5:13b is intoned by all creatures in heaven and on earth. The biblical reference is Psalms 41:13.[57]

Hymn and psalm texts from the Temple and Synagogue traditions used in Revelation (see 4:8, 11; 11:17, 18; 14:7; and 15:3-4) were "borrowed directly from the synagogue (sic, Jewish tradition) of the Greek-speaking Jewish world" and adapted to the early Church. The focus of these songs was to

> the holy and righteous God of Judaism which is extolled...in the synagogue liturgy as Creator and Sustainer of the world, and Judge of all.[58]

In Revelation 14:3 the "new song" is sung by the ζοα (zoa—"the creatures") and the elders. They represent Creation and the Church. This song is actually sung before them and, consequently, not by them. It is sung by the angels. Although the angels do not benefit from the redemptive work of Christ, they appear to be seriously concerned for the salvation of humanity (see Ephesians 3:10 and I Peter 1:12). The angels lead the "new song" which "the redeemed themselves have yet but imperfectly learnt."[59] It is not easily sung by the 144,000 either. The "music of the heart" (see Ephesians 5:19 and Colossians 3:16) cannot "be acquired without a receptivity which is a Divine gift."[60]

The "new song" symbolized Christ's completed work. This song attests to the fact that through his work he has purchased all people of all races: "new works of grace call forth new songs of praise."[61] The "newness" of this song is akin to "a qualitative sense of something previously unknown, unprecedented, [and] marvelous."[62]

---

[57]Lucetta Mowry, "Revelation 4-5 and Early Christian Liturgical Usage," *Journal of Biblical Literature*, 71(1952):77.

[58]Martin, *Worship in the Early Church*, 45-46.

[59]ASJ, 178.

[60]Ibid.

[61]Ibid., 82.

[62]Coleman, *Songs of Heaven*, 45.

The new song is characterized by "stainless souls" who produce "stainless beauty."[63] New songs are also mentioned in Psalms 33:3; 40:3; 96:1; 98:1; 99:9; and Isaiah 42:10. These songs may be "mystical songs unable to be learned by those who are not advanced in prayer,"[64] a reference to the saints who can "know" the songs of the angels as Job's daughters did (see *Testament of Job*).

In Revelation 5:9 and 14:3 the descriptive word of song is καινός (*kainos*—"new"). This adjective refers to character and form implying the new form and character which the eschatological songs will consist of. The Song of Moses celebrated the deliverance of the Jews from the hands of their oppressor; the "new song of Christ" in Revelation celebrates the redemption of the once-for-all atoning work of Jesus Christ.[65] Καινός (*Kainos*) is "not new in time...but new as to (its) form or quality, of different nature from what is constrasted as old."[66] It is the Greek word νέος (*neos*) which "signifies (something) new in respect of time, that which is recent; it is used of the young."[67]

The writer of the Apocalypse "draws heavily upon the periods of the most active miraculous activity in the Old Testament." God's omnipotence, omniscience and reality are recalled, and God's final victory is praised by the worshipers. "Visions and words of praise" recall God's previous deeds. But the doxological praise of Revelation does not end there. The Song of Moses is transformed into a new song. New acts of God are commemorated in new song.[68]

A "great chorus of believers" is pictured standing by a sea of glass (see Revelation 15:3-4). In their hands are harps of gold which they played "to accent their songs of praise." The Song of Moses is transformed into the Song of the Lamb.[69] Just as Moses delivered his people from the hands of Pharaoh, so the resurrected Lamb delivers his people from the hands of eternal damnation.

---

[63]IB, 469.

[64]J. Massyngberde Forde, ed., *The Anchor Bible: Revelation* (Garden City, NY: Doubleday and Company, Inc., 1975), 233.

[65]VED, 3:109.

[66]Ibid.

[67]Ibid.

[68]Ferrell Jenkins, *The Old Testament in the Book of Revelation* (Marion, IN: Cogdill Foundation Publications, 1972), 71.

[69]Coleman, *Songs of Heaven*, 122-124.

## Trumpet Call

Both the use of and the sound of the trumpet figure predominantly in the Apocalypse. The trumpet call is the foundation of trumpet melody, whether it be used as a royal fanfare or as a military signal.[70]

### Early Pagan

Many musical traditions of antiquity lay claim to having invented the trumpet. Altenburg hypothesizes a simple reason for this: a plethara of sizes, shapes, materials and performance practices existed for this instrument.[71] The Jewish tradition claims that Jubal invented it; others say the Egyptians or the Etruscans created it. The second century historian Pliny wrote that Piseus, an Etruscan king, invented it in the year 2951 of the creation of the world (or the year 260 before the founding of Rome).[72] Tarr states that the trumpet (Greek is σάλπινχ [salpinx], and Roman is lituus, tuba, buccina or cornu) was inherited from the Etruscans.[73]

The term trumpet comes from the Latin tremor, which literally means "a trembling or vibrating."[74] Tarr describes it as "a lip-vibrated aerophone."[75] The tone is produced via "a column of air that becomes "excited (i.e., caused to be set in vibration,...) by a player's lips...."[76] The majority of ancient trumpets were "short, straight instruments of wood, bronze or silver and used for both military and ceremonial purposes."[77]

The Etruscans contributed the use of brass instruments for military purposes,[78] and the Romans expanded this concept.[79] Sumerian straight trumpets were played by Assyrian soldiers.[80]

---

[70]THM. 35.
[71]EIHM, 6.
[72]Ibid., 3-4.
[73]Edward H. Tarr, "Trumpet," NGD, 19:214.
[74]HMI, 73.
[75]Tarr, "Trumpet," NGD, 3:639.
[76]MHBT, 21.
[77]Tarr, "Trumpet," NGD, 19:214.
[78]Homer Ulrich and Paul A. Pisk, A History of Music and Musical Style (New York, NY: Harcourt Brace and World, Inc. , 1963), 25.
[79]Hugh Milton Miller, History of Music (New York, NY: Barnes and Noble, Inc., 1960), 4.
[80]HMI, 73.

The Egyptian trumpet was made of a "yellow" metal. It was cone-shaped with a distinct mouthpiece and exhibited a "rather wide" bell. It was two feet in length and tuned similarly as the modern cornet.[81] Because the sound was so penetratingly loud and shattering, Egyptian police required that the trumpet could be played only in "barracks outside the city."[82] Plutarch commented that it sounded like an "ass's bray." An extant pictorial representation dated 1415 B.C.E. shows that it was used by soldiers. It was also used in the sacred worship of the Egyptian god Osiris.[83]

Extant Egyptian reliefs and paintings dating from the fifteenth century B.C.E. have been confirmed by the finding of two trumpets in the tomb of King Tutankhamen. Both trumpets have short expanding tubes with a funnel bell. The longer trumpet (58 cm.) is made of silver, and the shorter trumpet (49.4 cm.) is constructed of sheet bronze with partial gold plating. The bells are both engraved with the King's name and also the emblems of various successful military units of the time.[84]

The Assyrians used a trumpet similar to that of the Egyptians. An example in a Sennacherib relief shows a pair of trumpeters. One is playing while the other is resting.[85]

### Jewish

The Hebrew term for trumpet is *chazozrah*, not *jobel keren* (the Chaldean *shofar*). The *shofar* is variously translated to be a cornett, trombone or a rams horn (which Jubal invented).[86]

The trumpet was known by the time of Moses (born ca. 2372 B.C.E.). Yahweh commanded Moses (see Numbers 10:2) to construct two silver trumpets, and he gave one to each of Aaron's sons, Eleazar and Ithamar. The sons of Aaron used them to lead solemn religious ceremonies out of doors. Moses taught that the trumpet was to be used for only sacred purposes and, consequently, it was to be played only by the priests. It was stored in the "hut" of either Moses or Aaron.[87]

---

[81]Ibid., 100.
[82]Gerhard Friedrich, "Σάλπινχ (*Salpinx*—'Trumpet')," TDNT, 7:76.
[83]HMI, 100.
[84]BI, 53.
[85]Tarr, "Trumpet," NGDMI, 3:642.
[86]EIHM, 5.
[87]Ibid.

While Moses was commanded to use only two silver trumpets, the dedication of the Temple by Solomon witnessed a priestly ensemble of one hundred twenty trumpeters (see II Chronicles 5:12). Coupled with a song of praise, the trumpet ensemble signaled the moment when "the glory of God filled the house" (see II Chronicles 5:13).[88] Trumpets were depicted in the priestly insignia of the Temple. Representations of trumpets can be seen on the Arch of Titus, and trumpets are mentioned frequently in the Dead Sea Scrolls.[89]

In addition to using the trumpet at festive occasions, the Jews used the trumpet in their cultic sacrificial rites. It was used at both the burnt offering and the peace offering (see Numbers 10:10). When the trumpet sounded at the burnt offering, the worshipers cast themselves to the ground (see II Chronicles 29:27 and Sirach 50:16).[90]

Josephus described the *chazozrah* as an instrument "one ell long, chased [*sic*] from heavy metal, [an instrument] which expands gradually from the mouthpiece to the end in the form of a bell."[91]

According to Numbers 10:2, the trumpet was used by Moses to call the assembly together and "for the journeying of the camps" in the wilderness. In the Temple, three trumpet blasts indicated the commencement of the morning sacrifice. Blasts were also used at the end of Levitical chant to signal the moment when the worshipers were to prostrate themselves in the Temple. Thus, trumpet blasts or calls were used in Jewish practice to signal the beginnings of various events, whether in peacetime or in war.[92]

## Greek

Trumpet is signified in the Greek language as σάλπινχ (*salpinx*). As a verb, σάλπιζο (*salpizo*) means "to produce a blast on the trumpet." The trumpet is not a typical Greek instrument. Homer was familiar with it, but it "does not seem" to have been utilized by the Greek military.[93] Due to the lack of information concerning Greek use of the trumpet, it can be conjectured that (1) its use was overshadowed

---

[88]Friedrich, "Σάλπινχ (*Salpinx*—'Trumpet')," TDNT, 7:79.

[89]Tarr, "Trumpet," NGDMI, 3:642.

[90]Friedrich, "Σάλπινχ (*Salpinx*—'Trumpet')," TDNT, 7:79.

[91]EIHM, 5.

[92]Tarr, "Trumpet," NGDMI, 3:642.

[93]Friedrich, "Σάλπινχ (*Salpinx*—'Trumpet')," TDNT, 7:73.

by the use of the stringed (like κιθαρα (*kithara*—"harp") and wind
αὐλός (*aulos*—"flute") instruments, or (2) the trumpet was used in a
similar militaristic manner as the Romans used it. Oftentimes, music
in the two cultures is labelled Graeco-Roman.

## Roman
The Roman trumpet was an enlargement of the short trumpet. It was
typically two cubits long and had a mouthpiece which was separate
from the body of the instrument. The mouthpiece consisted of a cup,
a choke and a backbone made from bronze.[94]

Bate provides a more detailed picture of the Roman trumpet. He
claims that four different trumpet types existed:

(1) *Lituus*—a cylindrical conically shaped instrument which was
hooked like a letter "J." It was utilized by the calvary;

(2) *Tuba*—a conically shaped instrument which measured 46 inches
in length. It was used by foot soldiers;

(3) *Cornu*—a large horn that was gently tapered through 11 feet.
It was coiled, about three-and-a-half feet across, and was more
discriminately employed to sound fanfares at high-ranking
military activities; and

(4) *Buccina*—a simple bugle horn which was used "to mark the
four watches of the night" in camp. It was also used to sound
reveille.[95]

Flavius Josephus indicates that the instrument was as little as a cubit
in length.[96] It disappeared from Europe after the fall of Rome, but was
later reintroduced during the time of the crusades.[97]

## Early Church
The sound of the trumpet was used primarily to herald or announce the
beginning of events. The use of the trumpet in the period of the early

---

[94]BI, 57.

[95]Philip Bate, *The Trumpet and Trombone* (New York, NY: W.W. Norton, 1978), 90-103.

[96]Flavius Josephus, *The Works of Flavius Josephus*, taken from "Antiquities of the Jews," bk. III chap. XII, trans. by William Whiston (Nashville, TN: Broadman Press, 1974), 2:224.

[97]Tarr, "Trumpet," NGD, 19:214.

church is evidenced in Old Testament pseudepigraphal writings of the time. Examples of this are numerous. In *The Life of Adam and Eve* 22:1, the sound of the trumpet is used to mark the sayings of the Lord and to announce the Lord's coming into human presence. In *The Life of Adam and Eve* 37:1, the trumpet is used to indicate when the angels should stand: "While Seth was speaking to his mother, an angel sounded the trumpet and the angels who were lying on their faces stood up and cried out with a fearful voice, saying..."

Prophesying the birth of Jesus, *Apocalypse of Abraham* 31:1 says

> And then I will sound the trumpet out of the air, and I will send my chosen one, having in him one measure of all my power, and he will summon my people, humiliated by the heathen.[98]

Speaking of eschatological events, *Apocalypse of Zephaniah* utilizes the trumpet to herald and announce several events:

(1) trumpets herald the seers triumph over their accusers (see Revelation 9);
(2) trumpets herald the opening of heaven (see Revelation 10);
(3) trumpets call the saints to intercessory prayer (see Revelation 11); and
(4) trumpets introduce a discussion of the end-times (see Revelation 12).[99]

### In the Book of Revelation

The verb σάλπιζο (*salpizo*—"to trumpet") occurs frequently in the Book of Revelation. In I Corinthians 14:8, Paul refers to the military use of the trumpet metaphorically. He implies that if the use of tongues is not used in a clear manner the effort will have no effect. It would be tantamount to an unclear militaristic trumpet call which does nothing to prepare the troops for battle.[100] The voice of Christ's angel sounds as a trumpet blast. The trumpet blast "had already acquired [a]

---

[98]OTP, 1:704-705.
[99]Ibid., 1:498-499.
[100]Friedrich, "Σάλπινχ (*Salpinx*—'Trumpet')," TDNT, 7:86.

Christian association" in earlier New Testament passages (see Matthew 24:31 and I Thessalonians 4:16).[101]

When the "sound of the trumpet" is used in Revelation 1:10 and 4:11, the sound is not akin to a militaristic trumpet blast. Rather, the sound refers to the "loudness and indescribability of the tone." This sound is not made by an angel (see Revelation 5:2; 17:1; and 21:9). Neither is this the sound of the voice of the Son of Man (see Revelation 1:15). Instead, it is the voice that is "surely that of God Himself" (see Revelation 16:1 and 17).[102]

Revelation 18:22 contains the only hint that the trumpet is to be used as a musical instrument. When the final judgment on Babylon is proclaimed, the silent trumpeters are grouped with the flautists, harpists and other players.[103] The trumpet blast or call is primarily used as an introduction or an announcement of revelation.

### Summary
It is doubtful whether the trumpet was often used in the ancient world as a musical instrument. The Egyptian trumpets have "fundamentally only two notes, the basic and the tenth," though Kirby indicates a third tone two octaves above the basic.[104] Usage of the trumpet in the Book of Revelation supports its usage as a heralding device. The trumpet was reserved for use to make signals and to set rhythms.

The trumpet is used eschatologically in a similar fashion by both Judaism and the early church:

(1)  the trumpet announces the great judgment at the end-time;
(2)  the loud trumpet blast is heard in all the corners of the earth. When it occurs, the angels will assemble the elect from all parts thereof (see Matthew 24:31); and
(3)  the transforming of the living and the raising of the dead will occur at the sound of the trumpet.

---

[101]ASJ, 13.
[102]Friedrich, "Σάλπινχ (*Salpinx*—'Trumpet')," TDNT, 7:86.
[103]Ibid., 7:88.
[104]Ibid., 7:75.

The trumpet call is the eschatologically heraldic sound which will signal the end of the age. Friedreich believes that the sound which is made by the trumpet cannot be made by a human instrument.[105]

---

[105]Ibid., 7:87-88.

# 4

# Performing Groups

WITHIN the pages of the Apocalypse both vocal and instrumental musicians are described performing in a variety of groupings. An analysis of the various groupings follows.

## Soloists and a Small Ensemble

While soloists do not figure prominently in the Book of Revelation, a variety of vocal and instrumental ensembles are employed. Occasions for solo singing arise when solos are given to members of a larger ensemble. An example of this can be found in Revelation 6. Each of the four living creatures (ζῷαν—*zoan*) in turn say in a thunderous voice "Come!" Similarly, the ensemble of trumpeters mentioned in Revelation 8 are never heard playing together. While they are grouped together, each one individually heralds successive actions in turn.

A quartet comprises the smallest group of singers. The four living creatures (see Revelation 4:6, 8; 5:6, 8, 11, 14; 6:6; 14:3; and 15:7) are a blend of creatures, including cherubim (see Ezekiel) and seraphim (see Isaiah 6). Ezekiel's cherubim are of Babylonian origin and the seraphim are celestial beings, apparently of human form with six wings, but of unknown origin. They are positioned near the throne and their function is to carry the platform of God's throne which is similar to a chariot.[1]

The Jewish mind sees the cherubim and seraphim together. In his vision of heaven (see *I Enoch* 71:7 and 14:23), Enoch sees the

---

[1]IB, 12:403-404.

seraphim, cherubim and ophannim (the personification of the eyes on
the wheels of the chariot of God's throne) protecting the throne of God.
These creatures never sleep.[2]

## In the Book of Revelation
In Revelation 4:8, perpetual music is heard around the throne. It is
sung by the four living creatures who "never cease to sing." This is
owing to the fact that "at a certain stage loyalty and love inevitably
become lyrical, bursting into song." Although there may be different
types of churches, "no church exists of perpetual silence." God has
placed the four living creatures' "deathless melody" of eternal hope and
life into the heart of every Christian.[3]

In Revelation 4:9-11, the four living creatures join with the 24
elders to sing antiphonally to the Creator God. This song assures
humankind that God is in complete control over all of creation and that
His power will soon be finally evident.[4]

## Κορός (*Choros*—"Chorus")

One of the principal features of music or a music practice in the Book
of Revelation is the utilization of a chorus. Although the Greek word
for chorus (κορός—*choros*) does not specifically appear in the Book
of Revelation, its implementation is implied. The first allusion to the
chorus appears in Chapter 4:10, 11:

> the twenty-four elders fall down before him who is seated on the
> throne and worship him who lives for ever and ever; they cast
> their crowns before the throne, singing, 'Worthy art thou, our
> Lord and God, To receive glory and honor and power, For thou
> didst create all things, And by thy will they existed and were
> created.'

---

[2]Ibid., 12:404.
[3]Ibid., 12:403-404.
[4]Ibid., 12:405.

## Early Pagan
Evidence of early pagan choirs is virtually nonexistent. The earliest organized choirs occurred in Davidic times in the Jewish tradition, but no inofrmation of surrounding cultures of that time is extant.

## Jewish
Rabbinic sources have legends and visions which portray heavenly angelic choirs beginning their own songs of exultation in imitation of the Jewish community singing and praising God in the *Kedusha* and Exodus 15.[5]

The period of the kings of Israel and Judah finds the first signs of well-organized choral singing. In I Chronicles 15:16, three singers are found who were assigned the duty of signaling or leading the chorus. The use of cymbals and 14 instrumentalists (playing 8 psalteries and 6 harps) indicates that the singers were accompanied. This instrumentation became a standard for Jewish choral music accompaniment.[6] During Davidic times, 24 groups of 12 musicians (288 in all) whom Chenaniah had trained were appointed by the King. It is from these origins that a choir school was maintained by the successors of Chenaniah. This school continued training generation after generation of cantors and choristers. These Levitical choirs consisted primarily of men with boy apprentices, but probably no women.[7]

By exilic times, vocal music likely lacked the accompaniment of instrumentalists owing partly to small financial resources and the lack of skilled players. However, the model of the Temple choirs from earlier times still prevailed. Musical practice consisted of responsorial as well as antiphonal styles. Some of the Psalms have superscriptions which can be interpreted to mean that they were performed by a soloist (cantor) with a responding choir. Nehemiah 12:31-39 illustrates the practice of antiphony. By the first century, Philo of Alexandria described congregational antiphony in his *De vita contemplativa*, paragraph 29,

---

[5]TSB, 141.

[6]James G. Smith, "Chorus," NGD, 4:343. See also John W. Kleinig, *The Lord's Song: The Basis, Function and Significance of Choral Music in Chronicles* (Sheffield: JSOT Press, 1993).

[7]Ibid., 4:343.

They rise up together and...form themselves into two choirs, one of men and one of women, the leader chosen from each being the most honoured and most musical among them. They sing hymns to God composed of many measures and set to many melodies, sometimes chanting together, sometimes antiphonally... It is thus that the choir of the Therapeutae [a Jewish sect] of either sex—note in response to note and voice to voice, the deep-toned voices of the men blending with the shrill voices of the women...create a truly musical symphony.[8]

## Greek

The κορός (choros) finds its greatest early utilization in Greek tragic drama. Modern knowledge of Greek drama is based on the extant plays of three fifth-century B.C.E. Greek playwrights: Aeschylus, Sophocles, and Euripides. Of the more than 1,000 plays written between 500-400 B.C.E., only 31 survive. The plays of Sophocles are considered to be the most skillfully conceived—Oedipus Rex being his greatest. The plays of Sophocles developed Greek music to its highest form. The typical play contained the following sections:

(1) the prologue—which provides the background to the story;
(2) the παραδος (parados)—provides the entrance for the κορός (choros). It relays the exposition and establishes the mood of the play;
(3) a series of episodes—three to six episodes develop the story. They are separated by choral songs (στασιμα—stasima); and
(4) the exodus—provides the concluding scene in which the characters and κορός (choros) depart.[9]

The κορός (choros) served the dual purpose of singing and dancing and was commonly grouped in the following manner: (1) men, (2) women, (3) men and women, and/or (4) men and boys. The music which the κορός (choros) sang was characteristically monophonic in either a responsorial or antiphonal style. The singers were expected not only to sing, but to dance as well. Choral music was performed in

---

[8]Ibid.
[9]Oscar G. Brockett, History of the Theatre (Boston, MA: Allyn and Bacon, Inc., 1968), 13-14.

unison.[10] The κορός (*choros*) finds its Greek origins in the Periclean Age. It evolved from the religious and ceremonial performances of the sixth and fifth centuries B.C.E. The three principal types of choral dances found in Greek drama are:

(1) the *paean*—mentioned first in the *Iliad* (ca. 850 B.C.E.). It is used as an invocation to Apollo who was the god of healing;

(2) the *partheneia* (ca. 650 B.C.E.)—was performed by a women's chorus of Spartan virgins; and

(3) the *dithyramb* (ca. 600 B.C.E.)—consisted of a choreographic display which told the story of the fertility god Dionysus. This form of the choral dance ultimately led to the Greek tragedies and dramas of the fifth and fourth centuries B.C.E.[11] The leader of the κορός (*choros*) was referred to as "a corporate commentator."[12]

The κορός (*choros*) in Greek tragic drama spoke for conventional society, and assisted in enlightening the audience regarding the protagonistic problems of the particular play. It is also described as a group of actors "who stood aside from the main action of the play and commented on it."[13]

The pre-dramatic choruses could be as large as 600, whereas the dithyrambic chorus normally consisted of approximately 12 to 50 boys and men who were arranged in a circle surrounding an *aulos* player. Comedies most often employed either 24, 50 or 60 in the κορός (*choros*), while the dramas commonly employed less. The early dramas of Aeschylus utilized 12 in the chorus, while Sophocles employed 15. A κορός (*choros*) of 15 became the standard for the tragedies.[14]

Aeschylus' (525-456 B.C.E.) use of the chorus as a dramatic resource within the storyline of the myth was employed to intensify the importance of the crisis within the episodes. But when Aeschylus

---

[10]Warren D. Anderson, *Ethos and Education in Greek Music* (Cambridge, MA: Harvard University Press, 1966), 2.

[11]Smith, "Chorus," NGD, 4:341-342.

[12]Ibid., 4:342.

[13]Phyllis Hartnoll, editor, *The Oxford Companion to the Theatre* (London: Oxford University Press, 1972), 176.

[14]Smith, "Chorus," NGD, 4:342-343.

introduced a second actor, he consequently reduced the role of the chorus. Sophocles (ca. 495-406 B.C.E.) provided more balance between the actors and the chorus. The chorus in Sophocles' plays share the following characteristics:

(1) it plays a small part in the action of the play;
(2) its chief function was purely lyrical; and
(3) it was employed between the histrionic scenes (which now became "acts") in order to carry the dramatic rhythm.[15]

Music and the κορός (*choros*) share the following characteristics by the time of Euripides (484-ca. 406 B.C.E.):

(1) the music and chorus were more emotional and coincided more closely with the realism and the pathos of the plots;
(2) the chorus' role continued to diminish owing to the fact that the actors' roles were becoming more important. Non-tragic plots became more elaborate and important and resulted in the number of actors increasing to as many as 11 as seen in *Phoenician Women*; and
(3) eventually the music of the chorus was reduced to merely decorative filler.[16]

Sophocles' plays represent the high point in tragic drama. Consequently, the characteristics inherent in his works are used as the standard in the analysis to follow.

### Roman
Choral performances occurred in Rome on a grand scale. Roman theaters could seat as many as 12,000 spectators. Seneca wrote that there were often more performers than audience at the plays of his day. Brass instruments were frequently placed in the audience because there was no room on or offstage for them.[17]

---

[15]Hartnoll, *The Oxford Companion to the Theatre*, 404.
[16]Ibid.
[17]MSR, 412.

## Early Church

In Colossians 3:16 and James 5:13, the early church gave approval to the use of music in church services. The early church functioned initially as a Jewish sect and attempted to follow the precedent of its Jewish forbears. However, it did not have the financial wherewithal nor the physical facilities which its Jewish counterparts enjoyed. Thus, most of the first-century Christian music consisted of congregational singing.[18]

Specific references to the early church's use of choirs is nonexistent. However, patristic writers indicate that choirs were common in their day. Eusebius (C.E. ca. 260-ca. 340), the Bishop of Caesarea, indicates in his *Historia ecclesiastica*, that antiphonal singing was "still" practiced by the Christians of his day.[19] It can only be conjectured that since choirs are common in Greek and Jewish practice up to and through the first century and subsequently are alluded to in writings after C.E. 100, that some form of choir existed during the first century in the Christian community.

Choral music in the modern sense was probably not employed by the early church owing to the fundamental concept of κοινωνία (*koinonia* "fellowship"). Κοινωνία (*koinonia*) refers to the fellowhip, the oneness, which the early church experienced. The early church consisted of slave and free persons. To raise up or lift up one group of a congregation by assigning them a special act in worship was outside of the concept of a unified fellowship. Thus, congregational singing, as normative choral singing, included all worshipers equally (see Acts 4:24-30; I Corinthians 14:15-16:26; Ephesians 5:19; and Colossians 3:16).[20] Ending the Lord's Supper with a song of jubilation, Jesus portrayed a powerful illustration of the κοινωνία (*koinonia*) of gathering in worship as an affront to the struggles which lie ahead. Empty, rote worship has no meaning and cannot compare with this type of refreshing and vital worship.[21]

Owing to Jewish influence, it is conjectured that antiphonal and responsorial singing originated in the early church in and around

[18]Smith, "Chorus," NGD, 4:343.
[19]Ibid.
[20]William Shepherd Smith, *Musical Aspects of the New Testament* (Amsterdam: Vrije Universiteit te Amsterdam, 1962), 29, 35.
[21]IB, 7:576.

Jerusalem, and via the evangelical spreading of the Word had been spread to the four corners of the then-known world by the fourth century. The patristic record indicates that opinion was divided on the use of instruments as accompanimental aids because of their association with pagan festivals. Clement of Alexandria (C.E.ca. 150-ca. 220) censored the use of instruments, but this practice was later repealed by Didymus of Alexandria (C.E.ca. 313-338) who wrote that a psalm is "a hymn which is sung to the instrument called either the psaltery or cithara."[22]

## Summary
The chief characteristics of the chorus summarized from its origins follows.

   (1) In Jewish Music Practice, the chorus:
       (a)  was well-organized;
       (b)  used instrumental accompaniment;
       (c)  consisted of trained and skilled musicians;
       (d)  used antiphonal and responsorial techniques which were chanted or sung;
       (e)  consisted of large groups (in excess of 60 members each), primarily men with boys, occasionally women; and
       (f)  sang hymns to God.
   (2) In Greek Music Practice, the chorus:
       (a)  spoke for conventional society;
       (b)  commented on the action of the main plot;
       (c)  was 12 to 60 persons in size, primarily men or men and boys; and
       (d)  was lyrical and emotionally and physically dramatic.
   (3) In early church music practice, choral music:
       (a)  consisted primarily of congregational singing;
       (b)  shows no extant record from the first century that choirs, other than "congregational choirs," existed; and
       (c)  was probably unaccompanied.

---

[22]Ibid.

## In the Book of Revelation

Three choruses[23] are alluded to in the Book of Revelation.

*A Chorus Consisting of the Twenty-Four Elders.* This relatively small chorus is referred to in the following passages.

*Revelation 4:10-11:*
The twenty-four elders fall down before him who is seated on the throne and worship him who lives for ever and ever; they cast their crowns before the throne, singing, "Worthy art thou, our Lord and God, to receive glory and honor and power, for thou didst create all things, and by thy will they existed and were created."

*Revelation 5:8-9:*
And when he had taken the scroll, the four living creatures and the twenty-four elders fell down before the Lamb, each holding a harp, and with golden bowls full of incense, which are the prayers of the saints; and they sang a new song, saying, "Worthy art thou to take the scroll and to open its seals, for thou wast slain and by thy blood didst ransom men for God from every tribe and tongue and people and nation, and hast made them a kingdom and priests to our God, and they shall reign on earth."

*Revelation 11:16-18:*
And the twenty-four elders who sit on their thrones before God fell on their faces and worshiped God, saying, "We give thanks to thee, Lord God Almighty,who art and who wast, that thou hast taken thy great power and begun to reign. The nations raged, but thy wrath came, and the time for the dead to be judged, for rewarding thy servants, the prophets and saints, and

---

[23]A fourth choir is mentioned in Revelation 18 consisting of "Kings of the earth who committed fornication and were wanton with her . . ." (see 18:9-10) and "the merchants of the earth [who] weep and mourn for her, since no one buys their cargo any more" (see 18:11-20). But this choir is outside the scope of worship in the Book of Revelation; consequently, it is outside the scope of the present study.

those who fear thy name, both small and great, and for
destroying the destroyers of the earth."

*Revelation 19:4:*
And the twenty-four elders and the four living creatures fell
down and worshiped God who is seated on the throne, saying,
"Amen. Hallelujah!"

The κορός (*choros*) of 24 elders borrows features of the Greek
κορός (*choros*). It probably consisted of only men. Elements of
Jewish chorus origins are evident in the organization, theatrics, and
probable skill which the elders exhibit since they are robed similarly in
white garments and golden crowns. Their actions appear to be
choreographed, and it seems that they were able to play the harp.
Thus, their singing was probably accompanied by musical instruments.[24]
Just as Jewish chorus practice was directed primarily to a monotheistic
god, Yahweh, so is this music directed to God the Father/Creator and
to Jesus Christ, the Savior of the world.
      *A Second Chorus Numbering Thousands and Thousands in Heaven.*
This very large chorus consists of angels and the scriptural references
to it are as follows:

*Revelation 5:11-12:*
Then I looked, and I heard around the throne and the living
creatures and the elders the voice of many angels, numbering
myriads of myriads and thousands of thousands, saying with a
loud voice, "Worthy is the Lamb who was slain, to receive
power and wealth and wisdom and might and honor and glory
and blessing!"

*Revelation 7:9-12:*
After this I looked, and behold, a great multitude which no man
could number, from every nation, from all tribes and peoples
and tongues, standing before the throne and before the Lamb,

[24]Johannes Quasten, *Music and Worship in Pagan and Christian Antiquity*, translated
by Boniface Ramsey (Washington, D.C.: National Association of Pastoral Musicians,
1973), 72.

clothed in white robes, with palm branches in their hands, and crying out with a loud voice, "Salvation belongs to our God who sits upon the throne, and to the Lamb!"

And all the angels stood round the throne and round the elders and the four living creatures, and they fell on their faces before the throne and worshiped God, saying, "Amen! Blessing and glory and wisdom and thanksgiving and honor and power and might be to our God for ever and ever! Amen."

*Revelation 14:2 3:*
And I heard a voice from heaven like the sound of many waters and like the sound of loud thunder; the voice I heard was like the sound of harpers playing on their harps, and they sing a new song before the throne and before the four living creatures and before the elders. No one could learn that song except the hundred and forty-four thousand who had been redeemed from the earth.

*Revelation 19:1-3:*
After this I heard what seemed to be the loud voice of a great multitude in heaven, crying, "Hallelujah! Salvation and glory and power belong to our God, for his judgments are true and just; he has judged the great harlot who corrupted the earth with her fornication, and he has avenged on her the blood of his servants." Once more they cried, "Hallelujah! The smoke from her goes up for ever and ever."

*Revelation 19:6-8:*
Then I heard what seemed to be the voice of a great multitude, like the sound of many waters and like the sound of mighty thunderpeals, crying, "Hallelujah! For the Lord our God the Almighty reigns. Let us rejoice and exult and give him the glory, for the marriage of the Lamb has come, and his Bride has made herself ready; it was granted her to be clothed with fine linen, bright and pure"—for the fine linen is the righteous deeds of the saints.

In Revelation 7:9-12, the heavenly choir of angels joins with the four living creatures and the 24 elders who fall on their faces before the throne worshiping God. They respond with a seven-fold doxology beginning and ending with Amen. This counterpoint of praise represents "heaven's answer to earth's praise."[25]

The Book of Revelation is often labelled a book of doom and gloom. However, as Blevins[26] contrarily points out, it is a book of hope. Every generation of Christians from the early church has experienced persecution. The hope of every age is embodied within the spirit of the Book of Revelation.

> In spite of all the tragedy which it [the Book of Revelation] describes, it may be said to be one of the very happiest books ever written. The music of eternity sends its triumphant joy back into the life of time. The justification of glorious Christian music in this world is always justification by faith—... The writings of Paul also have this characteristic of bursting into song. You can judge an interpretation of the Christian religion by its capacity to set men [sic] singing. There is something wrong about a theology which does not create triumphant music.[27]

In Revelation 14:2, the sound which the Seer witnesses is "a voice like many waters and loud thunder heard in heaven." It is like "the sound of harpers playing upon their harps." The singers are not specifically identified in this passage, but if John considers the martyrs as being both in the heavenly and earthly Zion in this scene, then he could readily visualize the martyrs as the singers (see Revelation 7:10 and II Esdras 2:42).[28]

The "hallelujah" chorus (see Revelation 19:1-2, 3 and 6-8) is the expression of the great joy over the destruction of the wicked city of Rome. It is also heaven's rejoicing at the triumph over the final vestiges of evil on the earth. The term "hallelujah" (alleluia) comes

---

[25]IB, 12:420.
[26]RD, 136.
[27]IB, 12:420.
[28]Ibid., 12:468-469.

from the Hebrew term *hallel* ("to praise"). When it is combined with Yahweh it means "to praise God."[29]

The writer of the Apocalypse indicates that this angelic choir is represented by "a single voice." The choir's performance indicates a total "harmony of emotion and feeling" (let alone musical excellence) as they corporately "lift their song in antiphonal praise."[30] The angelic choir is intoning a song of praise to the Lamb, and it is "quite liturgical in character." The number of angels is reminiscent of those mentioned in Daniel 7:10 and I Enoch 40:1; they are beyond human calculation.[31]

Evidence of Greek κορός (chorus) practice is found in the positioning of this large choir "offstage" in heaven. Just as Greek choruses generally were not central to the onstage action, so is this κορός (chorus) positioned outside of the mainstream of the action. The use of expression is indicated by the nature of their "loud" singing. The κορός (chorus) appears to respond antiphonally to the κορός (chorus) of elders who appear closer to the action of the principal characters, and the message of their singing provides commentary on the storyline. Similar to the κορός (*choros*) of 24 elders, this κορός (*choros*) of angels is accompanied by instrumentalists on harps and they focus their attention on the completed action which Jesus Christ has accomplished in history.

*A Third Chorus Numbering Every Creature in Heaven and Earth.* The size of this κορός (chorus) appears to include all creatures ever created. The scriptural allusion to it follows.

*Revelation 5:13:*
And I heard every creature in heaven and on earth and under the earth and in the sea, and all therein, saying, "To him who sits upon the throne and to the Lamb be blessing and honor and glory and might for ever and ever!"

When the angelic response to God and the Lamb is ended, all creatures in the universe join in this doxology to the Godhead. This mighty outburst of praise ascribes eternal "blessing and honor and glory

---

[29]Ibid., 12:506-507, 309.

[30]Robert E. Coleman, *Songs of Heaven* (Old Tappan, NJ: Fleming H. Revell Company, 1975), 55.

[31]IB, 12:409.

and might" to the occupant of the throne and to the Lamb. The 24 elders prostrate themselves before the throne and the four living creatures end the doxology with an "Amen."

In Revelation 7:4-8, a choir of the Redeemed is mentioned. This choir allegorically is numbered to contain 144,000; it is made up of 12,000 from each of the 12 tribes of Israel. These 12 tribes are representative of all Christians who are the true Israel (see James 1:1 and I Peter 1:1).[32]

By literally becoming members of the Kingdom of God, this κορός (*choros*) does not merely represent and speak for conventional society: it is the Redeemed of conventional society. The size of the κορός (*choros*) has augmented the large choruses of Jewish tradition and performs the ultimate responsorial role. All of creation responds to the finished work of the Lamb. By the κορός' (*choros'*) immense size, it is very likely that it is highly organized and consists of dedicated and skilled performers.

**Summary**
The choir appears to function primarily as a responding mechanism to others in the text, specifically to God the Creator and Jesus Christ the Lamb. God and Jesus Christ are represented at various points in the text as "the voice of heaven" (see Revelation 10:8), "the voice of the temple" (see Revelation 16:1), and "the voice of the throne" (see Revelation 21:3).

A theological concept of the chorus in the Book of Revelation contains the idea of corporate participation in response to the "revelation" expressed by the Godhead in either a responsorial or antiphonal style. This includes physical posturing, although this characteristic is prominent only in the smaller choruses. The chorus of 24 elders appear to lead the larger choirs as the action in the text builds in a mighty crescendo of participation and sound; it initiates with the chorus of 24 elders singing, followed by an antiphonal response of the creatures of heaven, and culminates when these antiphonal forces participate in a joined response with the remainder of creation, including the Redeemed. Together they corporately direct their praise to the Godhead.

[32]Ibid., 12:419.

## Instrumental Music

Bales states that "instrumental music in worship is not authorized in the New Testament." [33] However, the Book of Revelation contains more instruments by name than the remainder of the New Testament, and would consequently challenge Bales' assertion. The instruments are partly used in the Apocalypse in conjunction with the joyful celebrations revolving around Christ's ultimate victory over Satan.[34]

Small ensembles of instrumentalists are used at various times throughout the Book of Revelation. The three specific groups are:

(1) a trumpet ensemble of seven (see Revelation 8 and 18:22);
(2) a harp ensemble (see Revelation 5:8, 14:2 and 18:22); and
(3) a flute ensemble (see Revelation 18:22).

These instruments are not intermingled in a mixed ensemble. The Greek musical style is maintained in order to express a single ethos.

The instrumental ensembles which fall within the realm of worship in the Apocalypse are the trumpet ensemble (see Revelation 8) and the use of harps by the 24 elders in Revelation 5:8. The other instrumental ensembles are not used in a conventional sense. Since the trumpet, flute and harp ensembles mentioned in Revelation 18:22 are not utilized in worship, they are outside of the scope of this study.

Passages in Revelation 5:8-13, 14:3, et al., portray a "heavenly celebration" which indicates that the author envisaged a highly ordered practice of music. The music of καθαρσις (katharsis) is taken for granted. The early church fathers were reluctant to allow instrumental music in their services because it "carried too many reminiscences" of pagan and Jewish temple cultic practices. The synagogue had banished all instrumental music because instrumental music partly represented mourning over the destruction of the temple.[35]

In the Jewish tradition it was common, however, for the instrumental musicians to serve in accompanimental roles or to play interludes. While admitting to no conclusive definition for the 70 odd

---

[33] James D. Bales, *Instrumental Music and New Testament Worship* (Scarcy, AR: James D. Bales, 1973), 9.
[34] David Appleby, *History of Church Music* (Chicago, IL: Moody Press, 1965), 20.
[35] TSB, 318.

occurrences of *selah* in the Book of Psalms, Sendrey suggests the following interpretation as a possibility. When the singers came to the marking *selah* in the text, it may have been an indication for the musicians to enter loudly with trumpets and percussion instruments and for the voices to cease. Because the main task of doing the music in the Temple services resided in the Levitical singers (I Chronicles 16:37, 40), it was only natural that a period of rest and recovery occur frequently during a long service. The periods between text singing "might have caused the resorting to instrumental interludes" indicated by the marking *selah*. Sendrey submits the following example although there is no evidence to connect this with *selah*.

> Ben Arza clashed the cymbal and the Levites broke forth into singing. When they reached a break in the singing they blew upon the trumpets and the people prostrated themselves; at every break there was a blowing of the trumpet and at every blowing of the trumpet a prostration. This was the rite of the daily Whole-offering in the service of the House of our God.[36]

Instrumental solo or ensemble music carrying a melodic line is not specifically mentioned nor alluded to in the Book of Revelation. Its use is reserved exclusively as a heralding device (see Chapter 3 of this study) or as accompaniment to singing. Specific reference to accompanied song in worship occurs in Revelation 5:13. Accompanying the hymns, responses, doxologies, prayers, and *Tersanctus* are instrumental music, incense, and ritual movements.[37]

### Harp Ensemble

The generic name for harp-like instruments is chordophone. By definition, a chordophone exists when a "plane of strings is perpendicular to a soundboard."[38]

---

[36]MAI, p. 150.
[37]IB, 12:410.
[38]Ann Griffiths, et al., "Harp," NGDMI, 2:131.

**Early Pagan**

Sumerian harps date from ca. 2800 B.C.E. The early Sumerian harp consisted of a plane of strings vertical to the soundboard with the body elongated at one end. The curved neck formed an arch. The boat-shaped resonators came in all sizes with up to six strings.[39]

The earliest extant harp from Mesopotamia dating ca. 2500 B.C.E. was located in the Royal Cemetery at Ur.[40] From ca. 1850 B.C.E. in Mesopotamia (the Old Babylonian period), the angular harp predominated and was played in two ways: when the strings were vertical the resonator rested against the player's body and both hands were used to pluck the strings; and when the strings were horizontal to the resonator, the resonator was held under the left arm and the strings were strummed or picked by a plectrum by the right hand. The left hand was used to dampen the strings.[41]

The arched harp of the Old Kingdom in Egypt contained a resonator which was shaped like a spoon or a spade. Bas-reliefs in tombs surrounding the Giza pyramids illustrate this type of harp. It was customarily played by a kneeling man who was joined in accompanying a singer by a flautist and double-parallel pipe player. However, in the tomb of Mereruka at Saqqara (Dynasty 6, ca. 2345-2181 B.C.E.), the Princess Seshseshat "plays to her husband on the harp and accompanies her own song."[42] A male ensemble of seven harpers can be viewed in the tomb of Ibi at Deir el-Gebrawi. By the time of the Egyptian Middle Kingdom, chamber groups tended to be smaller and contained more women. The resonator was deeper and more oval-shaped, like a ladle.[43]

The Egyptian New Kingdom harps illustrated the use of a wide variety of chordophones. They ranged from small portable harps with boat-shaped resonators that played on the shoulder to the giant harps. The giant harps were played by standing male musicians. An example of this can be found in the tomb of Rameses III in the Valley of the Kings.[44]

---

[39]Ibid., 2:133.
[40]Ibid.
[41]Ibid.
[42]Ibid.
[43]Ibid.
[44]Ibid.

The angular harp was so named because the body and the neck came together at an angle.[45] It appeared "schematically on a few later seals (after the third millenium) and on an incised stone of the second millenium from Megiddo of Palestine."[46] These were equivalent to the assymetrical lyres used by the Jews from 2000 B.C.E.

### Jewish

The Jewish harp was called a *kinnor*. It was similar to a lyre, called a κιθάρα (*kithara*) by the Greeks. It was made of wood, possibly cypress, and was shaped with curved outlines and horizontal crossbars. According to Flavius Josephus, the Jewish historian and Roman general born C.E. 37 in Jerusalem, it consisted of ten strings.[47] It was plucked with a plectron. It was tuned pentatonically without semitones through two octaves. It was not a solo instrument, but was preferably used as a "tool for singing" (see I Chronicles 16:42). Thus, its role was one of an accompanimental nature, unlike the trumpet and cymbal. The melodies of the *kinnor* were of a gay, happy nature, and, consequently, were not used for lamentation.[48]

### Greek

Greek musical practice did not mix instruments of different types within the same ensemble. To do this would be to confuse the ethos which the ensemble sought to portray.[49]

Sendrey found that in 283 B.C.E. Carinus produced a series of plays which utilized 100 trumpet players. Other groups used 100 horn players and 200 χοραυλός (*choraulos*) and πιθαυλός (*pythaulos*) players. These plays, well received in their day, were considered to be highlights of the year.[50]

---

[45]HMI, 79.

[46]Griffiths, "Harp," NGDMI, 2:133.

[47]Flavius Josephus, *The Works of Flavius Josephus* in "Antiquities of the Jews," Book VII, Chapter XII, paragraph 3, trans. by William Whiston (Nashville, TN: Broadman Press, 1974), 2:466.

[48]HMI, 107-108.

[49]MSR, 412.

[50]Ibid.

## Roman

Roman musical practice frequently mixed instruments of various types in performing ensembles.[51]

## Early Church

Little information is available regarding the use of the harp in the early church. During that era the lyre

> remained comparatively unblemished by use in idol worship and was employed more frequently in private homes, while the flute, tambourine, cymbal and all the other instruments were much more closely associated with pagan cults.[52]

However, no conclusive evidence exists to indicate that the lyre was used either as a solo instrument or an accompanimental instrument in the early church, apart from its use in the Book of Revelation.

## In the Book of Revelation

In Revelation 5:13 and 18:22 appear the "harpers" (Greek word κιθάραδον [kitharodon]) who play on the harp (κιθάρα [kithara]). This term also appears in I Corinthians 14:7; Revelation 5:8, 14:2 and 15:2. Today's equivalent would be a harpist.[53]

In Revelation 5:13, the 24 elders are seen holding harps while they sing. While it is not explicitly indicated that the 24 elders played harps, their use as accompaniment to their song is implied. Used in this manner, the sound which they produced was presumably of a chordal nature, not a melodic one.

## Trumpet Ensemble

### Early Pagan[54]

The trumpet functioned primarily as a solo instrument.

---

[51]Ibid.

[52]Quasten, *Music and Worship in Pagan and Christian Antiquity*, 73.

[53]Ralph Earle, *Word Meanings in the New Testament* (Grand Rapids, MI: Baker Book House, 1982), 460.

[54]See Chapter 3 of this study for a discussion of the early history of the use of this instrument.

**Jewish**

Numbers 10:1-2 and 9-10 contain the idea of "drawing Yahweh's attention towards his worshipers by a strong sound." The strong sound used by the Jews was that of the trumpet blast or call. Although this idea was primitive, the trumpet call was widely practiced in the early Jewish tradition. However, Elijah's later preaching refuted this concept theologically.[55] In I Kings 18:27, Elijah shouted to the priests of Baal to "Cry aloud: for he is a god; either he is talking, or he is pursuing, or he is in a journey, or per adventure he sleepeth and must be awakened."

The trumpet symbolically heralded the coming of the Lord (see Zephaniah 1:16; Zechariah 9:14; *Psalms of Solomon* 11:1; and *Apocalypse of Abraham* 31). And *Pseudo-Philo* 32:18 referred to singing accompanied by trumpets

> And when Deborah made an end to her words, she along with the people went up to Shiloh, and they offered sacrifices and holocausts, and they sang to the accompaniment of the trumpets. And when they were singing and the sacrifices had been offered, Deborah said 'And this will be as a testimony of trumpets between the stars and their Lord.' And Deborah came down from there and judged Israel forty years.

From Aaron's day, the two original silver trumpets were the priestly instruments associated with sacrifices and used only near the tabernacle. By the time of the Temple, trumpeters were separated from horn players who could only play outside the Temple. Priestly trumpeters stood in front in battle and at the sacrificial altar in the Temple stood on two pillars or stood near the Ark of the Covenant. The trumpeters' purposes were several: (1) to glorify God; (2) to show the Israelites were a holy people and soldiers of Yahweh; (3) to encourage the soldiers; (4) to unite prayers with sonority; and (5) to remind the people of the presence of Yahweh.[56]

**Greek**

Chapter 3 contains a discussion of this instrument in the Greek culture.

---

[55]HMI, 112.
[56]EIHM, 18.

## Roman

Tibia players (*tibicines*) constituted one of the most ancient professional groups at Rome. Their music was used to "render inaudible any maleficent noises" which occurred during the Roman sacrificial rites. It was also used to "banish evil spirits and to summon up benevolent deities." Music was also used at funerals, other ceremonies and at other sacrifices. While the music was occasionally accompanied by lyre players (*fidicines*), the tibia was the instrument traditionally used. The tibia was the national Roman religious instrument and originally consisted of "a bone pipe with three or four finger holes, and later, like the Greek aulos, [became] a double pipe reed instrument with two pipes made from ivory, silver or boxwood."[57]

Roman military music utilized trumpeters (*tubicines*) and horn players (*cornicines*). They originated as part of the constitutional reforms of the fifth century B.C.E. and are attributed to Servius Tullius.[58]

The trumpeters provided signals to "sound the alarm, break camp, attack or retreat." They also signalled changes of the watch and were played while on the march as well as at funerals and in triumphal and sacrificial processions. In battle, the combination of trumpet blasts and the "dark coarse noise of the horns" served to encourage the Roman army and to confuse the enemy.[59]

## Early Church

No record of the use of the trumpet either as a solo or ensemble instrument can be found in the early church, apart from its use in the Book of Revelation.

## In the Book of Revelation

Although the seven angels of Revelation 8 are given seven trumpets, they do not perform together as an ensemble. Rather, each one individually heralds the subsequent revelatory action in the text.

---

[57]Fleischhauer, "Rome," NGD, 16:147.
[58]Ibid., 16:148.
[59]Ibid.

The two original silver trumpets were used exclusively near the tabernacle which housed the Ark of the Covenant. In the Temple tradition, trumpeters were separated from horn players who were allowed to play outside of the Temple only. The priestly trumpeters of the Temple stood at the front in battle and during the sacrificial rite stood at the table on two pillars or near the Ark of the Covenant. Trumpets were used to glorify God, to show the Israelites they were a holy people and to show they were the soldiers of Yahweh, to encourage the soldiers in battle, to aid in prayer, and to remind the people of the presence of Yahweh.[60]

---

[60]EIHM, 18.

# 5

# Performance Practice

THIS chapter deals with the type of musical sounds made and the manner the sound is produced.

## Vocal

Reference to the types of sound made in the production of music in the Apocalypse are derived from the Greek word ψωνή (*phone*). It is used throughout the Book to represent both vocally and non-vocally produced sound. It can be literally translated to mean "a sound" or "a voice" and is often used to "address one by word of mouth."[1]

### Early Pagan
Music is as old as civilization itself. At the earliest stages of development

> music-making must have utilized, in a sing-song manner, sounds of different pitch. Out of such crude-sounding utterances came human song and even human speech which, according to some theories, developed from it laboriously over a long period of time.[2]

---

[1]VGNT, 680.
[2]MSR, 24.

The natural question arises: which came first, song or speech? Schneider believes that language came first.[3] However, it is likely speech is a "watered-down" version of song. Anthropology informs us that humanity sought to imitate the sounds of nature first. This theory assumes that humanity sang before it spoke.[4]

The origin of vocal sounds by the human voice, either spoken or sung, consists of a wide variety of theories. An early theory put forth by Herbert Spencer[5] suggests that speech and song appear to have originated from the same source. In summarizing Spencer's theory, Sendrey says

> singing was a primitive function of speech. The organs of speech, under the influence of emotion, create certain reflex actions, which manifest themselves in acts related to singing. The vocal peculiarities which indicate excited feeling, are those which especially distinguish song from ordinary speech.[6]

However, Spencer does admit that the distinctions between speech and song in early pagan times is still "hazy."[7]

Sendrey also summarized the opinions of Lombroso, Darwin, Buecher and Sachs concerning the origins of singing. It is Lombroso's[8] opinion that song originated in primitive dance. The onlookers, as well as the performers themselves, excited the dancers via collective vocal cheers. These cheers developed into a "sing-song" pattern."[9] From this earliest type of rhythmic chant came vocal sound production.[10]

Darwin attempted to relate the origin of singing with human courtship and mating. Buecher[11] hypothesized that vocal music began

---

[3]Marius Schneider, "Primitive Music," *New Oxford History of Music* (Oxford: Oxford University Press, 1984), 5.

[4]William James Durant, *The History of Civilization* (New York, NY: Simon and Schuster, 1954), 88.

[5]Herbert Spencer, "The Origin and Function of Music," in *Essays* (New York, 1904).

[6]MSR, 24.

[7]Ibid.

[8]Cesare Lombroso, *Klinische Beiträge zur Psychiatrie* (Leipzig, 1869), 145; see also Gerhard van der Leeuw, *Sacred and Profane Beauty*, trans. by David E. Green (Nashville, TN: Abingdon Press, 1963).

[9]MSR, 27.

[10]Ibid.

[11]Karl Buecher, *Arbeit und Rhythmus* (Leipzig, 1909).

early as a result of group-work activity. To break the tedium of work, early pagan societies used "accompanying rhythmical devices."[12] This included singing.

Curt Sachs[13] rejects all of these theories and other theories and concludes that their common mistake is their belief that music began from a single source. Sachs points out that

> music, bound to the motor impulses of our bodies to the vague images of our minds, and to our emotion in all its depth and width, eludes whatever attempt may be made to find a single formula.[14]

But he does agree that "music began with singing."[15]

**Jewish**
Traditional Jewish and Christian belief espouse a literal creation of the universe. When Adam and Eve were newly created by their Creator, it is assumed they could speak immediately. Likewise, as humankind was created in the image of God, just as God in Zephaniah 3:17 sang over creation, it is assumed that Adam and Eve could sing from the first day of their respective creation dates.

In the Jewish culture, ψωνή (*phone*) could be made by animals, nature, humankind, and by the Godhead. Examples of its usage are numerous:

(1)  ⌐Noise as in "claps of thunder" (Exodus 9:23, 29, 33);
(2)  "Roar" of great masses of water (Psalms 42:7, 93:3);
(3)  "Swish of rain" (I Kings 18:41);
(4)  "Rolling of an earthquake" (Ezekiel 37:7);
(5)  "Sound of steps" (Genesis 3:8);
(6)  "Trampling of horses" (Jeremiah 4:29);
(7)  "Rolling of wheels" (II Kings 7:6);
(8)  "Whistling of whips" (Nahum 3:2);

---

[12]MSR, 25-26.
[13]Curt Sachs, *The Wellsprings of Music* (Paris: The Hague, 1962), 16-21.
[14]MSR, 27.
[15]Ibid.

(9)  "Tumult of a large and excited crowd" (I Kings 1:40) or "city"
     (I Samuel 4:14; Ezra 23:42);
(10) "Rustling of wings of the cherubim on the throne chariot of
     God" (Ezra 1:24, 3:13, 10:5);
(11) "Sound of musical instruments, especially the ram's horn"
     (Amos 2:2; Ezekiel 33:4; Exodus 19:16, 20:18; II Samuel
     6:15, 15:10; I Kings 1:41; Jeremiah 4:21, 6:17, 42:14; Psalms
     47:5, 98:6; Job 39:24);
(12) "Sound of trumpets" (II Chronicles 5:13);
(13) "Sound of zithers" (Ezra 26:13);
(14) "Sound of flutes" (Job 21:12);
(15) "Sound of the bells" on the upper garment of the high priest
     (Exodus 26:13; Sirach 45:9);
(16) "Crying" (Isaiah 65:19; Psalms 6:8);
(17) "Lamenting" (Isaiah 4:14; Jeremiah 51:54);
(18) "Groaning" (Psalms 102:6);
(19) "Jubilation" (Isaiah 48:20); and
(20) God's revelation of himself (Psalms 29).[16]

In Apocalyptic writings, ψωνή (*phone*) is perceived as:

(1)  Noise and sound, like the roaring of many waters;
(2)  The voice of Man.  "Man's faculty of speech is designed
     especially for the service of God's praise";
(3)  The voice of the angels.  Their collective voice praises God
     with "one" voice (see *Apocalypse of Abraham* 18:2); and
(4)  The voice of God himself.  Thunder is sent by God and is
     separate from the revelation of the Word.  Lightning is a
     blessing or a curse from God.  And the "voices of thunder" are
     under the control of the angels in heaven.[17]

In Rabbinic Judaism, ψωνή (*phone*) never means "speech" or "word."
Rather, it is translated as:

(1)  Noise and sound, similar to a door opening;

---

[16]Otto Betz, "Ψωνή (*Phone*)," TDNT, 9:280-283.
[17]Ibid., 9:285-286.

(2) The human voice. The sound used by humans to communicate and considered to be an essential mark of the individual;
(3) Thunder. It comes from God as a universal declaration;
(4) The voice of God at Sinai (Exodus 19:16); and
(5) An anonymous voice from heaven. Following the destruction of the second temple and the last prophets Haggai, Zechariah and Malachi, Rabbinic Judaism believes that the Holy Spirit left Israel and substituted the voice of heaven in its place.[18]

Hellenistic Judaism interpreted the use of ψωνή (*phone*) in the following manners:

(1) Septuagint usage. Ψωνή (*Phone*) was limited to the oral sounds of living creatures. The revelation of God only occurs by the Word;
(2) Aristobulus (170-150 B.C.E.) warns against an "anthropomorphic view of [the] divine voice." He claims that the voice of God should be comprehended by its operation, not the spoken word. He views it as it was described by Moses when Moses described the "works" of Yahweh as "divine words";
(3) Josephus uses the concept of God's voice to "express more clearly the distance between God and man;" and
(4) Philo believes that among living creatures, only humankind has an articulate voice and it should be used to serve praise to God.[19]

**Greek**
In Greek usage, the term ψωνή (*phone*) is a sound "made by living creatures in the throat."[20] It could consequently be made by animals but was primarily an indication signifying the sound which humankind produced.[21]

---

[18]Ibid., 9:286-288.
[19]Ibid., 9:290-291.
[20]Ibid., 9:278.
[21]Ibid.

**Roman**
No information can be found on the types of sound produced in the
Roman world.

**Early Church**
In the early church, ψωνή (*phone*) was construed to represent the
following interpretations:

(1) Noise and sound. Similar to its usage in the Old Testament,
    ψωνή (*phone*) can also denote the "melody" of a musical
    instrument. Examples of this are flutes and zithers (I
    Corinthians 14:7) and the signal of trumpets (I Corinthians
    14:8);
(2) The human voice. The speech of human beings can make
    ψωνή (*phone*) which are "either agitated or moved by the
    Spirit" (Luke 23:23; Acts 7:57, 60, 26:24) and also which
    praise God (Luke 17:15, 19:37; Revelation 7:10); and
(3) The speech of angels, spirits or bearers of the Spirit.[22]

**In the Book of Revelation**
The Book of Revelation contains many occurrences of ψωνή (*phone*)
which represent a wide variety of uses. In Revelation 1:10, 4:1 and
8:13, ψωνή (*phone*) implies the noise of the sound of trumpets. In
Revelation 10:3, it is a "calling"[23] that sounds like the roar of a lion.
In Revelation 7:10, ψωνή (*phone*) refers to the sound made by the
human voice.[24]

Ψωνή (*Phone*) is produced by the speech of angels, spirits or
bearers of the Spirit as witnessed in Revelation 6:10. The souls of the
martyrs cry out with a loud voice. It is their desire that God reign
down retribution on those who have caused them pain and persecution
(this is similar to the soul of Abel "lamenting in the realm of the
dead").[25] Angels praise God in Revelation 5:12 in a way in which it

---

[22]Ibid., 9:292-293.
[23]Ibid.
[24]Ibid.
[25]Ibid., 9:293.

will be heard on earth (see also Revelation 8:13, 14:7, 9, 18 and 18:2).[26]

In the Apocalypse, ψωνή (*phone*) can also represent the voice of God. In Revelation 10:3, the seven voices of thunder, which reply in speech to the cry of an angel, are not written down because they cannot be translated. The thunders represent the voice of God as witnessed in Psalm 29:3-9. However, the inarticulate thunder of God exists in the Book of Revelation with the very understandable words of the Son of Man like the sound of the trumpet in Revelation 1:10-12. In eschatological fulfillment, God's speaking through nature and angelic creatures is replaced by the directives of the Son of Man "in plerophorous [a variety of] expressions the signs of the theophany at Sinai are transferred to the world-shaking catastrophe of the last judgment."[27]

The ψωνή (*phone*—"sounds and voices") produced by the participants in musical worship in the Book of Revelation are made by two groups. The first group is comprised of the Godhead or agents thereof, principally the angels. The type of sound produced by this group can be called **revelatory**. The second group consists of all creatures of creation who recognize the Godhead. Their primary musical and worship activity is **response** to their God. This group is comprised of the martyrs, the four living creatures (who represent all of creation), the 24 elders and the angels of heaven (see Appendix). Notice that only the angels can serve in both categories.

*Voice* (as revelation—see Revelation 1:12). The voice from heaven is often anonymous.[28] The heavenly voice "seldom gives revelation or elucidation."[29] Most often this voice provides:

(1) imperatives or commands to its hearers (see Revelation 1:11, 10:4, 8, 14:13);
(2) instructions to the angels as to the next action which they need to undertake in the "heavenly drama" (Revelation 9:13, 16:1); or

---

[26]Ibid.
[27]Ibid., 9:296.
[28]Ibid., 9:282.
[29]Ibid., 9:296.

(3)   the final assertion to the completion of the eschatological act
(Revelation 11:15, 12:10, 16:17, 21:3).[30]

*Voice (ψωνή [phone]) of a sound of many waters* (as
revelation—see Revelation 1:15 and 14:2; as response—see Revelation
19:6).   In Revelation 1:15, this sound is reminiscent of the sound of
God's voice in Ezekiel 43:2.[31]  The voice portrays the radiant glory of
God.

*Great loud voice of an angel* (as revelation—see Revelation 5:2, 7:2,
10:3, 14:7, 14:9, 14:15, 14:18 and 19:17).  This sound is made by a
strong angel.  Perhaps this angel was one among the celestial order of
angels.  Ford conjectures that this angel might be Gabriel whose name
means "God is my strength."[32]   This sound conveys the paramount
importance of the message of God.[33]   The authority to wield such a
weighty message could only be given by the Godhead.[34]

*Great loud voices of angels, four living creatures and 24 elders* (as
response—see Revelation 5:11).   These corporate voices create a
"blending of divine, human and angelic sounds in response to the
crowning glory of the Godhead."[35]

*Voice in the midst* (as revelation—see Revelation 6:6).  Swete asserts
that "from the midst of the [ζῷα] zoa" comes "what sounds like a
voice, the protest of Nature against the horrors of famine."[36]

*Great loud voice of martyrs* (as response—see Revelation 6:10).
The cry of the martyrs is for God to avenge their blood.  They petition
God to perform just judgment.  It is also a cry of haste.  It is imploring
the speedy coming of eschatological fulfillment.  This type of cry of the
righteous sufferers has frequently been sent up to heaven throughout
time.[37]   Every generation of martyrs since the first century has "called

[30]Ibid.

[31]IB, 12:376.

[32]J. Massyngberde Ford, ed., *The Anchor Bible:  Revelation* (Garden City, NY:
Doubleday and Company, Inc., 1981), 85.

[33]Martin Kiddle, *The Revelation of St. John,* from the *Moffett New Testament
Commentary* series (New York, NY:  Harper and Brothers Publishers, 1940), 96.

[34]Ford, *The Anchor Bible: Revelation,* 117.

[35]Ibid., 233.

[36]ASJ, 87.

[37]Isbon T. Beckwith, *The Apocalypse of John* (Grand Rapids, MI:  Baker Book
House, 1979), 526.

aloud for judgement [*sic*] on the pagan world"[38] for their sacrificed lives.
*Great loud voice of all creation* (as response—see Revelation 7:10). Gelineau suggests that

> when the Book of Revelation describes the many groups which sing Amen, Alleluia, Holy [presumably the *Sanctus* found in Isaiah 6] and the other hymns to God and the Lamb, the author is using his own experience as a model for the practice of heaven. The canticles in the opening chapters of Luke, and those passages of Paul which are definitely hymns, witness to the creativity of the early Christian communities. It is quite by chance that we learn that Paul and Silas, when in prison at Philippi, spent the night hours 'praying and singing hymns to God' (see Acts 16:25).[39]

Swete describes their response as "the polyglott [*sic*] [multi-lingualed] multitude shouts [-ing] its praises as with one voice."[40] To cry in this way is equal to giving an Emperor, such as Caesar Domitian, one's loyalty.[41]
*Great loud voice out of heaven* (as revelation—see Revelation 9:13, 10:4, 10:7, 10:8, 11:2, 11:15, 12:10, 14:13 and 18:4). This voice is a single, set apart voice which seems to proceed from the horns of the Golden Altar mentioned in Revelation 8:3. It is perhaps the voice of an angel standing above the altar with a golden censer or the voice could represent the saints' prayers. This solitary voice declares the desire of the Church through-out all the ages.[42] It is difficult to pinpoint the author of this voice out of heaven. In Revelation 11:15, this same great loud voice in heaven may belong to the ζῷα (*zoa*) who represents all of creation. Revelation 12:10 does not attribute the great loud voice to either the angels or the ζῷα (*zoa*). Swete believes it to be the voice of one of the elders. But in Revelation 18:4, the great

---

[38]ASJ, 90.

[39]J. Gelineau, "Music and Singing in the Liturgy," *The Study of Liturgy*, Cheslyn Jones, Geoffrey Wainwright and Edward Yarnold, eds., second edition (New York, NY: Oxford University Press, 1992), 498.

[40]ASJ, 101.

[41]Ibid., 101.

[42]Ibid., 120.

loud voice is either the voice of God Himself or the voice of one of the angels representing Him.[43]

*Great loud voice as a lion roars* (as revelation—see Revelation 10:3). The lion is a recurring symbol in the Graeco-Roman world. It represented a sun deity who ruled the world, put an end to evil, and placed the dead into the security of the next world. For the Jewish mind, the lion represented Yahweh's power and the power of the Torah.[44] Consequently, the type of sound produced was one which was very authoritative and powerful.

*Great loud voice out of the shrine* (as revelation—see Revelation 16:1). This voice also illustrates the strength of God's voice. Yet, a parallel reference, in Deuteronomy 28, speaks of a "mystical voice coming out of the high heavens."[45]

*Great loud voice from the throne* (as revelation—see Revelation 16:17, 19:5 and 21:3). When the classical prophets received the Word of God, they ordinarily did not mention that the specific voice of God spoke to them. This was due to the fact that the prophets perceived themselves to be God's voice.[46]

*Great loud voice of a crowd in heaven* (as response—see Revelation 19:1). Swete believes that these shouts of triumph are from a crowd in heaven. He believes that the crowd consisted of an angelic host (*ochlos polus*).[47] Contrarily, Beckwith calls this an "anticipative chorus" with all of the heavenly hosts doxologically praising their God because he has visited justice to the beast and the "slayer of the saints."[48] This antiphonal response is expressed by the four living creatures, the 24 elders and "all the orders of heavenly beings ranged before and round about the Almighty." Both the "higher and lower orders" of creation sing antiphonally.[49]

### Summary
The Godhead, as Creator, relates in a discernably audible manner to Creation via a lowly, human mechanism called ψωνή (*phone*). Vocal

---

[43]Ibid., 141, 154 and 228.
[44]Ford, *The Anchor Bible: Revelation*, 88.
[45]Ibid., 260.
[46]Betz, " Ψωνή (*Phone*)," TDNT, 9:283.
[47]ASJ, 242.
[48]Beckwith, *The Apocalypse*, 720-721.
[49]Ibid.

φωνή (*phone*) can only be produced by air passing through a throat. Characteristic of revelatory vocal φωνή (*phone*) is the empowered strength and clarity of its tone. While prophets in the Old Testament were able to "speak" for Yahweh, only angels will be able to be sanctioned to carry the Godhead's message in eschatological time.

Responsorial vocal φωνή (*phone*) can be expressed by groups as small as a quartet on the one hand and by legions upon legions of all types of creatures on the other. Yet, the type of φωνή (*phone*) which they collectively declare is heard as a single voice. Even multi-lingualed responses sounded simultaneously will be discerned as a single, unified voice.

## Non-Vocal (including Instrumental)

### In the Book of Revelation
The types of non-vocal φωνή (*phone*) produced in the Revelation can be categorized into two groups. One group consists of the sounds of nature and the other group are sounds produced by musical instruments. The musical instruments utilized in the Apocalypse in worship are the harp and the trumpet.

*Great loud voice as a trumpet* (as revelation—see Revelation 1:10-11). This great loud voice rings out as "clear and incisive as a trumpet note." The sound thus produced is "clear, thrilling and ominous."[50] At Sinai, God broke the silence with the voice like a trumpet and it was excrutiatingly loud. At the morning rite, the great door of the Jewish Temple was opened by the signal of a trumpet. The year of Jubilee was ushered in by the call of a silver trumpet. Similarly, the trumpet blast in the Revelation will herald the "Apocalypse of our Savior."[51]

*Voice as of a trumpet* (as revelation—see Revelation 4:1). Interestingly, the Seer first hears the voice, as a far-off voice, and then sees the one speaking.[52] This sound is like that which is mentioned in I Corinthians 14:8; I Thessalonians 4:16; and Hebrews 12:19. It is a Sinai motif taken from Exodus 19:16-19 and 20:18.[53]

---

[50]Kiddle, *The Revelation*, 11, 80.
[51]J. A. Seiss, *The Apocalypse* (New York, NY: Charles C. Cook, 1909), 2:70.
[52]IB, 12:54.
[53]Ibid., 12:70.

*Out of the throne came forth lightnings and voices and thunders* (as
revelation—see Revelation 4:5). Similar phenomenon accompanies
other theophanies (see Exodus 19:16; Ezekiel 1:13; *Apocalypse of
Abraham* 17; and I Enoch 14:11, 17) as in this passage. The sound
emanates from the throne and displays the "awesome majesty of
God."[54]   A loud voice or other great noise often occurs with
Christophanies as well.[55]

In Revelation 4:5, the Greek word  ψωνή (*phone*) is used to
represent a type of sound in nature called βροντή (*bronte*). In this
context it means "thunder." In the plural it could mean "peals of
thunder."[56] In this passage it means "sounds" or "rumblings."[57]

In Psalm 29, thunder is not merely a natural phenomenon. Rather,
it serves as the "rumbling, majestic voice of God."[58]  According to
Betz, in Apocalyptic literature, the "sound, size and color" of claps of
thunder are typically exaggerated. Psalm 29 describes the voice of God
as does the theophany of thunder at Sinai (see Exodus 20:18; Hebrews
12:18).[59]  The display of lightnings, voices and thunders from the
throne illustrate the Creator's power to "destroy the Creation which
denied his laws."[60]

These sounds indicate that the throne is a throne of judgment and
that God's wrath will proceed from it. Similar to Yahweh preparing
to visit Egypt's sins on her, he "sent thunder (voices), and hail, and
fire ran along upon the ground"[61] (see Exodus 19:16). When Yahweh's
wrath was kindled against the Philistines, he "thundered with a great
thunder on that day..., and discomfited them, and they were smitten
before Israel" (I Samuel 7:10).[62]

[54]Ibid., 12:403.

[55]Ibid., 12:374.

[56]Ralph Earle, *Word Meanings in the New Testament* (Grand Rapids, MI: Baker Book
House, 1982), 460.

[57]Ibid.

[58]Betz, " Ψωνή (*Phone*)," TDNT, 9:283.

[59]Ford, *The Anchor Bible: Revelation*, 97.

[60]Kiddle, *The Revelation*, 85.

[61]Seiss, *The Apocalypse*, 1:245.

[62]Ibid.

In John 12:28-29, when a voice from heaven spoke to Jesus, some in the crowd thought that it had either thundered or an angel had spoken to Jesus.[63]

*Sound as of harpers* (as response—see Revelation 5:8, 15:2). Just as incense is associated with the office of the priest, similarly the harp is associated with the prophets. In I Samuel 10:5, Samuel relayed to Saul that "thou shalt meet a company of prophets coming down from the high place, with a psaltery and a tabret, and a pipe, and a harp before them, and they shall prophesy." Similarly, the six sons of Jeduthun prophesied with a harp (see I Chronicles 25:3). In Psalm 49:4, David says "I will open my dark sayings upon the harp."[64] In Revelation 5, the prophetic harps and prayers of incense are held and performed by the worshipers of the Lamb. They remind the Lamb of all the prayers, songs and prophesies which have come before. When the Lamb takes up the Book of Life, he seals the pledge of the Godhead to save them and consequently assures the Redeemed of their long-awaited reward.[65] The type of sound produced by the κιθάρα (*kithara*) are accompanimental.

*Great loud voice of an eagle* (as revelation—see Revelation 8:13). This proclamation of a highly dramatic nature is rendered by a bird of bad omen. This is verifiable in both the scriptures and cultural superstitions.[66] The type of sound produced by the bird captures the attention of all who hear it.

*Sound of thunders* (βροντῆς *[brontes]*) (as revelation—see Revelation 14:2; as response—see Revelation 19:6). The sounds of Revelation 14:2 are not made by the 144,000, but by a heavenly crowd.

In contrast to the angelic host of Revelation 19:1, the voice in Revelation 19:6 is the voice of the "Universal Church"[67] (see Revelation 7:9). These "sound(s) of the collective praise of the Church" in the writer's ears are like "the din of a vast concourse, the roar of a cataract (waterfall or flood)"[68] (see Revelation 1:15, 14:2), or

---

[63]Ford, *The Anchor Bible: Revelation*, 159.
[64]Seiss, *The Apocalypse*, 1:290.
[65]Ibid.
[66]Kiddle, *The Revelation*, 153.
[67]ASJ, 177.
[68]Ibid.

the roll of thunder (see Revelation 6:1, 10:3). The words are discernable. This hallelujah, the fourth one sung in Chapter 19, is thanksgiving to God because he has set up His Kingdom.[69]

## Summary

Revelatory sounds in the Book of Revelation are made by the trumpet and nature. The types of sounds which the trumpet and nature make are majestic, articulate, authoritative and powerful. In contrast to these decidedly punctuated sounds are the non-vocal sounds produced by those who respond. These accompanimental, non-vocal sounds blend well and are harmonious with the vocal sounds made by the worshipers.

### Performance Practice—Manner Sound is Produced

This section will analyze how the vocal and non-vocal sounds are produced.

## Vocal

Ψωνή (*Phone*) can be performed by the human voice in a variety of ways. It can be:

(1)  "Uttered" (Amos 1:2; Proverbs 2:3, 8:1);
(2)  "Called aloud" (Jeremiah 4:16, 12:8, 22:20);
(3)  "Lifted up" (*Jubal* 9:7);
(4)  "Lifted up in joy and rejoicing" (Isaiah 24:14);
(5)  "Raised" (Genesis 39:15, 18; Isaiah 13:2); and
(6)  A "great loud" voice (Genesis 39:14; I Samuel 28:12; II Samuel 15:23, 19:5; I Kings 8:55, 18:27; II Kings 18:28; Isaiah 36:13; Ezekiel 8:18, 11:13; Proverbs 27:14; Ezra 3:12, 10:12; Nehemiah 9:4; II Chronicles 32:18).[70]

When ψωνή (*phone*) is used in the above ways it helps the reader to identify the speaker. It signifies the manner of dealings between the Godhead and Creation. In Psalm 19:2, the ψωνή (*phone*) of the angels declares the glory of God. But Isaiah 6:3 indicates that humankind cannot hear the cries of the seraphim as they never cease to

---

[69]Ibid.
[70]Betz, "Ψωνη (*Phone*)," TDNT, 9:281.

praise God. Yet, the ψωνή (*phone*) of the seraphim are "so loud that they cause the lintels of the temple to shake."[71]

The strength of the ψωνή (*phone*) of angels is similar to Yahweh's use of angels in the Old Testament:

(1)   the roaring of a lion (Revelation 10:3; Amos 1:2; Hosea 11:10); and

(2)   the noise of many waters (Revelation 1:15, 14:2, 19:6; Ezekiel 1:24, 43:2).[72]

The voice of heaven can be regarded as "angelic speech" by some and as a "clap of thunder" by others.[73]   Singing, as the response of humankind, has a unique role in the Christian liturgy because it combines pure music with the word which has been revealed.   The revealed word is the worshiper's "confession of faith in Christ" that "all music can indeed be religious or sacred, but only that music is specifically Christian which articulates the Christian faith."[74]

Wainwright reports that B. Fischer believes that the early church did not sing the psalms.   Rather, they read them as though they were only scriptural lessons.   This conclusion is disputed by J. D. Crichton in *Christian Celebration: The Prayer of the Church* (G. Chapman, 1973), pp. 59-61.[75]   Crichton points out that the Hebrew and Greek languages do not have separate words in their respective vocabularies for "music," per se.   The distinction between singing and speaking was far less wide in the ancient world than it is today in the present century.   From the earliest times, when speech turned into poetry in a public setting, rhythm and melody were naturally incorporated.[76]   Gelineau illustrates the continuum which exists in vocal ψωνή (*phone*) from speech to chant to song:

---

[71]Ibid., 9:282.
[72]Ibid., 9:294.
[73]Ibid.
[74]Gelineau, "Music and Singing in the Liturgy," *The Study of Liturgy*, 443.
[75]DOX, 211.
[76]Gelineau, "Music and Singing in the Liturgy," *The Study of Liturgy*, 444.

Continuum from Word to Music—

(1) Ordinary speech;
(2) Proclamation (cantillation);
(3) Meditation (psalmody);
(4) Chant;
(5) Hymn (lied);
(6) Acclamation (develops from the human cry);
(7) Vocalise and/or jubilus
    (including the use of melodic instruments).[77]

As previously discussed, both views are correct according to recent scholarship. In the synagogue, psalms were not sung, but only taught and read. In early church worship—following the example of the worship in the Temple—psalms were sung.

Two characteristics of singing in the early church were that one must be filled with the Holy Spirit, and the singing must be the expression of a conscious faith.[78] All musical action in a liturgical context consists of a "significant" human act, a symbolic and ritual context, and a given musical form.

The main characteristic of singing in Christian worship is "to act as a support for the words."[79] That is, the music, as a means, should serve the text (the end). The term which defines this role of music is logogenic as opposed to pathogenic.[80] The actual performance should look for real human and religious dimensions which provide "significance to the musical activity" in question.[81]

**In the Book of Revelation**
    Say (λέγω [lego]) (as revelation—see Revelation 1:11, 1:17, 4:1, 6:6, 7:2, 9:14, 10:4, 10:8, 11:12, 11:15, 12:10, 14:7, 14:8, 14:9, 14:13, 14:18, 16:1, 16:5, 16:17, 18:4, 19:5, 19:17, 21:3; as

---

[77]Ibid., 450-454.
[78]Ibid., 445.
[79]Ibid., 450.
[80]Pathogenic music describes the situation that exists in melismatic music in which the text is delivered in a highly florid, emotional manner.
[81]Gelineau, "Music and Singing in the Liturgy," *The Study of Liturgy*, 450.

response—see Revelation 4:8, 4:10, 5:5, 5:9, 5:11, 5:13, 5:14, 6:1, 6:3, 6:5, 6:7, 6:10, 7:10, 7:12, 11:16, 15:3, 19:1, 19:4, 19:6). λέγω (*Lego*) can be translated in a variety of ways:

(1) "I say or speak";
(2) "I speak of";
(3) "I mean";
(4) "I tell"; and
(5) "I command."[82]

In Revelation 2:1 and 8, λέγω (*lego*) is also used as a "formal and solemn phrase to introduce the edicts of Emperors and magistrates" (see also Matthew 5:34, 39; Romans 2:22).[83] When λέγω (*lego*) is used as revelation via the voice of the Godhead or an agent thereof, it is used in the imperative and implies a command. This use can be seen in Revelation 10:8 when the voice commands the Seer to take the scroll from the angel.[84] In Revelation 11:15, a loud voice proclaims that which was previously hidden in the silence after the opening of the last seal. And in Revelation 12:10, the voice is sounded in a proleptic [anticipated] manner.[85]

The doxological praise of the 24 elders in Revelation 4:10-11 is different from the praise ascribed to the Godhead by the four living creatures. The 24 elders address God, and the praise is based on God's work in creation. The ζῷα (*zoa*) praise God for his divine attributes. Later in Revelation 5, the 24 elders will praise the Lamb for his work in redemption.[86]

*Sing* (αδω [*ado*]) (as response—see Revelation 5:9, 14:3, 15:3). The Greek word αδω (*ado*) literally means "to sing" or "to celebrate" something.[87] In the period of the early church, αδω (*ado*) could dually represent both the spoken word and song. The era did not differentiate between the two: the distinction between them was "fluid."[88]

---

[82]VGNT, 372.
[83]Ibid.
[84]Kiddle, *The Revelation*, 173.
[85]Ibid., 207, 233.
[86]Robert H. Mounce, *The Book of Revelation* (Grand Rapids, MI: William B. Eerdmans Publishing Company, 1977), 139, 147.
[87]Heinrich Schlier, "Αδω (*Ado*)," TDNT, 1:163-164.
[88]Ibid.

In Revelation 5:9, 14:3 and 15:3 appears the phrase αδειν οδαν (*adein odan*—translated "to sing songs"). This same language appears in Colossians 3:16 and Ephesians 5:19. Both Ephesians 5:19 and Revelation 5:13 include the word λαλειν (*lalein*—"to say"). Revelation 5:9 reads αδουσιν οδαν καιναν λεγοντες (*adousin odan kainan legontes*—"they sing song a new saying"). This verse contains both the verbs "sing" and "say." However, λέγω (*lego*) appears most frequently without αδω (*ado*) throughout the remainder of the Book of Revelation. Because the construction of the formula of Revelation 5:9 is similar to that of the other λέγω (*lego*) passages in Revelation, it can be conjectured that λέγω (*lego*), broadly defined, can include the act of singing.[89] The practice of chant refers to the process of furnishing words and sentences with "the most phonetic inflexion."[90] Three types exist:

(1)   Plain recitation (spoken);
(2)   Echonesis (semi-musical recitative); and
(3)   Cantillation (regular musical chant).[91]

Consequently, λέγω (*lego*) can be interpreted broadly to include "to sing."

A preference for the high voice can be found in the ecclesiastical chant which was essentially carried over from the synagogue tradition where the cantor had "an almost monopolistic influence."[92] The high voice was desired because it was "flexible and capable of the elegant delivery of melismatic lines."[93] The musicians who performed classical Greek music developed a "speech melody" (λογοδες μελός [*logodes melos*]) which consisted of a "system of tonic accent distinguished by actual variations in pitch. Among the symbols devised by Alexandrian scholars the acute accent mark indicates an original heightening, the grave accent a lowering and the circumflex a combined

[89]Ibid., 1:164.
[90]TSB, 104.
[91]Ibid.
[92]Owen Jander, "Singing," NGD, 17:339.
[93]Ibid.

rise and fall."[94] Consequently, pitch accent may have had a part in shaping melodic lines.

*Proclaim* (καρυσσο [*karusso*]) (as revelation—see Revelation 5:2). The common usage of καρυσσο (*karusso*) in the period of the early church was "to announce" as in a public announcement.[95]

*Cry* (εκραζό [*ekrazo*]) (as revelation—see Revelation 7:2, 10:3, 14:14, 18:2, 19:17; as response—see Revelation 7:10). In Romans 9:27, this same word was used for the crying of the prophet Isaiah. It was also used in conjunction with the "fervent prayer of the Spirit in the hearts of men" (see Galatians 4.6).[96]

*Spoke* (ελαλεο [*elaleo*]) or uttered (as revelation—see Revelation 10:3, 10:4). This sound is "a low sound, like the lowing of an ox" (see Job 6:5; I Kings 6:12) or the "growl of thunder."[97] Coupled with this low or deep voice is the fact that it is extremely loud in volume. The sound probably does not convey understandable words.[98] This sound is not a cry of fear or distress but a "shout of power."[99] Its sound draws the awe-inspiring attention of its hearers. It serves in this passage as a signal. No words were uttered, although a reply was at once forthcoming.[100]

*Rejoice* (Χαιρόυσεο [*Chairouseo*])...*and are glad* (ευθραινεο [*euthraineo*]) (as response—see Revelation 11:10). The root χαιρό (*chairo*) means "to rejoice"[101] and is a very common opening in letters from the period of the early church (see Acts 15:23, 23:26; James 1:1). It is used as a "mutual greeting" as in the following example: "Greeting (χαιρό [*chairo*]), my Lord Apion."[102]

*Responsory* (as response—see Revelation 5:9-14, 11:15-18, 16:4-7, 19:5-8). The simple idea of expressing a common thought through repetition by a large group of people occurred from the earliest times in the Jewish culture as well as other ancient groups, primarily the

---

[94]Warren D. Anderson, *Ethos and Education in Greek Music* (Cambridge, MA: Harvard University Press, 1966), 3.
[95]VGNT, 343.
[96]Ford, *The Anchor Bible: Revelation*, 99.
[97]Ibid., 158-159.
[98]Ibid.
[99]Seiss, *The Apocalypse*, 2:129.
[100]ASJ, 127.
[101]VGNT, 682.
[102]Ibid.

Orientals. The Babylonian-Assyrian liturgy contained formulas of acclamation which were likely sung and were used as an introduction to various ceremonies. The oft-repeated refrains in Assyrian hymns were likely sung responsorially by a priest as the precentor and answered by a choir.[103]

Responsorial and antiphonal singing met the sociological needs for groups of people to bond.

This trend...is manifest wherever religiously bent people are grouped together in a common social environment. If religion is to be considered one of the strongest cementing powers of collective life and communal consciousness, singing in joint religious manifestations must be adjudged the same binding force.[104]

The role of music in Egyptian religious cultic practice was of the highest significance. Soloists intoned hymns to which choirs answered responsorially.[105]        Babylonian hymns and psalms were sung responsorially by priests and congregations. They heavily influenced the Jewish psalm writers.    When the Jews were deported from Babylonia by King Nebuchadnezzar (see Nehemiah 7:67), they continued the Babylonian practice of responsorial singing as well as the singing of psalms and lamentations.[106]

As much as it appears that pagan influences weighed heavily on the formulation of a Jewish musical tradition, it should not be over-emphasized. The religious institutions of the other ancient peoples were markedly very dissimilar to the patriarchal religion of the chosen people of Yahweh.[107]

In the realm of Jewish music, responsorial psalmody can be defined as "the chanting of a psalm by alternation between a soloist (cantor), who sings a verse or verses, and a chorus (congregation or choir), who sing a refrain ("respond").[108] It was both a style of performance and

---

[103]MSR, 166-167.

[104]Franz Lietner, *Der gottesdienstliche Volkgesang im jüdischen und christlichen Alterum*, trans. by Alfred Sendrey (Freiburg: i. B., 1906), 38.

[105]MSR, 41.

[106]Ibid., 53.

[107]Ibid., 138.

[108]Thomas H. Connelly, "Responsorial Psalmody," NGD, 15:759.

a formal structure. An example of responsorial music occurred at the Exodus. Following the Israelites crossing of the Red Sea, the responsive singing of the Jewish women and the Song of Moses praised Yahweh for his mighty salvatory deliverance. This act of responsorial singing was heavily influenced by the Egyptian culture.[109]

The psalmody referred to in the Talmud was responsorial in character as opposed to antiphonal. Present-day scholarship has recently established that the psalms were originally composed for a cultic purpose—"the response of a group to a leader in prayer is a fundamental and universal manner of worship."[110]

Early Christian writers, like Tertullian and Egeria, mention the use of responsorial music in their respective worship practices. From their comments, it can be conjectured that perhaps "a natural continuity of responsorial psalmody"[111] originated from Jewish tradition. Logically, in time it likely passed through the first-century early church to later Christian liturgical use.[112]

*Antiphony* (as response—see Revelation 4:8-11, 5:9-14, 7:9-17, 19:1-4). Antiphonal singing was the dominating musical force at Egyptian festivals. It was performed by choral groups which consisted of dancing men and women. Frequently, young men marched in procession and sang songs until, "possessed by the spirit,"[113] they began to prophesy in honor of their bull-shaped god Apis.[114] Sacred music was performed by a special guild of temple singers and musicians. The tradition was passed orally and was revered because of its "effect upon the human soul."[115] The Assyrians performed hymns antiphonally and illustrate well the fact that both antiphonal music and responsorial music were used long before it was recorded in the Old Testament Jewish culture.[116]

Although no precise reference alludes to antiphony in the Old Testament, antiphonal psalmody is implied in Exodus 15:21; Numbers

---

[109]MSR, 87.
[110]Connolly, "Responsorial Psalmody," NGD, 15:759.
[111]Ibid.
[112]Ibid.
[113]MAI, 40.
[114]Ibid.
[115]Ibid.
[116]Ibid., 46.

10:35; 21:17;[117] I Samuel 18:7; Ezra 3:10-11; and Nehemiah 12:31-42.
Antiphonal psalmody consists of the "chanting of a psalm by two choirs
or half-choirs in alternation, commonly with an added refrain-like text
called an antiphon."[118]
    Antiphonal singing was part of the original official liturgy in the
Temple and became an oft-used form in sacred musical performances.
Antiphonal singing was also mentioned in connection with funeral
observances (see II Samuel 1:19, 25, 27; and II Chronicles 35:25).[119]
Antiphonal singing was the Jewish tradition's greatest early contribution
to the development of music.

## Summary
The use of λέγω (*lego*) in the Apocalypse contains the spectrum of
vocal sound production, from declamatory speech to sung song. Λέγω
(*Lego*—"to say"), καρυσσο (*karusso*—"to proclaim"), εκαζό
(*ekrazo*—"to cry"), and ελαλεό (*elaleo*—"to speak or utter") are
manners in which revelatory vocal ψωνή (*phone*) are produced in the
Book of Revelation.
    Eschatological fulfillment, as witnessed in the Book of Revelation,
indicates that responsive creation replies to the acts of the Godhead via
a more mannered speech, i.e., song. The singing in the time of the
early church could be expressed by αδω (*ado*—"to sing") as well as
λέγω (*lego*—"to say"). In contrasting balance to the declamatory
ψωνή (*phone*) of the Godhead, the praise of Creation will be
responsorial and antiphonal singing given in a spirit of glad
χαιρουσεο (*chairouseo*—"rejoicing").

## Non-vocal (including instrumental)
Instruments have been kept out of the church throughout the ages
largely on socio-historical grounds. But Gelineau proposes that "a
balanced attitude to instrumental music sees the instrument as an
extension of the human voice and body."[120] When people accompany
their singing or perform pure instrumental music, it widens their

[117]Ralph P. Martin, *Worship in the Early Church* (Grand Rapids, MI: William B.
Eerdmans Publishing Company, 1964), 40.
    [118]Thomas H. Connolly, "Antiphonal Psalmody," NGD, 1:481.
    [119]MAI, 168.
    [120]Gelineau, "Music and Singing in the Liturgy," *The Study of Liturgy*, 444.

capacity for song.[121] An analysis of non-vocal music in the Book of Revelation follows.

*Having harps* [presumably to play them] (as response—see Revelation 5:8, 15:2). In Revelation 5:8, the harps, which the 24 elders play, serve as a pacifying accompanimental force which blends harmoniously with their song. The harps are "held" to the players' breast by the left hand. The strings are strummed by the right hand.

When the martyrs acquire harps in Revelation 15:2, it can be conjectured that the harps are played in a similar manner. The martyrs' harps, however, could be played in a different manner because they are called God's. harps and accompany the song which "no one else can learn." Kiddle suggests that "the celestial harmony is now complete, [with] the diapason closing full on [Redeemed] man."[122]

*...in order that they might trumpet (σάλπιζσ—salpizo)* (as revelation—see Revelation 8:1, 6). No two of the trumpets are alike and "there is a gradual rising" from the first until the last.

> One touches the ground, the trees, and the green grass. Another touches the sea, the ships, and the creatures of the sea. A third touches the rivers and the springs of water. A fourth touches the sun, moon, and stars. A fifth breaks open the door of separation between earth and hell. A sixth unlooses the dreadful army of horses and horsemen, the seven thunders, and the mighty struggle and murder of the two witnesses. And the last brings on 'the battle of the great day of God Almighty.'[123]

This description illustrates a great deal of order and forethought. When the scripture says "they prepared themselves that they might trumpet," it is not referring to mere technical performance practice. It is referring to the "deliberate adjustment among themselves [the angels] of the place and subject which each one was to take in the work" of the end-times.[124] The sounds made in succession are not "haphazard" sounds. Ετοιμαζο (*Etoimazo*—"readymaking") is used to imply the

---

[121]Ibid.
[122]Kiddle, *The Revelation*, 266.
[123]Seiss, *The Apocalypse*, 2:40.
[124]Ibid.

"pre-determinations"[125] of actions which follow the necessary rehearsals before the action is to take place.[126]

The voice of the trumpet is the most significant voice mentioned in the scriptures. In early Old Testament times, it was described as a strong and loud cry which was sounded only for special events. In Revelation 8, the number of trumpets is seven: a complete and perfect ensemble. These trumpets are not mere copies of those that came before throughout history. The trumpets in the Book of Revelation are the prototypes. The Old Testament trumpets are copies of the heavenly trumpets which the Seer witnessed in his vision.[127]

*Trumpeted* (as revelation—see Revelation 8:2, 8:7, 8:8, 8:10, 8:12, 9:1, 9:13, 11:15). In Revelation 8:2, 6, 7, 8, 10, 12, 13; 9:1, 14; 10:7; and 11:15, the trumpet stands "by itself, separate and complete."[128] It is used in scripture because of its "loud, piercing and far-reaching sound." The purpose of the trumpet blast is "to demand the attention of all men [sic] in view of a matter of urgent importance."[129]

In Revelation 8:7 appears the word "sounded" (Greek verb is σάλπιζο [salpizo]) which comes from the noun σάλπινχ (salpinx) which means "trumpet." In this passage, sounded means "to sound a trumpet."[130]

According to the account of Plutarch, "certain Egyptian delta towns" disliked the sound of the trumpet because it sounded like an "ass's bray."[131] Baines conjectures that the sound consisted of "a series of powerful blasts on a pitch roughly corresponding to the lower sound" of a trumpet.[132]

The angels which perform the trumpet calls are seven in number. Ford supposes them to be:

(1) Uriel—the "Fire of God";
(2) Raphael—"God has healed";

---

[125]Ibid., 2:42.
[126]Ibid.
[127]Ibid., 2:22-25.
[128]IB, 266.
[129]Ibid.
[130]Earle, *Word Meanings*, 460.
[131]BI, 56.
[132]Ibid.

(3) Raguel—the "Friend of God";
(4) Michael—"Who is like God";
(5) Sariel—the "Prince of God";
(6) Gabriel—"God is my strength"; and
(7) Remiel—the "Thunder of God" or the "Height of God."[133]

*Being about to trumpet* (as revelation—see Revelation 8:13, 10:7). The trumpet was primarily used to sound an alarm, but in later centuries, in Christian liturgical use the trumpet came to be a priestly instrument.  In the Book of Revelation, it serves primarily as a heralding instrument.[134]  In this passage, the trumpet introduces the "acts of God" which are "cosmic disturbances uncontrollable by man."[135]

## Summary
The sounds of both the harp and the trumpet are likely produced according to commonly accepted earthly practice.  The harp is strummed and the trumpet is played with pursed lips by blowing air through a narrow shaft.  Due to the nature, however, of the song which "no one can learn," it is possible that the martyr's accompanimental harps are played in a completely unknown way.  Because the present age has no clue as to the physical nature of their "heavenly bodies," it is impossible to conjecture as to the manner in which the martyr's harps might be played.

Sciss makes a point of stressing the "readiness" with which the angel's prepare to trumpet.  Eschatological fulfillment requires a meticulously worked out plan.  So too, does the music which accompanies it.

## Postures of Performance

An important element in the production of the types of sounds recorded in the Book of Revelation is the physical posture from which they are made.  Unfortunately, little research has been done in this area.

---

[133]Ford, *The Anchor Bible: Revelation*, 130.
[134]Ibid., 132.
[135]Ibid., 146.

**In the Book of Revelation**

*Sitting* (as response—see Revelation 4:4, 11:16). The 24 elders are angelic kings, "a rank in the heavenly hierarchy."[136] They are kings owing to the fact that they are wearing robes and crowns and they are sitting on thrones about the throne of God.[137]

*Before [facing] the throne (and round the throne)* (as response—see Revelation 4:6, 5:11, 14:3). "In the midst"[138] of the throne connotes an orchestral circular area which is reminiscent of a Greek amphitheater. In the Greek theater, the speaking place of the gods was situated on the perimeter of the stage, whereas in the Book of Revelation, it dominates the center of the stage. Surrounding it are stone seats which serve as small thrones. They were carved out of stone and reserved for important personalities.[139] In the Book of Revelation these seats are occupied by the 24 elders. Throughout the drama of heavenly worship, the 24 elders assume standing, sitting and kneeling positions.

The martyrs or Redeemed mentioned in Revelation 7 are seen facing the throne. While they are not "joined to the throne," they are in its presence. Consequently, they occupy a place near the throne,[140] perhaps even nearer than the angels.[141]

*Fall before* (as response—see Revelation 4:10, 5:8, 5:14, 11:16, 19:4). The 24 elders prostrate themselves before the throne, and cast their crowns before the throne and praise the Godhead.[142] Owing to the fact that the elders are holding harps, it is highly unlikely that when they "fell down" to worship they prostrated to their bellies. Rather, it is perhaps more likely that they went to their knees and bowed. This would provide them the freedom to accompany themselves on the harp.

*Standing* (as response—see Revelation 5:6). A literal translation of the text indicates that the angels stood in a circle around the throne. No mention is made of a standing posture of the four living creatures, the 24 elders nor the martyrs.

---

[136]Beckwith, *The Apocalypse*, 498.
[137]Ibid.
[138]Ford, *The Anchor Bible: Revelation*, 70.
[139]Ibid.
[140]Seiss, *The Apocalypse*, 1:448.
[141]Ibid.
[142]Mounce, *The Book of Revelation*, 139.

**Summary**

Very little material concerns itself with the physical posturing of the responsorial groups around the throne in the Book of Revelation. While it is typical to sit or stand erect in order to play the trumpet and to sing, little instruction is provided in the text of Revelation regarding this. The most notable inference regards the playing of the harp. In Revelation 5:8, while holding harps, the 24 elders "fall down" and worship before the Lamb. They clearly cannot prostrate themselves on the ground and accompany their singing with the harp. It is more likely that they bowed on their knees

# 6

# A Theology of Music for Worship

THIS chapter sets forth a theology of music for worship derived from the Book of Revelation. In order to accomplish this task, this chapter will synthesize the purely musical elements found in worship in the Book of Revelation and provide a manner in which to deal with the music from both a theological and worship context.

**Background—Theology Becomes Ritual**
The six dimensions of the religious experience advanced by Ninian Smart are:

(1) Ritual;
(2) Mythological;
(3) Doctrinal or theological;
(4) Ethical;
(5) Social; and
(6) Experiential.[1]

In the development of religions, what was done via ritual probably occurred before it was determined what was said (myth). But ritual and myth are linked because it can be supposed that "the myth is

---

[1]Ninian Smart, *The Religious Experience of Mankind* (New York, NY: Charles Scribner's Sons, 1976) 7-12.

already implicit in the ritual."[2]  Wainwright agrees and adds that worship in a Christian context is

> the point of concentration at which the whole of the Christian life comes to ritual focus... Into the liturgy (of the ritual) the people bring their entire existence so that it may be gathered up in praise.[3]

Wainwright includes in his definition of worship both Smart's ritual and myth.[4]  Theology typically is developed following ritual and myth in order to describe those activities.

Theology is the discipline which "investigates and systematizes knowledge concerning the phenomenon of God."[5]  Systematic theology seeks an orderly progression of this knowledge and thereby approaches a scientific study.  However, in a true sense "theology can never be a science, because it does not recognize the supreme law of science, namely reason as the final arbiter."[6]

Theology relies ultimately on faith.  Zerbe agrees with Brunner's assessment and purports that theology, whether systematic, polemical, or other, "is neither historical, Biblical, polemical and dialectic."[7]  Unfortunately, in order for polemical theology to refute reason, it must employ reason to do it.[8]  Theology spreads the vision of the Christian community by articulating its message and the vision of theology experiences a singular consummating objective in worship.[9]

As this study was begun, this writer had concluded that the type of theology of music which would result would be entirely systematically reasoned.  But, as the study progressed, he has found it to be systematic also in a "practical" sense.  This study has identified the music for worship in the Book of Revelation and analyzed it according to:  (1) the forms of music;  (2) the performing groups;  (3) the

---

[2]John MacQuarrie, *God-Talk* (New York, NY:  Harper and Row, 1967), 19.
[3]DOX, 8.
[4]Ibid., 9.
[5]ATM, v.
[6]Alvin Sylvester Zerbe, *The Karl Barth Theology* (Cleveland, OH:  Central Publishing House, 1910), 244.
[7]Ibid.
[8]Ibid.
[9]DOX, 9.

types of sounds the performers make; and (4) how they make those sounds. This analysis is essentially practical but does not imply a "pragmatic" study as defined by Smart. Smart refers to pragmatic theology as theology or ritual aimed at "the attainment of certain experiences"[10] via human response. This is in contradistinction to "sacred ritual" which he describes as being "directed toward a holy being, such as God."[11] The practical theology which follows can be aligned with the doing of sacred ritual. It is directed solely at the Godhead. Also, while this "theology" is derived from the Book of Revelation, this "theology" is rooted in and relies on the entire biblical record—Genesis to Revelation. Christian theology must be placed in its full historical continuum.

All of the great religions developed through theophanies. In Judaism, Moses witnessed the presence of God at Mt. Sinai. Elijah was able to challenge the priests of Baal at Mount Carmel when he called down Yahweh's fire from heaven. Even in Jesus' day, his followers witnessed many of his signs and miracles. But in the following current age, it seems that a "non-religious secularized environment"[12] has taken hold wherein the supernatural has been limited to indwelling finite believers. In the future eschatological time of final judgment, which the Book of Revelation deals with, supernatural manifestations again reappear.

Zerbe asserts that both Barth and Brunner believe that religious education cannot begin with what people do in practicing their faith. Rather, religious education must be approached from the perspective of what the Godhead has done, is doing, or will do,[13] or, perhaps, what the Godhead allows humankind to do in religion. In the Book of Revelation, the visions which the writer unveils to the reader are glimpses of what the Godhead allows all of creation, including humankind, to do in terms of eschatological worship. The place of music in worship can be summarized as follows:

Music is in some strange and mystical way a credential of God. We come into some place where sacred songs fall upon our

---

[10]Smart, *The Religious Experience of Mankind*, 7.
[11]Ibid.
[12]MacQuarrie, *God-Talk*, 19.
[13]Zerbe, *The Karl Barth Theology*, 267.

spirits, and a transformation begins within us. We do not argue. We seek no syllogism. But there comes a sense of God, a consciousness of his holy presence. What does this?... is it the inevitable creed of music, recited in the temple of the soul? Is it the confession of faith, set in the harmony of God's own making? The theologian, without being dogmatic, will not hesitate to reply affirmatively, and to declare that the song of God is an evidence of the God of song.

...Music can have no higher function than this—of taking its large and persuasive place in the program of God's holy temple and of thus preparing us for that city in which the seer beholds 'no sanctuary" simply because the habit of worship has so trained the heart that all the world becomes 'Bethel,' the house of God.[14]

While it presupposes submission to God, worship, in its highest sense, is not supplication for needs, or even thanksgiving for blessings, but "the occupation of the soul with God himself."[15]

## A Theology of Music for Worship

A summary listing of the chief characteristics of music in worship derived from the Book of Revelation forms the basis of a proposed theology of music. They are:

**(1) A continuum of vocal sound ranges from declamatory speech to sung word as revelation and response mechanisms.**

"Liturgical music serves one purpose—to support the text."[16] Similarly, the music of the Book of Revelation serves to support the eschatological worship of God. Revelation of the Godhead is generally expressed by declamatory speech in the Book of Revelation, whereas the worshipers' responses appear to consist of the continuum from declamation to singing.

**(2) A mandate exists for the saints to continue the *Imago Dei* process by creatively composing new songs of praise.**

---

[14]Ibid., 68.
[15]Robert E. Coleman, *Songs of Heaven* (Old Tappan, NJ: Fleming H. Revell Company, 1980), 58.
[16]ATM, 11.

Through the end of the age, humankind is exhorted to fulfill the
process of creation. For the use of music in worship, this means that
worshipers are to continue to create new musical compositions.
Although the work of Christ was completed at Calvary, the saints are
to persevere to the end of time. Characteristic of the martyred saints
in the Book of Revelation is the utilization of their own "new" songs
as they doxologically praise the Godhead. These fresh examples of
song imply that the martyred saints are continuing to grow in their
responses to the near-completed eschatological work of the Godhead.

(3) **Instrumental accompaniments (specifically, timbres which
blend with the human voice) are used to aid in the vocal response
to the Godhead.**

The Book of Revelation assumes that the Godhead is most satisfied
with the vocal sounds produced by the creaturely device known as
"speech" (including song). But the worshipers, whether they be the
saints or the 24 elders, are allowed to augment their utterance of praise
via non-vocal means. In the Apocalypse, the distinctive timbre of the
harp in worship blends harmoniously with the worshipers' collective
voices. It should be noted that the instrumental support does not
supplant the importance of the words of the text nor does it contain a
mixture of diverse instruments. The instrumental ensemble contains a
singular type of instrument which blends with the voice. This supports
the Greek idea of ethos. The careless mixing of instrumental timbres
could destroy the single affection of the moment. Also, only the
worshipers as responders use instrumental accompaniment, and the
instruments are presumably the handiwork of their own invention.

(4) **Instrumental heralding (specifically, the trumpet call) is used
to announce the revelation of the Godhead.**

Only the angels, as agents of the Godhead, are called upon to play
the trumpet. Used in a priestly context, trumpets are symbols of the
Godhead. As heralding revelatory devices, trumpets appear in an
ensemble, but are not used in the ensemble in a conventional manner.
Rather, they are used singly in succession. The natural question arises
"why could not a single angel blow the same trumpet seven times?"
This study has shown that the angels appear most frequently as a group,
perhaps to provide a well-balanced and unified social order. Just as the
church is made up of many members who need to band together, so
too, the angels, as agents of the Godhead, can function in a more
balanced and complete manner as a group.

(5) The exhibition of emotion in the performance of the music exists owing to the use of a variety of Greek verbs such as say, sing, rejoice, cry, and a variety of sounds from nature. Examples of the sounds of nature are the sound of many waters and the sounds of thunder.

Dramatic expression is conveyed throughout the various dialogues in the Book of Revelation. The Godhead expresses Godself through an assortment of voices, primarily of nature. God employs the human "cry" in only one passage. Although these voices are understood by the hearers, some of whom are human, the respective voices' characteristic timbres are basically taken from animate and inanimate nature. Contrarily, the responses of the worshipers are primarily manifest via the sound and timbre of the human voice. But even in that, the continuum of vocal human sound from declamation to sung song is evident.

Human beings exist of two components: mind and emotion. To separate them would detract from the balance which God intended. It is important that each exist in order to provide balance.[17] This is true not only for contemporary worshipers, but it will continue to be important for eschatological worshipers. Eschatological worshipers, as evidenced in the Apocalypse, display a dramatic excitement in their doxological praise of the Godhead.

(6) The postures for the performance of music in worship involve more that just sitting and standing.

Just as singing, speech and sounds of this old earth seem to continue on in the Seer's glimpse into the future, so apparently, our "new" physical bodies display characteristics of our "old" bodies. The worshipers appear around the throne in a variety of human postures: sitting, standing, kneeling and falling down. These physical posturings represent the worshipers' attitudes before and around the throne. Coupled with these positions is the idea of facing and coming before the throne. It seems important for the worshipers visibly to be able to see the object of their worship. Consequently, the "new" body will be able to withstand the "blinding" glory and splendor of the Godhead. So too, it appears, our new "personhood" perhaps will be subject to the gravitational forces of the New Jerusalem.

---

[17]Calvin M. Johansson, *Music and Ministry* (Peabody, MA: Hendrickson Publishers, Inc., 1986), 64-65.

(7)  The music of worship includes the use of the sounds of nature from all creation, both animate and inanimate.

The revelation of the Godhead utilized the entire gamut of vocal and non-vocal sounds known to all of creation.   Coupled with the theophanies of thunder, et al., is the anthropomorphism of the angel's, as agent for the Godhead, exclusive use of a human being's  "cry." Based on evidence in the Book of Revelation, only expressions of revelation by the Godhead, or its agents, can be accompanied by all animate and inanimate sounds of nature from all creation.   The worshipers of the Apocalypse express themselves via the primary means of vocal production.  Only instrumental accompaniment is optional for these worshipers.  Instrumental solos as a response are not found in this eschatological worship.

(8)  A sense of unity [κοινώνια (*koinonia*)] is perceived via the dynamics of antiphonal and responsorial response by the various groups.

The use of a variety of choirs and ensembles in the Apocalypse portrays the responsorial creatures assembled in like-kind groupings. They respond in an orderly and balanced manner which witnesses the totally complete, uncompromising unity of all of the Godhead's creation.  Worship in the Apocalypse is "genuinely congregational" and inclusively unites variegated levels of creation into a sea of doxological praise to the Godhead.[18]

The assorted musical ensembles are well-organized, well-rehearsed and, consequently, well-prepared.    And the preparedness extends beyond  mere  musical  considerations;  the  ensembles  are  well-choreographed also.

(9)  Old προσκυνέο (*proskuneo*), motivated by reverential fear of  a  vertical  master-to-slave  nature,  merges  with  a  new προσκυνέο (*proskuneo*), motivated by love of a horizontal host-to-guest nature.  Theology becomes doxology as the solemn act of worship.

The master/slave mentality of the relationship between Yahweh and his chosen people loses primacy.  It is superseded by the host/guest relationship which Jesus displayed between himself and his followers. The de-emphasis of physical prostration in the new προσκυνέο (*proskuneo*) allows for ἀγάπη (*agape*) love to be manifest as the

---

[18]Evelyn Underhill, *Worship* (New York, NY:  Harper and Row, 1936), 98.

primary motivator of the doxological praise of the Godhead. This overriding characteristic of spiritual love predominates the worship of the Godhead. It is supported by the full spectrum of humankind attributes: emotive musical expression, the social unity of musical ensembles, the mental assertion of the musically creative will, and the physical actions of human posturings in musical performance. The gamut of eschatological worship is in perfect doxological balance as the worshipers respond to the consummated actions of the Godhead in history.

(10) Music dramatically involves all the senses of humanity and all the collective resources available in all Creation.

The music in worship found in the Apocalypse illustrates well the counterpoint of all of the forces of creation: humankind versus the heavenly hosts versus all other living creatures; the redeemed of humankind versus the unbelievers; the new earth versus the old; and the new music versus the old music. Ritual ties "speech, gesture, rhythm and agreed ceremonial"[19] into the activity of humankind worship. It results in uniting humankind's physical, mental and emotional components in a socially unifying response to its focus.[20] Within this entirely balanced system exists music which appeals to all the senses of all creation. To all creation this "new" music appeals to all levels of animate and inanimate consciousness: mental, emotional, physical, social and spiritual and others which humanity cannot presently fathom.

The music for worship in the Book of Revelation is a means whereby the worshipers lose themselves in the total adoration of the Godhead. To "lose themselves in worship" does not imply a loss of the worshipers' relational position to the Godhead. Rather, it implies that any of the worshipers' wrong motivations for worship are suppressed entirely. The highest form of the worshipers' spiritual love is poured out to the Godhead in doxological praise.

---

[19]Ibid., 37.
[20]Ibid.

## Synthesizing a Theology of Music for Worship

According to Adey, there are three primary types of hymns.[21] They are:

(1) Objective, which "offers praise or beseeches mercy for all...(or) conveys teaching to believers."[22] Humanity is invited to shed all its worldly distinctions and concerns in favor of adoration to the Godhead. Objective hymnody consists primarily of songs of praise;

(2) Subjective, which contains a "core of objective assertions"[23] and is typically sung in the first person. Gospel hymnody is basically embodied in this category; and

(3) Reflexive, which lends itself to idolatry because it "hovers on the edge of ecclesiology."[24] This type of hymnody is evidenced textually by phraseologies which speak of the actions of the worshipers. Reflexive texts which survive from long ago are those which are able to detach their message from contemporary issues.[25]

The above categorizations regarding hymns can be generally applied to worship encounters. One can experience worship in the following three ways: (1) actually "doing" worship (objective), as in doxologically praising the Godhead; (2) personalizing worship (subjective); and (3) talking about what the worshiper does in worship (reflexive).

Θεός (*Theos*) is God; "ology" (from λογος *logos*) in "theology" connotes a reflection or a study as in the study of a science. Thus, "theology" is the study or science of knowing God. But theology was not originally intended to be a reflexive study. Rather, just as the term mythology originally meant the actual doing or recital of myth, so too,

---

[21]Lionel Adey, *Hymns and the Christian "Myth"* (Vancouver: University of British Columbia, 1986), 7, and its sequel, *Class and Idol in the English Hymn* (Vancouver: University of British Columbia Press, 1986). In his two books, Adey enumerates a total of 15 types, of which the three mentioned here are primary.

[22]Ibid.

[23]Ibid.

[24]Ibid.

[25]Lionel Adey, *Hymns*, 7.

theology was first practiced as the "solemn utterance about God Himself."[26] So, it was not at first reflexive. Theology originally consisted of the act of knowing God, and thus in reverence bowing before God.

Before theology was developed, ritual and myth were the actual recital of worship to a deity based on oral tradition. From this foundation, theology evolved to interpret and codify the actual practices. Through the ages, an aspect of theology has reflexively become the study of the recital of worship. Liturgical theology is rooted in thought. And thought is perhaps tertiary, subsequent to the primary action and secondary vocalization of it.[27] The actions of humankind's doing something has historically occurred prior to their reflection upon the same. Gerhard van der Leeuw said

There is no basis for doing what theology might perhaps wish to do, and give words an exclusive or even a preferred position in the relationship of man to the 'other,' in the religious sense... Words do not even represent the original form of human expression. For the first work was a gesture... Gesture is not only...an elucidation of the word, but is its predecessor... The words are secondary.[28]

The history of music in worship from Genesis leading up to the Apocalypse has come full cycle and reverts to ritual and myth once again. And in the context of the Book of Revelation this theology of music for worship becomes a doxological worship, the highest form of sacred ritual. The music in worship in the Apocalypse is always objective. It is a proto-typical expression of actually doing worship. Consequently, a theology of music for worship set in the doxological context of the Apocalypse must in the end not be a study, as this study has been, but must become, paradoxically, the actual doing of music in

---

[26]Wilhelm Staehlin, "The Church Hymn and Theology," *Response: In Worship—Music—The Arts* , I/1(1959):26.

[27]Paul Waitman Hoon, *The Integrity of Worship* (Nashville, TN: Abingdon Press, 1971), 87.

[28]Gerhard van der Leeuw, *Sacred and Profane Beauty*, trans. by David E. Green (Apex ed: Nashville, TN: Abingdon Press, 1963), 124.

worship. The glimpse into eschatological time does not tell us what our future will bring but actually shows us what it is.

The Cappodician theologians of the Patristic period sought to contemporize the experiences of eschatology. In the fourth century a group of three theologians, Saint Basil and his brother Saint Gregory of Nyssa and their friend Saint Gregory of Nazianzus, formulated Orthodox Christian doctrine and were known as the Cappadocian theologians. All three were educated in secular disciplines, yet are more well remembered today for their mystical Christian doctrines. St. Gregory of Nyssa inherited the mysticism of Origen which was based on the Alexandrian Jewish-Christian traditions of Philo, Clement and Plutinos.[29] St. Gregory of Nyssa's theology was "dynamic and progressive; it is [was] set on an endless journey.[30] For the Cappadocian theologians, theology was not a reflexive study; rather, it consisted of actually "travelling towards the infinite, towards the vision of the divine, which ancient sages and modern-day contemplators have both sought after."[31] The doing of theology consists of "the ascent or perpetual growth of the soul"[32] and is bound up in εpektasis (*epektasis*)—which literally means "the tension, extension and stretching out towards the Immovable."[33]

This way of looking at theology is consistent with Old Testament theology. Old Testament theology does not consist of a reflexive study of the Israelites knowing Yahweh. Rather, Yahweh dealt with the Old Testament Jews in a linear manner which is rooted in historical encounters. Although Israel was tied to the cyclical course of nature, she was bound up with specific historical events with Yahweh. As successive generations remembered these prior historical encounters, they represented more than mere reflection. These past dealings literally became actualized in each new generation. Only as the assembled community recited its festive rituals did Israel, as Yahweh's chosen people, come into being. Each commemoration placed the contemporary Jewish nation into the historic situation to which the

---

[29]See Saint Gregory of Nyssa, *Commentary on the Song of Songs*, trans. by Casimir McCambley (Brookline, MA: Hellenic College Press, 1987), 7.

[30]Ibid, 1-3.

[31]Ibid., 3.

[32]Ibid, 13.

[33]Ibid., 13. See also Thomas Hopko, *All the Fulness of God* (Crestwood, NY: St. Vladimir's Seminary Press, 1982).

festival in question was related. When Israel ate the Passover, she "was doing more than merely remembering the Exodus: she was entering into the saving event of the Exodus itself and participating in it in a quite 'actual' way..."[34]

Just as the contemporary Jew brings the **"past"** to the **"present,"** Christians are exhorted by Christ to remember the Last Supper by taking the **"present"** back to the **"past"** (αναμνεσις—*anamnesis*). Why then, should one not **use the music of the "future" as found in the Book of Revelation in the "present" Age?**

This concept of theology aligns with Pike's theology of music. If music is "a product of the mind in time, embodying in material form the fluctuating spiritual states of the soul,"[35] then it needs to be used as a positive means to assist finite humanity in reaching his or her unattainable "perfection" in this life. In its pure state, the mind seeks the unification of all the disparities of life. The mind seeks an ordered whole. Music provides the mind an ordered microcosm of life.[36]

The Godhead is both the "FIRST CAUSE" and the "FINAL END"[37] of the past, present and future. Pike indicates that

> His (God's) plans will evolve regardless. To those who chose to willingly participate, progress will be easier. Man [*sic*] can use his mind to praise and contemplate God, but he can also use this same faculty for trivial and even obscene things.[38]

As an ordered microcosm of life, music has "more undeveloped potentialiary [*sic*] for spiritual expression than any other art."[39] Christians have been given the attitude of prayer which assists them in contemplating the multitudinous aspects of the Godhead. The church's use of music seeks to relay these thoughts: "music is the was [sic] we should like life to be, a glimpse of that world where all strife ends."[40] In approaching that eschatological journey in this lifetime, the

---

[34]Gerhard von Rad, *Old Testament Theology: The Theology of Israel's Prophetic Tradition*, trans. by D. M. G. Stalker (Edinburgh: Oliver & Boyd, 1965), 104.

[35]ATM, 48.

[36]Ibid., 69.

[37]Ibid, 88.

[38]Ibid.

[39]Ibid., 94.

[40]Ibid.

worshiper can transcend not only his or her finiteness but even the music itself. Pike states that music is purposeful only if it serves as a means of knowing the Godhead. The primary purpose and function of music in worship in the Book of Revelation is to know God.[41]

But how then do music and worship interrelate? Music is "an expression of life"[42] or a form of life, whereas worship is a "celebration of life"[43] or a dramatization of life. Music and worship share several characteristics. They both contain the idea of moving forward. This involves flow and movement. Music is more suggestive, it acts as a stimulant. Both possess inherent spiritual qualities. While music is an "autonomous"[44] art, worship is primarily an end in itself. The common end which both music and worship seek is the doing of worship itself. The medium of music and worship becomes worship itself. The medium of music and worship becomes the worshipers own offering. The meaning of music is spiritual, whereas the meaning of worship lies in "an awareness of and reverence for the Ultimate Reality in a universe which is fundamentally spiritual."[45] The ultimate purpose for both music and worship is communion between person and God. This is accomplished through the social characteristics of music and the intensely "corporate" character of worship.[46]

Following on Wright's ideas, Smart says of worship that it:

(1) is a relational activity;
(2) expresses the superiority of the Focus (the Godhead) to the worshiper via ritual;
(3) "performatively sustains" or is part of the power of the Focus;
(4) is an experience which is expressed by the numinous and the object of worship is then perceived to be awe-inspiring;
(5) involves a Focus which is transcendent, or unseen;

---

[41]Ibid.

[42]Taken from a summary of music and worship by LeRoy Evert Wright, "The Place of Music in Worship." Ph.D. dissertation, Northwestern University, Evanston, IL, 1949, 329-343.

[43]Ibid.

[44]Ibid.

[45]Ibid.

[46]Ibid.

(6) displays the superiority of the Focus over the worshiper. This gap of power is infinite wherein the worshiper has no relative merit apart from that which the Focus ascribes; and

(7) involves praise by the worshiper which is addressed directly to the Focus.[47]

This study has shown biblically that Smart's concept of worship has been met.

Although this study has shown that non-vocal, non-texted music is not used in the Apocalypse's worship as a responsive mechanism, the early church, including the Patristic period, utilized a Christian theology which consisted of all types of praise and liturgy.[48] The following legend illustrates the relationship between liturgy and theology: Fra Egidio, of the order of St. Francis, was cornered one day by a "most learned theologian with an array of profound propositions." The theologian's logical arguments never seemed to cease. Brother Egidio waited to reply until he was sure his opponent was through. "Then, taking a flute from the fold of his robe, he played out his theological answer in song!"[49]

In the totality of humanity's responsive efforts to the Godhead, Wainwright shows the interrelationships between the sacred and secular life experiences. He focuses on three themes: life, doctrine and worship.[50] Wainwright is able to divide our very existence into these tight little bundles because of the great disparity which can separate them this side of eternity. The Book of Revelation, however, shows how all three can and will be fused together eschatologically. We should not assume a futilistic attitude because of our inability totally to fuse them all now. Rather, our spirits should contrarily gain energy as we seek and try to serve God doxologically in worship for the hope which shall one day be.

The corporate expression of worship, including music in worship, represents the "total orientation of life towards God" and it is expressed via "stylized liturgical action and spontaneous common praise."[51] The

---

[47]Smart, *The Concept of Worship*, 26, 41, 44, 51, 75.
[48]Jean Leclercq, "Theology and Prayer," *Encounter*, 24(1963):62.
[49]Hoon, *The Integrity of Worship*, 90-91.
[50]DOX, 217.
[51]Underhill, *Worship*, 84.

Book of Revelation portrays an idealized form of Christian worship wherein all of the "sensible accompaniments of an ordered cultus— music, song, incense, ritual movements and prostrations—are all there and already taken for granted." [52] The picture of eschatological worship "stretches back to the very beginnings of...worship" and consequently links the past with the future.[53]  For "doxology is at the beginning (in the past and in the present) and at the end (in the future) of all striving for unity."[54]

---

[52]Ibid., 92.
[53]Ibid.
[54]DOX, 290.

# 7

# Implications for Today's Church Musicians and Worship Leaders

IS the music for worship which the writer of the Apocalypse portrays a true glimpse into eschatological music for worship? Was the music which humanity had fashioned up to the time of the Revelation actually so similar to what the Seer foresaw? Was the couching of it in terms of the past and present the only way in which the Seer could relate his visions to finite humanity? How do we interpret apocalyptic music for use today? This chapter seeks to begin to answer these queries by setting forth some applications and considerations for the contemporary church musician and worship leader based on the present study of the music utilized in the eschatological worship of the Book of Revelation.

Admittedly, the music in the Book of Revelation is performed eschatologically by redeemed and perfect humankind as well as the other sinless creatures of heaven and earth. How could it be possible to develop a theology of music for worship from it in order to enlighten or assist church professionals in the present century? The music cannot be matched in human standards this side of eternity. Yet, the music of the contemporary church is rooted historically primarily in the Jewish and pagan traditions, music traditions which sometimes had very high standards, and abysmal standards at other times. Additionally, the contemporary church is musically richer by the blending of Catholic and Protestant traditions. With this rich past on the one hand and the high ideals of music in worship which the Book of Revelation portrays eschatologically on the other, how can the contemporary church

135

musician sit idly by and say that neither affects him or her? Regardless of whether one believes in the Jewish concept of a chosen people's encounter with its Creator in linear time, or the Greek world's encounter with everyday life in a cyclical pattern, or even the spiral progression of Christianity in this period of Grace,[1] contemporary Christianity is historically tied to its past and eschatologically pulled into its future. The recorded lessons which the contemporary church has experienced in the past and the eschatological glimpses it has received of the future must be analyzed, codified and then utilized, if possible.

Should earthly music of the present time strive for the heavenly sound as portrayed in the Apocalypse? The writer of the Apocalypse heard from heaven music which was perfect and complete, and at best a wishful dream for human beings. But the writer also knew that "the heavenly music can so sing in human hearts that all the world is changed."[2] Christianity's quest to follow the Master's command to "be holy" demands nothing less of all Christians than willfully to strive for perfection in this life. This is true within the realm of music in worship, too. A key to advancing church music rests in the worshipers' individual and collective attitudes. The moment that worshipers even think of snubbing either their own, or more likely, another's music in worship, they have destroyed the act of worship. Fortunately, each new day that the Lord provides in this life gives a fresh opportunity to "better it" the next time.

Historical Christian worship is couched in terms of an "eschatological tension."[3] The fourth-century church sought to worship via its credal dictum of "one, holy, catholic and apostolic Church." Christians have sought to fashion their life-styles after the words of the Bible for 2,000 years. But when it has come to finding guidelines for the doing of music in worship, few have found substantial assistance from the New Testament, especially from the last book of the New Testament. Church musicians and worship leaders throughout the history of the church have bemoaned the fact that the New Testament has so little to say concerning the use of music in worship. These leaders have set varying degrees of high standards for the use of music

---

[1]James Blevins, *Revelation* (Atlanta, GA: John Knox Press, 1984), 7-8.
[2]IB, 12:405.
[3]DOX, 121-122.

in worship based often on nonscriptural bases. Coincidentally, many of these same standards have been the highest standards for secular music as well.

This study has sought to analyze the use of music in worship in a bona fide book of the New Testament. For contemporary church music and worship to aspire to this "perfect" representation is not entirely out of the reach of the contemporary worshiper. Perhaps the Godhead allowed this glimpse of eschatological perfection in the music of worship specifically for us to seek after. While music can create barriers within the church, music has the ability to break down denominational, racial, and ethnic barriers. Perhaps the Godhead provided the church this glimpse of eschatological music to aid the Holy Spirit in assembling an ecumenical community. A key to ecumenicity could be found in the church's musical doxology in corporate worship.

The ten points of musical theology for worship derived from the Book of Revelation as summarized and synthesized in Chapter 6 of this study are discussed in a contemporary context as follows. This chapter is a think-piece stemming from the prior chapter's "decalogue" of music for worship characteristics in the Book of Revelation—the following discussion suggests a beginning springboard of ideas which hopefully the reader will be able to continue in future thought, dialogue and studies. Placing eschatological music and worship standards in our "sights" can provide a measuring stick of where we are in the present age and point us to a direction for the future.

**(1) A continuum of vocal sound ranges from declamatory speech to sung song as revelation and response mechanisms—logogenic versus pathogenic music.**

As a responsive mechanism, music in the church today is performed typically in only one manner: lyrical singing. However, music in the Apocalypse is probably performed in ways ranging from singing to chanting to declamation. Perhaps the church today could broaden its concept of performance practice by encouraging its composers to provide a wider repertoire of non-sung vocal music and perhaps an opportunity to "rediscover" lost non-lyrical repertoire. Examples of non-sung vocal music consist of works performed by declaiming or chanting ensembles.

Only the words of the music of Revelation survive today. Perhaps this fact bears witness to the fact that the music from the first century is primarily logogenic. Otherwise, if the actual music had been of critical importance for worship, would not the church leaders have sought some sure long-term way of preserving it, even though it appears to have been beyond their means? Or would not the Godhead have seen to its being maintained through some other way? A lesson in this for the contemporary church worship leader is that the music utilized in revelatory and responsive worship should be primarily logogenic. Music should be a means, not an end, to relate the revealed Λόγος (*Logos*), i.e., Jesus Christ, in worship.

This argument, however, suggests that there is perhaps something inherently suspect in pathogenic music. But does not pathogenic music allow the responder in worship the opportunity to transcend his or her finiteness for a moment of mystical and emotional worship? Is not this perhaps one way in which our spirits groan in unutterable doxology to the Godhead? In order for pathogenic music to be viable in worship, perhaps the worshiper has to have reached potentially a certain "level" in his or her pure worship pilgrimage. Otherwise, pathogenically driven music as response invariably could be judged according to its aesthetic merit, and thereby be limited as a means to worship.

Can the musical adoration which worshipers lift up to the Godhead "pass over the linguistic horizon into silence."[4] Music begins and ends with silence; on silence is layered patterned or unpatterned sound. Perhaps church musicians could give more thought to the idea of offering up worshipful silence to the Godhead. The words which we cannot utter, which only the Spirit knows, perchance could be given more purposeful direction and import in the musical expressions of praise which we lift up each week.

(2) **A mandate exists for the saints to continue the *Imago Dei* process by creatively composing new songs of praise.**

Christians are commanded to "grow in grace" (II Peter 3:18). How can one grow in grace when presumably the total grace of God is showered on a Christian from his or her conversion? The answer can be found from the Christian's perspective. Growing in grace is partly quenching the Holy Spirit less on a moment-by-moment basis. When a Christian actively seeks to quench the Holy Spirit less each moment,

<hr>

[4]Ibid., 39.

he or she grows in his or her perception of an increasing amount of grace from the Godhead. When a Christian actively seeks to quench the Holy Spirit less, he or she can experience a long-term growth which culminates in his or her passing from this world into the next. The climb would be ever upward in seeking to follow the command to be "holy," as Christ is holy (I Peter 1:15-16). John Wesley said that church music, specifically hymns, could assist the worshiper "as a means of raising or quickening the spirit of devotion; of confirming his faith; of enlivening his hope and of kindling and increasing his love to God and man."[5]

A certain way to grow in grace is to incarnate the *Imago Dei* principle pointed out by Johansson.[6] An application of this concept for the Christian community of every age is to exhort its composers to continue to create new music for worship. The mandate is clearly supported by evidence found in the Book of Revelation. The saints of God are singing new songs which no one else can learn or discern apart from the Holy Spirit's understanding. Johansson tells the contemporary church that "the church music program needs to take active steps to widen and deepen the church's scope of influence in the artistic realm.[7]

But Johansson goes on to caution the church that not all "new" music can or should be acceptable. His criterion of acceptable "new" music is that

'New' means nothing if it is not creative (that which breaks new ground imaginatively and with integrity). Much of the religious 'new' is a commercialized variety of afterthought, a warmed-over version of pop music's last frontier, the wake of everchanging fads, a copy of its nonchurch counterpart. Often, so-called contemporary religious music has not the slightest relationship to Biblical creativity.[8]

---

[5]John Wesley, *A Collection of Hymns for the Use of the People Called Methodists* (London: John Mason, 1779), Preface.

[6]Calvin M. Johansson, *Music and Ministry: A Biblical Counterpoint* (Peabody, MA: Hendrickson Publishers, Inc., 1986), 21-27.

[7]Ibid., 19.

[8]Ibid.

Today's church music composer can do nothing less than to pursue his or her calling to compose fresh, ever-new praise for worship. Part of the creative artistic process falls on the performer of the music also. As interpreters of the musical score, church musicians, as performers, are actively carrying forward the λόγος (*logos*) by means of fresh, creative energy which seeks to put forth both the Creator's and the creator's wishes.

Creating new songs should not be limited, however, to thoroughly written-out musical compositions. Well thought-out spontaneity can occur regularly within the context of church music for worship. The four living creatures which represent all living creatures never cease to give praise to the Godhead. This possibly implies that newly improvised songs are being composed alongside their learned, well-rehearsed praise.

The emphasis which music schools place on the performance of the memorized "classics" needs to be balanced with church musicians who are able to express extemporaneous musical thoughts effectively as well. Examples of well thought-out spontaneity can be found primarily in today's charismatic and Afro-American churches. Often, time is provided for the congregation to share testimonies intermingled with spontaneous outbursts of song. The worship leader moves on with the service when he or she "feels moved by the Spirit" to do so. Church music schools can devote class time in experiential worship practices which incorporate spontaneous as well as memorized choruses and other music within the context of the greater whole of worship.

**(3) Instrumental accompaniments (specifically, timbres which blend with the human voice) are used to aid in the vocal response to the Godhead.**

The use of instrumental accompaniment is possible in today's church based on its use in the Book of Revelation. However, it is used within three very specific guidelines: (1) The worshiper must utilize the accompaniment without even the slightest thought of its secular connotation. Is this possible in today's world? Can we so condition our minds and spirits so as totally to suppress worldly connotations? Although the rhetorical answer to this question is "no," another question needs to be asked. What worshiper can cleanse totally his or her heart in order to worship at all? Because the answer to this is a decided "no," the question begs to be asked "why should Calvinistic thinking prevail regarding the use of instrumental accompaniment in worship?"; (2) Instrumental accompanimental music in the Book of Revelation is composed of a single timbre. This implies a single affection. Is there room in church music for orchestral accompaniments with mixed timbres? Can contemporary orchestral accompaniment relay a single affection?; and (3) Evidence in the Book of Revelation suggests that instrumental accompaniment is desirable if it does not dominate the text. Accompaniment acts in a manner that supports the logogenic character of the music.

**(4) Instrumental heralding (specifically, the trumpet call) is used to announce the revelation of the Godhead.**

Instrumental heralding is used in the Book of Revelation as an announcement of pending revelation. So too it can be used in the church today in a similar manner. The use of an instrumental ensemble or a soloist before a revelatory event can be recommended based on its usage in the Book of Revelation. But the question arises "Can revelatory instrumental heralding, as evidenced in the Apocalypse, be employed in worship in the contemporary church as a non-heralding responsive mechanism?" Although the Book of Revelation does not allow for the responsive use of "pure" music, the Christian experience historically supports its practice in many traditions.

**(5) The exhibition of emotion in the performance of the music exists owing to the use of a variety of Greek verbs such as say, sing, rejoice, cry, and a variety of sounds from nature.** Examples of the sounds of nature are many waters and the sounds of thunder.

The music of Revelation is full of emotion. The worshipers are actively desiring to express their heart-felt, nay, life-felt, gratitude to the near-completed work of the Godhead. The saints have endured so much pain and sorrow throughout the cyclical course of history that they lose themselves in worship. But this ecstatic adulation of the Godhead is not entirely without order. Evidence in the Book of Revelation indicates that it is and can be well-planned, well-rehearsed and well-performed. This is spoken of in Proverbs 16:1-3, which exhorts humankind to devise a plan, commit it to God and have faith that God will bless it.

But alongside well-planned order exists perhaps spontaneity. Raymond Bailey speaks of four manners of praying:

(1) entirely spontaneous praying;
(2) planned spontaneous praying;

(3) well thought-out praying which is not spontaneous except in its conception; and

(4) written out prayers.[9]

These manners of praying can be directly applied to the performance practice of music for worship. Music for worship can range from spontaneity on the one hand to entirely written-out compositions on the other. Most churches across Christendom display a tendency for one or perhaps two of the above characteristics. But how many churches actively seek for a consistent balance of this continuum within their services?

Many Christians' experience of music in worship could basically be categorized almost exclusively as "well-thought out." No room for spontaneity is desired, let alone considered. Consequently, the music tends to be performed generally in a mechanical manner. Perhaps a lesson can be learned from "charismatic" brothers and sisters who display a wide range of physically vocal emotions in their services. Why cannot the church literally "shout" spontaneously in worship? Why cannot the church literally "whisper" spontaneously in worship? At the other end of the spectrum, why cannot the church write out a musical liturgy to be used by the people? Does it have to bore ones' spirits? The music which is used in worship needs to cover the range of emotions which we experience in everyday living. If it does not, perhaps we have limited our potential for worship.

Worship is a celebration of life. As a microcosm of life, then, it should contain the full gamut of all the good that makes up life. This includes the wide range of emotions which humanity experiences. Until worshipers can couple this range of emotion with the added preparatory experiences (ranging from spontaneity to fully written-out types of music in worship), perhaps they cannot hope to experience the freedom which comprises the doxological worship evidenced in the Book of Revelation.

(6) **The postures for the performance of music worship involve more than just sitting and standing.**

A clear mandate is provided the church musician to employ all human postures in worship: from sitting to standing to kneeling to

---

[9]Taken from class notes in a class taught by Dr. Raymond Bailey in the fall of 1987 at Southern Baptist Theological Seminary, Louisville, KY.

lying prostrate on the floor. Worship demands the total range of all human posture including interpretive or litugical dance. Restrictively sitting or standing alone inhibits worshipers from experiencing the total spectrum of worshipful encounter. The actions of the participants and revelers in worship are not haphazard, but quite planned and orderly. In the Book of Revelation, these posturings tend to be choreographed.

Religious ritual contains the idea that the Godhead is hidden to the worshiper's eyes. In primitive pagan thought it was believed that if one was seen by another, the one seen would lose his or her power. In historic Christianity, God is hidden (*Deus absconditus*).[10] But not so in the Book of Revelation. In eschatological fulfillment, all of the redeemed of Creation shall come before the very face of the Godhead in worship. However, on this side of eternity, perhaps the only revealed face of the Godhead which we can see are those we rub shoulders with in the choir, in the church and in the remainder of creation during the week.

The creaturely posturings which we employ in worship should betray the expectation of the continuing revelation of the Godhead. How dare worshipers slouch! How can one expect to be worshipfully responsive, spiritually fed, mentally stimulated, emotionally restored and socially responsible if one is physically lackadaisical in his or her musical posturings in the worship experience?

The concept of coming round the throne also carries the idea of symmetry in worship. Worship in heaven will not consist of responsive creatures lined up in pews. Eschatological worship will perhaps exhibit the neo-classic posturing or positioning of the orchestra around the conductor who led from the harpsichord in the midst. This circular concept of posturing in worship also will perhaps not only be two-dimensional: it may be three-dimensional!

(7) **The music of worship includes the use of the sounds of nature from all Creation, both animate and inanimate.**

Revelation is expressed audibly in the sounds made by all of Creation. The divine Λόγος (*Logos*) is not limited to mere human speech. Its production and timbre can be couched in all types of the sounds of human-made instruments and of nature, too. Why not utilize the sound of thunder in worship? It could accompany the revealed Λόγος (*Logos*), or even speak revelation apart from the Word. The

---

[10]DOX, 33.

sermon, scripture reading and revelatory music could be accompanied
by a variety of sounds and sights from nature, like lightning, the roar
of a lion, or of a waterfall. Even technological laser light shows could
be used! Ascribing the classification of musical keys or modes to
certain smells might have merit. Maybe the Dorian mode could best
be described by the smell of cinnamon. A "smell" study could parallel
Scriabin's and Rimsky-Korsakov's independent colorization of the
major and minor modes in Western music. Synchronizing musical
"colors" with the colors of the church year is a possibility. This could
be broadened into a general study of the use of the other non-musical
senses, i.e., taste, touch and sight, in the practice of worship in the
Apocalypse and/or worship in general, which has roots in the "higher"
traditions of the church.

Part of the job description of humanity is the task of using the
natural creation properly.[11] Although natural creation is "used" in a
revelatory manner in the Book of Revelation, humankind should not
lose sight of the fact that humanity is charged with the stewardship of
creation. When Christians care for creation, they are responding by
"fulfilling a priestly function on behalf of creation" and "when they
give God thanks and praise [for it], they are [also] fulfilling a priestly
function on behalf of Creation."[12] Consequently, humanity needs to
assume the lead in "assisting" creation in responding to the Godhead.
In worship this can be seen through the Eucharist. Wainwright states
that participation by the saints in the communion meal presupposes a
commitment to "the proper use of the earth's resources."[13] But this
does not necessarily pertain to the sounds of nature unless one hears the
cracking in the fraction of "the breaking of the bread" and the liquid
sounds in "the pouring of the blood."

**(8) A sense of unity is perceived via the dynamics of antiphonal
and responsorial responses by the various groups.** Is music ever
divisive? Is it always unified in the Book of Revelation?

Choirs are disappearing from many churches today. Robert
Hayburn reports that "everyone is making music in the church, except

---

[11]Ibid., 23-24.
[12]Ibid., 25.
[13]Ibid., 32.

trained musicians:"[14]   many churches today exclusively use the congregational choir in worship. This trend runs counter to the biblical norm found in Revelation. Evidence in the Book of Revelation does not support the absence of smaller choral ensembles from worship. Rather, this study has shown a balance in the use of  congregational groups and large and small choral ensembles in worship.

The choirs of eschatology are very well organized.   The early historical mandate for this is found in the choirs of the Jewish Temple. Today's choirs can be no less planned for, rehearsed nor seasoned in performance.

The church musician in the present century is exhorted via the evidence of the Book of Revelation to use music responsorially and antiphonally.   By and large, high traditions, charismatic and Afro-American churches implement these styles more consistently than their small, average church-size counterparts.   Even though the average church is only 200 members strong, with an average choir attendance of five to fifteen percent of the congregation, antiphonal singing is possible. If a single church's choir is small, why not sing antiphonally with the congregation as choir or join with another church in antiphony?   Why should local congregations in the same region, or even across the country, not become acquainted?   It is already possible and being done via large-screen teleconferencing.

An inherent characteristic of the use of choirs in the Book of Revelation is the fellowship and community which they enjoy. Although potentially divergent groups join together, they can and do so in "perfect" harmony.   The eschatological choir shares a fraternity which the contemporary choir can emulate.   Just as the Christian sacraments are enjoyed corporately,[15] so too, the choir in the church cannot exist apart from considering themselves and performing as a cohesive, unified team in concert "with," to," and sometimes "for" one another.

Music has the ability to break down all types of barriers, not the least of which are racial, ethnic, and denominational.   Utilization of church music in worship is a positive means by which to evangelize an unsaved world and a positive way for Christians of all traditions to

---

[14]Robert Hayburn, *Papal Legislation of Sacred Music* (Collegeville, MN:   The Liturgical Press, 1979), 408.

[15]DOX, 142.

unify. Just as Wainwright states that the "implied vocation of the church is to catholicity,"[16] so too should our choirs be a blending-pot of the diversity of our congregations and churches. The choirs in the church should be a microcosm, a cross-section, of the local and universal congregation just as the eschatological choirs will be very diverse, yet unified in their purpose and mission.

(9) **Old προσκυνέο (*proskuneo*), motivated by reverential fear of a vertical God-to-slave nature, is merged with a new προσκυνέο (*proskuneo*), motivated by love of a horizontal host-to-guest nature. Theology becomes doxology as the solemn action of worship.**

Many Christians were "saved" or converted at an early age in a "fire and brimstone" atmosphere owing to a guilty conscience and the fear that he or she might "go directly to hell" should he or she die without knowing Jesus. Although the Apostle Paul does not encourage this means of salvation in Philippians 1:15-18, he does come to the conclusion that "at least they are saved." But Paul does imply that coming to know the Lord with the principal motivation of genuine heartfelt love is to be desired. So, too, should our music in worship be motivated by this ἀγάπη (*agape*) love. The music of our worship should be able to lift us up into a spiritual love in order that we might become lost in doxological praise of the Godhead's work in all of eternity, both historical and eschatological.

The highest form of doxological praise is objective in character: it is not subjective nor reflexive. It is admittedly impossible for the church this side of eternity to practice only the objective form of worship. This is partly owing to the fact that as finite growing human beings, persons are often striving for more educatively. Consequently, worship of the Godhead will necessarily at times be reflexive. While objective worship in its highest doxological sense cannot be practiced by mere "saved" mortals this side of eternity, the contemporary church must constantly seek this unattainable goal. To avoid futility in this quest, the church must firmly rest in its eschatological hope in the completed work of the Godhead.

Matthew 22:37-40 provides us Jesus' summarization of the law:

---

[16]Ibid., 133.

And he said to him, 'You shall love the Lord your God with all
your heart, and with all your soul, and with all your mind. This
is the great and first commandment. And a second is like it,
You shall love your neighbor as yourself. On these two
commandments depend all the law and the prophets.'

Certainly, the obviously necessary element in Christan worship is to
vertically praise the Godhead for its revealed and promised mighty acts
in history. But perhaps those of us able-bodied saints who claim to be
able to worship "quite well thank you" week after week by watching
their favorite televangelist are missing out on the fulness of Christian
worship. "The second (commandment) is like unto the first:" equal to
the **vertical** praise with which worshipers respond to the Godhead is the
**horizontal** "rubbing of shoulders" with those in the pew. Part of the
fulness of Christian worship is the responsibility of Christians to
encourage those in and out of the faith to want to seek to praise the
Godhead. By showing up to corporate worship regularly Christians can
minister to "the least of all." Insofar as we exhort and encourage our
fellow brothers and sisters to praise God, we have done it unto the
Godhead, and thus we are fulfilling the full vision of προσκυνέο
(*proskuneo*) spoken of by the writer of the Apocalpyse.

(10) **Music dramatically involves all the senses of humanity and
all the collective resources available in all Creation.**

The Creator and redeemed Creation commune in a relational activity
called worship. And true worship expresses life as a whole.[17] Many
times church musicians are handicapped by the limited musical
resources available in the local church. But the Book of Revelation
exhorts us to break those bonds which cloud our view and rise up to
grab hold of every human, spiritual, emotional, physical, financial and
natural resource which is available in order to assist our music to serve
its worship goal. The church professional must realize that all Creation
is the music of life. To restrict one's choir to only sung song in four
balanced parts accompanied by a pipe organ or a Steinway piano is not
all that there is to music. Music is more. It is much more. It is the
energy of all of Creation! It is perhaps that bridge which will in part
carry finite, physical creation to its final destiny with the Godhead.
The music of our worship and worship itself should drive us through

---

[17]DOX, 16-20.

all of life. Wainwright argues that "the ethical acknowledgment of Christ's sovereignty in everyday living is secondary to the religiously primary acknowledgment of Christ as Lord in the context of worship."[18]

One reason that our church choirs may often appear apathetic and unmotivated is because its leaders have failed to provide balance in the music program. Granted, the scriptures have often been neglected and thus had little to say concerning music in worship in past times. However, contemporary church musicians and worship scholars are providing more scripturally-based tangibles which we dare not ignore any longer.

The doing of worship should be driven by the sacrificial love which the worshipers purposefully return to the Godhead. The old adage "the Spirit is willing, but the flesh is weak" should no longer be an allowable excuse. Individuals need willfully to be more responsible; they need to comprehend consciously that they will be held individually responsible for their actions or inactions in worship as in life.

Perhaps until one encounters dramatic balance in worship, one cannot be transformed by the worship. Part of becoming lost in worship is not just "knowing" the Godhead but in actually "conforming" to the image of the Godhead. This will not change our relational position before the Godhead, but will free us from the shackles of our finiteness. Doxological worship, rooted in the motion of Christianity's most characteristic rituals, is transforming in character.[19]

Christianity's personhood is as much spiritual as physical. Yet Christianity is often consumed with its seemingly sole attention on its physical state. Contemporary church music has the potential, as it is empowered by the Holy Spirit to take Christianity's mind off its physical condition and vivify its spiritual souls. Although this appears to be possible only on an eschatological level, finite humanity has been provided a model for music in worship in the end-times. Christianity was perhaps given this glimpse of future worship so that it may imitate it this side of eternity. Granted, this imitation may be only for fleeting moments in periodic worship; Christians may only transcend their physicality for short-lived moments in time as they hope for their final

[18]Ibid., 48.
[19]Ibid., 121.

eschatological consummation as true members of the church—the bride of Christ. But that is realized eschatology whereby each worshiper is being transformed little by little into his or her individual and collective fullest dimensions as the *Imago Dei* is played out in doxological praise.

# Appendices

# Appendix A

## Historical Timetable

The following timetable illustrates the various early cultures which coexisted simultaneously:

| Mesopotamia | Egypt | Crete/Greece |
|---|---|---|
| Sumerians | Old Kingdom | Early Crete |
| -2040 B.C.E. | -2160 B.C.E. | -2100 B.C.E. |
| | | |
| Babylonians | Middle Kingdom | Middle Crete |
| 2040-1750 B.C.E. | 2160-1580 B.C.E. | 2100-1580 B.C.E. |
| | | |
| Kassites | New Kingdom | Late Crete |
| 1740-1160 B.C.E. | 1580-1090 B.C.E. | 1580-1400 B.C.E. |
| | | |
| Assyrians | Nubians | Dorian migration |
| 1160-625 B.C.E. | 1090-663 B.C.E. | 11th Cen. B.C.E. |
| | | |
| Babylonians | | |
| 625-538 B.C.E. | | |
| | | |
| Persians | Saites | Classic Period |
| 538-331 B.C.E. | 663-382 B.C.E. | 6-4th Cen. B.C.E. |
| | | |
| Greeks | Greeks | Alexander |
| 331- B.C.E | 332- B.C.E. | 336-323 B.C.E. |

**Romans**

| | |
|---|---|
| 509-27 B.C.E. | The Republic |
| 509-264 B.C.E. | The Early Republic |
| 27- B.C.E. | Power in Emperor aided by Senate |

# Appendix B

## Dates of Early Playwrights, Philosophers and Theologians

| Person | Principal writings |
|---|---|
| Aeschylus ca. 525-456 B.C.E. | Wrote 90 plays, seven extant, including: *Supplicant Maiden; Persians; Seven Against Thebes; Prometheus; Agememmnon; Choephoroe;* and *Eumenides* |
| Sophocles ca. 495-406 B.C.E. | Wrote over 125 plays, seven extant, including: *Ajax; Antigone; Trachinine; Oedipus the King; Electra; Philoctetes;* and *Oedipus at Colonus* |
| Euripides ca. 480-380 B.C.E. | Wrote over 80 plays, 19 extant, among them: *Cyclops; Rhesus; Alcestis; Bacchantes; Iphegenia at Aulis; Medea; Hippolytus; Trojan Women; Helen;* and *Orestes* |
| Aristophanes ca. 445-380 B.C.E. | Wrote 40-60 plays, eleven survive, among them: *Clouds; Lysistrata; Frogs;* and *Plutus* |
| Socrates 469-399 B.C.E. | Wrote nothing of his own. A Greek philosopher and teacher of Xenophon and Plato. |

153

Plato
    468-347 B.C.E.    *The Seventh Letter; Lives; Republic (Books I-X);*
                            *Apology;* and *Laws (Books I-XII)*

Aristotle
    384-322 B.C.E.    A pupil of Plato; wrote *Logic* and *Politics.*

Aristoxenus
    350- ? B.C.E.    *Harmonic Elements*

Seneca
    C.E. ca. 5-65    *Dialogues; De clementia; De beneficiis;* and
                     *Tragedies*

Plutarch
    C.E. ca. 46-120    Over 60 writings extant

Tacitus
    C.E. ca. 55-117    *The Annals* and *The Histories*

Claudius Ptolemy Origen
    C.E. ca. 100-178    *Harmonics*

Pliny the Younger
    C.E. ca. 61-113    Ten books of letters

Saint Basil
    C.E. ca. 329-379    *Rule,* a Cappadocian theology

# Appendix C

## Song Texts

Various authors mentioned throughout the study have identified different hymn texts in the Book of Revelation. They are:

Cullman        5:9; 5:12; 5:13; 12:10-12; 19:1-2; and 19:6;

Harris         4:8-11; 5:9; 7:10; 11:17-18; 12:10-11; 15:3; and 15:4b;

Church, Mulry  1:5-8; 4:11; 5:9-11; 5:12-13; 11:17-18; 12:10-12; 15:3-4; 18:22-23; 19:1-9; 22:16-17; and 22:20; and

Wainwright     4:8; 4:11; 5:9; 5:12; 5:13; 7:10; 7:12; 11:15; 11:17; 12:10-12; 15:3; 19:1-8; 21:3-4.

Other hymn texts in Revelation identified by this writer are:

7:12; 7:15-17; 13:10; 14:7; 14:8; 14:9-11; 16:5-6; 16:7.

Obviously, little consensus exists concerning hymn texts in the Book of Revelation. As per this author, the following are hymn texts in the Revelation:

*Revelation 1:5-8:*
   And from Jesus Christ the faithful witness, the first-born of the dead, and the ruler of kings on earth. To him who loves us and has freed us from our sins by his blood, And made us a kingdom, priest to his God and Father, to him be glory and dominion for ever and ever. Amen.

155

Behold, he is coming with the clouds, and every eye will see him, everyone who pierced him; and all tribes of the earth will wail on account of him. Even so. Amen.

"I am the Alpha and the Omega," says the Lord God, who is and who was and who is to come, the Almighty.

*Revelation 4:8:*
Holy, holy, holy, is the Lord God Almighty, who was and is and is to come!

*Revelation 4:11:*
Worthy are thou, our Lord and God, To receive glory and honor and power, For thou didst create all things, And by thy will they existed and were created.

*Revelation 5:9:*
Worthy are thou to take the scroll and to open its seals, For thou wast slain and by the blood didst ransom men for God, From every tribe and tongue and people and nation, And hast made them a kingdom and priests to our God.  And they shall reign on earth.

*Revelation 5:11:*
To him who sits upon the throne and to the Lamb be blessing and honor and glory and might for ever and ever!

*Revelation 5:12:*
Worthy is the Lamb who was slain, to receive power and wealth and wisdom and might and honor and glory and blessing!

*Revelation 7:10*:
Salvation belongs to our God who sits upon the throne and to the lamb!

*Revelation 7:12*:
Amen!  Blessing and glory and wisdom and thanksgiving and honor and power and might, Be to our God for ever and ever! Amen.

*Revelation 7:15-17*

Therefore are they before the throne of God, And serve him day and night within his temple; And he who sits upon the throne will shelter them with his presence.

They shall hunger no more, Neither thirst any more; The sun shall not strike them, Nor any scorching heat,

For the Lamb in the midst of the throne will be their shepherd, And he will guide them to springs of living water; And God will wipe away every tear from their eyes.

*Revelation 11:15*:

The kingdom of the world has become the kingdom of our Lord and of his Christ, and he shall reign for ever and ever.

*Revelation 11:17-18*:

We give thanks to thee, Lord God Almighty, Who art and who wast, That thou hast taken thy great power and begun to reign.

The nations raged, but thy wrath came, and the time for the dead to be judged, For rewarding thy servants, the prophets and saints, And those who fear thy name, both small and great, And for destroying the destroyers of the earth.

*Revelation 12:10-12*:

Now the salvation and the power and the kingdom of our God and the authority of his Christ have come, For the accuser of our brethren has been thrown down, Who accuses them day and night before our God.

And they have conquered him by the blood of the Lamb, And by the word of their testimony, For they loved not their lives even unto death,

Rejoice then, O heaven and you that dwell therein! But woe to you, O earth and sea for the devil has come down to you in great wrath, Because he knows that his time is short!

*Revelation 13:10:*

If any one is to be taken captive, To captivity he goes; If any one slays with the sword, With a sword must he be slain.

*Revelation 14:7:*

Fear God and give him glory, For the hour of his judgment has come; And worship him who made heaven and earth, The sea and the fountains of water.

*Revelation 14:8:*

Fallen, fallen is Babylon the great, She who made all nations Drink the wine of her impure passion.

*Revelation 14:9-11:*

If any one worships the beast and its image, and receives a mark on his forehead or on his hand, He also shall drink the wine of God's wrath, Poured unmixed into the cup of his anger, And he shall be tormented with fire and sulphur in the presence of the holy angels, And in the presence of the Lamb.

And the smoke of their torment goes up for ever and ever; And they have no rest, day or night, These worshipers of the beast and its image, And whoever receives the mark of its name.

*Revelation 15:3-4:*

Great and wonderful are thy deeds, O Lord God the Almighty! Just and true are thy ways, O King of the ages!

Who shall not fear and glorify thy name, O Lord? For thou alone art holy. All nations shall come and worship thee, for thy judgments have been revealed.

*Revelation 16:5-6:*

Just art thou in these thy judgments, Thou who art and wast, O Holy One. For men have shed the blood of saints and prophets,

And thou hast given them blood to drink. It is their due!

*Revelation 16:7*:
Yea, Lord God the Almighty, True and just are thy judgments!

*Revelation 19:2*:
Hallelujah! Salvation and glory and power belong to our God, For his judgments are true and just; he has judged the great harlot who corrupted the earth with her fornication, And he has avenged on her the blood of his servants.

*Revelation 19:3*:
Hallelujah! The smoke from her goes up for ever and ever.

*Revelation 19:6-9*:
Hallelujah! For the Lord our God the Almighty reigns.

Let us rejoice and exult and give him the glory, For the marriage of the Lamb has come, and his bride has made herself ready;

It was granted her to be clothed with fine linen, bright and pure.

*Revelation 21:3-4*:
Behold, the dwelling of God is with men. He will dwell with them, and they shall be his people, and God himself will be with them; He will wipe away every tear from their eyes, and death shall be no more, Neither shall there be mourning nor crying nor pain any more, For the former things have passed away.

# Appendix D

## References to Music

| Musical Reference | Passage in the text of the Book of Revelation |
|---|---|
| "loud voice like a trumpet" | 1:10 |
| "saying (say, said)" | 1:22, 27; 5:9, 12, 13, 14; 6:1, 3, 5, 7; 7:3, 12, 13, 14; 9:13; 10:4, 8; 11:15, 17; 12:10; 13:4; 14:8, 13; 16:4, 17; 17:1, 7, 15; 18:10, 21; 19:4, 9; 21:3, 5, 6, 9; 22:6, 9, 10, 17, 20 |
| "voice like the sound of many waters: | 1:15; 14:2; 19:6 |
| "if any one has an ear, let him hear" | 3:22; 13:9 |
| "First voice, speaking to me like a trumpet, said" | 4:1 |
| "twenty-four elders" | 4:4,10; 5:8; 11:16; 19:4 |
| "voices" | 4:5; 6:6 |
| "sing(ing)" | 4:8,10 |
| "proclaiming with a loud voice" | 5:2 |
| "harp" | 5:8 |
| "sang (sing) a new song" | 5:9; 14:3 |

|                              | Passage in the text of |
| Musical Reference            | the Book of Revelation |

| Musical Reference | Passage |
| --- | --- |
| "I heard...voice of many angels numbering myriads and myriads and thousands and thousands...saying with a loud voice" | 5:11-12 |
| "cried (crying) out with a loud voice:" | 6:10; 7:10; 8:13: 10:3; 18:18, 19 |
| "calling" | 6:16 |
| "called with a loud voice:" | 7:2 |
| "silence" | 8:1 |
| "seven trumpets" | 8:2; 8:6 |
| "seven trumpets and ready to blow them:" | 8:6 |
| "blew the trumpet" | 8;7, 8, 10, 12; 9:1, 13; 11:15 |
| "trumpets" | 8:7, 8, 10, 12; 9:1, 13; 9:1, 13, 14; 11:15 |
| "blasts of the other trumpets" | 3:13 |
| "called out with a loud voice, like a lion roaring" | 10:3 |
| "when he called out, the seven thunders sounded" | 10:3, 4 |
| "trumpet call to be sounded:" | 10:7 |
| "heard a loud voice from (in) heaven" | 10:8; 11:12, 15; 12:10; 14:13; 16:1; 18:4 |
| "like the sound of loud thunder:" | 14:22 |
| "sound of harpers playing on their harps:" | 14:2 |
| "no one could learn the song" | 14:3 |
| "said (saying) with a loud voice" | 14:7, 9 |
| "calling (called) with a loud voice" | 14:15, 18 |

| Musical Reference | Passage in the text of the Book of Revelation |
|---|---|
| "sing the Song of Moses" | 15:3 |
| "heard a loud voice from the temple" | 16:1, 17 |
| "cried (crying)" | 16:7; 19:3, 6 |
| "called out with a mighty voice" | 18:1 |
| "weeping and mourning aloud" | 18:15 |
| "cried (crying) out" | 18:18, 19; 19:5 |
| "mighty voice of a great multitude in heaven crying" | 19:1, 5, 6 |
| "like the sound of mighty thunderpeals" | 19:6 |
| "with a loud voice he called" | 19:17 |
| "heard a great voice from the throne" | 21:3 |

# Appendix E

## Old Testament Pseudepigrapha

In order to use the Old Testament Pseudepigraphy to provide a picture of the early church, Charlesworth poses the question: "How can I [we] be certain that the Pseudepigrapha is earlier than the New Testament [era]?" Although the answer is "fraught with imprecision," he categorizes the literature in the following manner:[1]

**Pseudepigrapha too late for early church research:**
3 Enoch;
Apocalypse of Ezra;
Questions of Ezra;
Apocalypse of Sedrach;
Apocalypse of Daniel;
Testament of Isaac;
Testament of Jacob;
Testament of Solomon;
Testament of Adam;
History of Joseph;
Syriac Menander; and
Slavic Pseudepigrapha (the Old Testament Pseudepigrapha preserved only in slavic).

Charlesworth further indicates that one must not use Christian redactions that predate C.E. 150 because they cannot adequately convey the intellectual mind and world of early Judaism or the early church. These documents include:

---

[1]James Hamilton Charlesworth, *The Old Testament Pseudepigrapha and the New Testament* (Cambridge: Cambridge University Press, 1985), 31-43.

163

Testament of Twelve Patriarchs;
History of the Rechabites;
Martyrdom and Ascension of Isaiah;
Hellenistic Synagogal Prayers; and
4 Ezra (also known as 5 and 6 Ezra) to the Sibylline Oracles.

**Old Testament Pseudepigrapha suitable for early church research:**
*Apocalyptic Literature and Related Works—*
    Jewish and pre-Christian:
        1 Enoch;
        The Jewish Sibyllines; and
        The Treaty of Shem.
    Probably Jewish and pre-Christian:
        Apocrypha of Ezekiel; and
        Apocalypse of Zephaniah.
    Composed from earlier Jewish traditions and in the decades
following the destruction of the Temple in C.E. 70:
        4 Ezra;
        2 Baruch; and
        3 Baruch.
*Testaments—*
    Jewish and pre-Christian:
        Testament of Twelve Patriarchs;
        Testament of Job; and
        Testament of Moses.
*Expansions of the Old Testament—*
    Probably Jewish and pre-Christian:
        Letter of Aristears;
        Jubilees;
        Martyrdom of Isaiah;
        Life of Adam and Eve; and
        Lives of the Prophets.
    Jewish and basically contemporaneous with New Testament writings:
        Joseph and Aseneth;
        Pseudo-Philo;

4 Baruch; and
Jannes and Jambres.
*Wisdom and Philosophical Literature—*
Pre-Christian:
Ahigar; and
3 Macabees.
Basically contemporaneous with New Testament writings:
Pseudo-Phocylides; and
4 Macabees.
*Prayers, Psalms and Odes*
Jewish and pre-Christian:
5 more psalms of David;
Prayer of Manasseh; and
Psalms of Solomon.
Basically contemporaneous with New Testament writings:
Hellenistic Synagogal Prayers;
Prayer of Joseph;
Prayer of Jacob; and
Odes of Solomon.
*The Supplement—*
Philo the Epic Poet;
Theodotus;
Ezekiel the Tragedian;
Fragments of Pseudo-Greek Poets;
Aristobulus;
Demetrius the Chronographer; and
Aristeas the Exegete.

# Appendix F

## Music According to Use as
## Revelation or Response

**Performance Practice--Type of Sound Made**

|  | REVELATION | RESPONSE |
|---|---|---|
| *Vocal* | | |
| Voice | 1:12 | |
| Voice of a sound of many waters | 1:15; 14:2 | 19:6 |
| Great loud voice of an angel | 5:2; 7:2; 10:3, 17:7; 14:9, 15, 19; 19:17 | |
| Great loud voice of angels, four living creatures and 24 elders | | 5:11 |
| Voice in the Midst | 6:6 | |
| Great loud voice of martyrs | 6:10 | |
| Great loud voice of all creation | | 7:10 |
| Great loud voice out of heaven | 9:13; 10:4, 7, 8 11:2, 15, 12:10; 14:13; 18:4 | |

166

|  | **REVELATION** | **RESPONSE** |
|---|---|---|
| Great loud voice as a lion roars | 10:3 | |
| Great loud voice out of the shrine | 16:1 | |
| Great loud voice from the throne | 16:17; 19:5; 21:3 | |
| Great loud voice of a crowd in heaven | | 19:1 |

*Non-vocal*
*(including instrumental)*

|  | **REVELATION** | **RESPONSE** |
|---|---|---|
| Great loud voice as a trumpet | 1:10-11 | |
| Voice as of a trumpet | 4:1 | |
| Out of the throne came forth lightnings and voices and thunders | 4:5 | |
| Sound as of harpers | | 5:8; 15:2 |
| Great loud voice of an eagle | 8:13 | |
| Sound of thunders | 14:2 | 19:6 |

**Performance Practice--Manner Sound is Produced**

|  | **REVELATION** | **RESPONSE** |
|---|---|---|
| *Vocal* | | |
| Say (λέγω [*lego*]) | 1:11, 17; 4:1; 5:5, 9, 11, 13; 6:6; 7:2, 9:14; 10:4, 8; 11:12, | 4:8, 10; 5:14; 6:1, 3, 5, 7, 10; 7:10, 12; 11:16; |

|  | REVELATION | RESPONSE |
|---|---|---|
|  | 15; 12:10; 14:7, 8, 9, 13, 18; 16:1, 5, 17; 18:4; 19:5, 17; 21:3 | 15:3; 19:1, 4, 6, |
| Sing (αδω [ado]) |  | 5:9; 14:3; 15:3 |
| Proclaim (καρυσσο [karusso]) | 5:2 |  |
| Cry (εκραζό [ekrazo]) | 7:2; 10:3; 14:14; 18:2; 19:17 |  |
| Spoke (ελαλεό [elaleo]) or uttered | 10:3, 4 |  |
| Rejoice (χαιρόυσεο [chairouseo]) ...and are glad (ευθραινεο [euthraineo]) |  | 11:10 |
| Responsorial |  | 5:9-14; 11:15-18; 16:4-7; 19:5-8 |
| Antiphonal |  | 4:8-11; 5:9-14;7:9-17; 19:1-4 |
| *Non-Vocal (including Instrumental)* |  |  |
| Having harps |  | 5:8; 15:2 |

|  | **REVELATION** | **RESPONSE** |
|---|---|---|
| ...in order that they might trumpet (σάλπιζο [*salpizo*]) | 8:1, 6 | |
| trumpeted | 8:3, 7, 8, 10, 12; 9:1, 13; 11:15 | |
| Being about to trumpet | 8:13; 10:7 | |

*Postures of Performance*

| | | |
|---|---|---|
| Sitting | | 4:4; 11:16 |
| Before the throne | | 4:6; 5:11; 14:3 |
| Fall before | | 4:10; 5:8, 14; 11:16; 19:4 |
| Standing | | 5:6 |

# Appendix G

## References to Music—
## Greek to English

**Reference   Passage (Greek to English transliteration with translation[1])**

1:10   σάλπιγγος
       *salpiggos*
       (of a trumpet)

1:11   λεγούσής
       *legousas*
       (saying)

1:12   ψωνήν
       *phonan*
       (voice)

1:15   ψωνή αὐτοῦ ὡς ψωνή ὑδάτων πολλῶν
       *phona autou os phona udaton pollon*
       (voice of him as a sound waters of many)

---

[1]Alfred Marshall, *The Inter-Linear Greek-English New Testament* (London: Samuel Bagster and Sons Ltd., 1958); and Kurt Aland, et al., editors, *The Greek New Testament* (Stuttgart: United Bible Societies, 1983), third edition. When discrepancies occurred between Marshall and Aland, deference was given to Aland.

**Reference** **Passage**
1:17     λέγων
        *legon*
        (saying)

3:9     προσκυνήσουσιν  ἐνώπιον  τῶν  ποδῶν
        *proskunasousin*  *enopion*  *ton*  *podon*
        (they shall worship  before  the  feet

        σου
        *sou*
        of thee)

4:1     ψωνή  ἡ  πρώτή  ἦν  ἤκουσα  ὡς
        *phona*  *a*  *prota*  *an*  *akousa*  *os*
        (voice  first  which  I heard  as of

        σάλπιγγος  ...  λέγων
        *salpiggos*  ...  *legon*
        a trumpet  ...  saying)

4:4     εἴκοσι  τέσσαρες  πρεοβυτέρους
4:10    *eikosi*  *tessaras*  *presbuterous*
5:6     (twenty-four  elders)
5:8
5:11
5:14
11:16
14:3

4:5     ψωναί  καί  βρονταί
        *phonai*  *kai*  *brontai*
        (voices or sounds and  thunders)

4:6     τέσσαρα  ζῶα
4:8     *tessera*  *zoa*
5:6     (four  living creatures)
5:8
5:11

**Reference  Passage**
5:14
6:6
14:3
15:7

4:8                                    λέγοντες
                                       *legontes*
                       ([four living creatures] saying)

4:10          πεσοῦνται              καί
              *pesountai*            *kai*
              (will fall [the 24 elders] and

                       προοκυνήσουσιν ... λέγοντες
                       *proskunasousin* ... *legontes*
                       they will worship ... saying)

5:2                          κήρύσσοντα ἐν  ψωνῇ
16:1                         *karussonta*  *en*  *phona*
              ([an angel] proclaiming  in  voice a great

                       μεγάλή
                       *megala*
                       loud)

5:5          καί  εἷς ἐκ  τῶν πρεςβυτέρων  λέγει
             *kai*  *eis ek*  *ton*  *presbuteron*  *legei*
             (and  one of  the  elders          says

                       μοι
                       *moi*
                       to me)

5:8          ([four living creatures and 24 elders]

                       ἔπεσαν  ἔχοντες ... εκαστος κιθάραν
                       *epesan*  *echontes* ... *ekastos*  *kitharan*
                       fell       having   ... each one  a harp)

**Reference Passage**

5:9   καὶ  ᾄδουσιν  ᾠδὴν  καινὴν  λέγοντες
      kai  adousin  odan  kainan  legontes
      (and they sing  song  a new  saying)

5:11  καὶ  ἤκουσα  ψωνὴν  ἀγγέλων  ...
      kai  akousa  phonan  aggelon  ...
      (and I heard  a sound  angels  ...

      [and 4 living creatures and 24 elders]

      ... καὶ  ἦν  ὁ  ἀριμμὸς  αὐτῶν
      ... kai  an  o  arimos  auton
      ... and was the number  of them

      μυριάδες  μυράδων  καὶ  χιλιάδες
      muriades  murisdan  kai  chiliades
      myriads  of myriads  and  thousands)

5:12  χιλιάδων  λέγοντες  ψωνῇ
      chilisdon  legontes  phona
      of thousands saying  voice

      μεδάλή
      megala
      with a great loud)

5:13  καὶ  πᾶν  κτίσμα  ὃ  ἐν  τῷ οὐρανῷ
      kai  pan  ktisma  o  en  to ourano
      (and every creature which  heaven

      καὶ  ἐπὶ  τῆς  γῆς καὶ  ὑποκάτω
      kai  epi  tas  gas kai  upokato
      and  on  the  earth and  underneath

      τῆς  γῆς  καὶ  ἐπὶ  τῆς  θαλάσσής
      tas  gas  kai  epi  tas  thalassas
      the  earth and  on  the  sea

**Reference  Passage**

...  λέγοντας
...  *legontas*
...  saying)


5:14        ([four living creatures and 24 elders]

            ἔπεσαν    καὶ  προσκυνήσαν
            *epesan*   *kai*  *proskunasan*
            fell       and   worshiped)

6:1                            λέγοντος  ὡς
                               *legontos*  *os*
            ([four living creatures] saying    as

            ψωυή          βροντῆς
            *phona*        *brontas*
            with a sound  of thunder)

6:3         ἤκουσα   τοῦ  δευτέρου ζῴου
            *akousa*   *tou* *deuterou*  *zoou*
            (I heard   the  second      living creature

            λέγοντος
            *legontos*
            saying)

6:5         ἤκουσα   τοῦ  τρίτου ζῴου
            *akousa*   *tou* *tritou* *zoou*
            (I heard   the  third   living creature

            λέγοντος
            *legontos*
            saying)

**Reference** **Passage**

6:6    καί ἤκουσα ὡς ψωνὴν ἐν μέσῳ
      *kai akousa os phonan en meso*
      (and I heard as a voice in the midst of

      τῶν τεσσάρων ζῴων
      *ton tessaron zoon*
      the four living creatures

      λέγουσαν'
      *legousan*
      saying)

6:7    ἤκουσα ... τοῦ τετάρτου ζῴου
      *akousa ... tou tetartou zoou*
      (I heard ... the fourth living creature

      λέγοντος
      *legontos*
      saying)

6:10    καί εκραζαν ψωνῇ μεγάλῃ
      *kai ekrazan phona megala*
      (and they cried voice with a great loud

      λέγοντος
      *legontes*
      saying)

6:15    καί οἱ βασιλεῖς τῆς γῆς καί οἱ
      *kai oi basaleis tas gas kai oi*
      (and the kings of the earth and the

      μεγιστᾶνες καί οἱ χιλίαρχοι
      *megistanes kai oi chiliarchoi*
      great men and the chiliarchs

**Reference   Passage**

καὶ  οἱ  πλούςιοι καὶ  οἱ
*kai   oi   plousioi   kai   oi*
and  the  rich men  and  the

ἰσχουροὶ  καὶ  πᾶς   δοῦλος  καὶ
*ischuroi   kai   pas    doulos   kai*
strong men  and  every  slave    and

ελεύθερος
*eleutheros*
free man)

7:2      καὶ  ἔκραζεν                    ψωνῇ
         *kai   ekrazen   [allou   aggelon]  phona*
         (and he cried    [another angel]   voice

         μεγάλή              τοῖς  τέσσαροιν
         *megala             tois   tessarsin*
         with a great loud to     the  four

         ἀγγέλοις  ...  λέγων
         *aggelois  ...  legon*
         angels    ...  saying)

7:10     καὶ  κράζουσιν  ψωνῇ   μεγάλῃ
         *kai   krazousin   phona   megala*
         (and  they cry    voice   with a great loud

         λέγοντες
         *legontes*
         saying)

7:11, 12                εἰστήκειςαν ...
                        *eistakeisan   ...*
         ([and angels] stood         ...

**Reference  Passage**

καὶ  ζῷαν            ἔπεσαν ...
*kai  zoan            epesan ...*
and  living creatures fell    ...

καὶ  προσεκύνήσαν ... λέγοντες
*kai  prosekunasan  ... legontes*
and  worshiped       ... saying)

8:2      ἑπτά  ἀγγέλους ... ἐδόθησαν
  8:6    *epta  aggelous  ... edothasan*
         (seven angels    ... there were given

αὐτοῖς  ἑπτὰ σάλπιγγες
*autois  epta  salpigges*
to them seven trumpets)

8:6                          ἡτοίμεσαν
                             *atoimasan*
(Seven angels with seven trumpets prepared

αυτους    ἵνα
*autous    ina*
themselves in order that

σάλπισωσιν
*salpisosin*
they might trumpet)

8:7    καὶ ὁ  πρῶτος  ἐσάλπισεν
       *kai    protos   esalpisen*
       (and the first    trumpeted)

8:8    καὶ ὁ  δεύτερος  ἄγγελος  ἐσάλπισεν
       *kai o  deuteros  aggelos   esalpisen*
       (and the second  angel     trumpeted)

**Reference  Passage**

8:10        καὶ ὁ τρίτος ἄγγελος ἐσάλπισεν
            *kai o tritos aggelos esalpisen*
            (and the third angel trumpeted)

8:12        καὶ ὁ τέταρτος ἄγγελος ἐσάλπισεν
            *kai o tetartos aggelos esalpisen*
            (and the fourth angel trumpeted)

8:13        σάλπιγγος τῶν τριῶν ἀγγέλων τῶν
            *salpiggos ton trion aggelon ton*
            (trumpet of the three angels

            μελλόντων σάλπιζειν
            *mellonton salpizein*
            being about to trumpet)

9:1         καὶ ὁ πέμπτος ἄγγελος ἐσάλπισεν
            *kai o pemptos aggelos esalpisen*
            (and the fifth angel trumpeted)

9:13        καὶ ὁ ἕκτος ἄγγελος ἐσάλπισεν
            *kai o ektos aggelos esalpisen*
            (and the sixth angel trumpeted)

            καὶ ἤκουσα ψωνὴν μίαν ἐκ
            *kai akousa phonan mian ek*
            (and I heard voice one out of

            τῶν τεσσάρων κεράτων τοῦ
            *ton tessaron keraton tou*
            the four horns of the

            θυσιαστήρίου τοῦ χρυσοῦ
            *thusiastariou tou chrusou*
            altar golden

**Reference Passage**

τοῦ ἐνώτιον τοῦ Θεοῦ
*tou enotion tou Theou,*
before     God),

9:14    λέγοντα   τῷ    ἕκτῳ   ἀγγέλῳ   ὁ   ἔχων   τὸν
         *legonta*    *to*     *ekto*    *aggelo*    *o*   *echon*   *ton*
         (saying   to the   sixth   angel       having   the

         σάλπιγγα
         *salpigga*
         trumpet)

10:3    καὶ   ἔκραζεν   ψωνῇ    μεγάλῃ             ὥσπερ
         *kai*   *ekrazen*   *phona*   *megala*          *osper*
         (and cried       voice    with a great loud   as

            λέων   μυκᾶται   καὶ   ὅτε    ἔκραζεν
            *leon*    *mukatai*   *kai*   *ote*    *ekrazen*
            a lion    roars      and   when   he cried

            ἐλαλήσαν        αἱ   ἑπτὰ   βρονταὶ
            *elalasan*        *ai*   *epta*   *brontai*
            spoke or uttered   the   seven   thunders

            τας   ἑαυτῶν      ψωνῆς
            *tas*   *eauton*       *phonas*
            the   of themselves   voices)

10:4    καὶ   ἤκουσα   ψωνὴν   ἐκ   τοῦ   οὐρανοῦ
         *kai*   *akousa*   *phonan*   *ek*   *tou*   *ouranou*
         (and   I heard   a voice   out   of      heaven

            λέγουοαν
            *legousan*
            saying)

**Reference  Passage**

10:7    ψωνῆς    τοῦ    ἐβδόμου    ἀγγέλου    ὕταν
        *phonas*   *tou*   *ebdomou*   *aggelou,*   *otan*
        (voice   of the   seventh    angel,     whenever

        μέλλῃ        σάλπιζειν
        *mella*        *salpizein*
        he is about to trumpet)

10:8    καὶ    ἡ    ψωνὴ    ἦν    ἤκουσα    ἐκ    τοῦ
        *kai*   *a*   *phona*   *an*   *akousa*   *ek*   *tou*
        (and   the   voice   which   I heard   out of

        οὐρανοῦ ...   λέγουσαν
        *ouranou* ...   *legousan*
        heaven   ...   saying)

11:10   καὶ    οἱ    κατοικοῦντες    ἐπὶ τῆς   γῆς
        *kai*   *oi*   *katoikountes*    *epi tas*   *gas*
        (and   the   ones dwelling    on the   earth

        χαίρουσιν    ἐπ᾿    αὐτοῖς
        *chairousin*    *ep*    *autois*
        rejoice      over   them)

11:12   καὶ    ἤκουσαν    ψωνῆς    μεγάλῆς    ἐκ
        *kai*   *akousan*    *phonas*   *megalas*    *ek*
        (and   they heard   voice    a great loud   out

        τοῦ    οὐρανου    λεγούοής    αὐτοῖς
        *tou*   *ouranou*    *legousas*    *autois*
        of     heaven     saying     to them)

11:15   καὶ    ὁ    ἔβδομος᾿    ἄγγελος    ἐσάλπιζεν    καὶ
        *kai*   *o*   *ebdomos*    *aggelos*    *esalpisen*   *kai*
        (and   the   seventh     angel     trumpeted    and

**Reference   Passage**

|  |  |  |  |
|---|---|---|---|
| ἐγένοντο | ψωναί | μεγάλαι | ἐν τῷ |
| *egenonto* | *phonai* | *megalai* | *en to* |
| there were | voices | great loud | in |

| | |
|---|---|
| οὐρανῷ | λέγοντες |
| *ourano,* | *legontes* |
| heaven, | saying) |

11:16, 17

|  |  |  |  |
|---|---|---|---|
| προσσικύνήσων | ιῷ | Θεῷ | λεγοντες |
| *prosekunasan* | | *to Theo,* | *legoutes* |
| (24 elders worshiped | | God, | saying) |

12:10

|  |  |  |  |
|---|---|---|---|
| καὶ | ἤκουσα | ψωνὴν μεγάλής | ἐν τῷ |
| *kai* | *akousa* | *phonan megalan* | *en to* |
| (and | I heard | voice a great loud | in |

| | |
|---|---|
| οὐρανῷ | λέγοντες |
| *ourano* | *legousan* |
| heaven | saying) |

14:2

|  |  |  |  |  |
|---|---|---|---|---|
| καὶ ἤκουσα | ψωνὴν | ἐκ | τοῦ οὐρανοῦ | ὡς |
| *kai akousa* | *phonan* | *ek* | *tou ouranou* | *o* |
| (and I heard | a sound | out of | heaven | as a |

|  |  |  |  |  |  |
|---|---|---|---|---|---|
| ψωνὴν | ὑδάτων | πολλῶν | καὶ | ὡς | ψωνὴν |
| *phonan* | *udaton* | *pollon* | *kai* | *os* | *phonan* |
| sound | waters | of many | and | as | a sound |

|  |  |  |  |  |
|---|---|---|---|---|
| βροτῆς | μεγάλής | καὶ | ἡ | ψωνή |
| *brontas* | *megalas* | *kai* | *a* | *phona* |
| thunder | of great loud | and | the | sounds |

| | |
|---|---|
| ἤν | ἤκουσα |
| *an* | *akousa* |
| which | I heard was |

**Reference   Passage**

ὡς  κιθαρῳδῶν  κιθαριζόντων ἐν
*os   kitharozon   kitharizonton   en*
as    of harpers    harping        with

ταῖς  κιθάραις  αὐτῶν
*tais  kitharais  auton*
the    harps     of them)

14:3    καὶ  ᾄδουσιν  ᾠδὴν  καινήν ... καὶ
        *kai  adousin   odan   kaivan ... kai*
        (and  they sing  song   a new  ... and no

        οὐδεὶς  ἐδύνατο  μαθεῖν  τῆς  ᾠδὴν
        *oudeis  edunato   mathein  tan  odan*
        man     could     to learn  the  song

        μὴ  αἱ  ἑκατόν
        *ma  ai  ekaton*
        except the  hundred

        τεσσεπάκοντα  τέσσαρες  χιλιάδες ...
        *tesserakonta   tessares  chiliades ...*
        and forty-four            thousands ...)

14:7                    λέγων  ἐν  ψωνῇ
                        *legon   en  phona*
        ([another angel] saying  in  voice

        μεγάλῃ
        *megala*
        a great loud)

14:8                    ἠκολούθησεν  λέγων
                        *akolouthasen   legon*
        ([and a second angel] followed        saying)

**Reference  Passage**

14:9                                     ἠκολούθησεν    λέγων
                                         akolouthasen    legon
([and a third angel] followed            saying

                    ἐν ψωνῇ   μεγάλὴ
                    en phona   megala
                    in voice   a great loud)

14:13    καὶ   ἤκουςα   ψωνῆς   ἐκ τοῦ οὐρανοῦ
         kai   akousa    phonas   ek tou ouravou
         (and  I heard   a voice   out of heaven

                    λέγοντες
                    legousas
                    saying)

14:15                                    κράζων ἐν  ψωνῇ
                                         krazon   en phona
([another angel] crying                  in   voice

                    μεγάλη
                    megala
                    a great loud)

14:18                                    ἐψώνήσεν ψωνῇ
                                         ephonasen  phona
([another angel] he spoke                voice

                    μεγαλη          ... λέγων
                    megala          ... legon
                    in a great loud ... saying)

15:3     καὶ  ἄδουσιν  τὴς ὠδὴν Μωϋσέως  τοῦ
         kai   adousin   tas odan  Mouseos   tou
         (and they sing  the song of Moses    the

**Reference Passage**

δούλου  τοῦ  Θεοῦ καὶ  τὴν  ὠδὴν
*doulou   tou   Theou kai   tan   odan*
slave    of    God   and   the   song

τοῦ  ἀρνίου  λέγοντες
*tou   arniou,   legontes*
of the lamb,    saying)

16:5    καὶ  ἤκουςα  τοῦ  ἀγγέλου  τῶν  ὑδάτων
     *kai   akousa   tou   aggelou   ton   udaton*
     (and I heard   the   angel   of the waters

λέγοντες ... καὶ  ἤκουσα τοῦ
*legontes ... kai   akousa   tou*
saying    ... and  I heard  the

θυσιαστηρίου  λέγοντες
*thusiastariou    legontes*
altar        saying)

16:17   καὶ  ἐζῆδθεν  ψωνὴ  μεάλή      ἐκ
     *kai   ezalthen   phona   megala       ek*
     (and came out  a voice a great loud out of

τοῦ  ναοῦ  ἀπὸ  τοῦ  τρόνου
*tou   naou   apo   tou   thronou*
the   shrine  from   the   throne

λέγουσα
*legousa*
saying)

18:2    καὶ  ἔκραζεν ἐν ἰσζυρᾷ  ψωνῇ  λέγων
     *kai   ekrazen  en  ischura   phona   legon*
     (and he cried  in   a strong  voice   saying)

**Reference** **Passage**

18:4 καὶ ἤκουσα ἄλλήν ψωνήν ἐκ τοῦ οὐρανοῦ
*kai akousa allan phonan ek tou ouranou*
(and I heard another voice out of heaven

λέγουσαν
*legousan*
saying)

18:22 καὶ ψμνὴ κιθαρωδῶν ιαὶ μουσικῶν
*kai phona kitharodon kai mousikon*
(and sound of harpers and of musicians

καὶ αὐλήτῶν καὶ σάλπιστῶν
*kai aulaton kai salpiston*
and of flutists and of trumpeters)

19:1 ... ἤκουσα ὡς ψωνήν μεγάλήν
... *akousa os phonan melalan*
(... I heard as voice a great loud

ὄχλου ...
*ochlou ...*
crowd ...)

πολλοῦ ἐν τῷ οὐρανῷ λεγόντων
*pollou en to ourano legonton*
(of a much in heaven saying)

19:4 ([and 24 elders and four living creatures]

προσεκύνσαν Θεῷ ... λέγοντες
*prosekunasan to Theo ... legontes*
worshiped God ... saying)

19:5 καὶ ψωνὴ ἀπὸ τοῦ θρόνου ἐξῆλθεν
*kai phona apo tou thronou ezalthen*
(and a voice from the throne came out

**Reference**   **Passage**
                λέγουσα
                *legousa*
                saying)

19:6       καί ἤκουσα ὡς ψωνὴν ὄκλου πολλοῦ
          *kai akousa os phonan ochlou pollou*
          (and I heard as a sound crowd of a much

          καί ὡς ψωνὴν ὑδάτων πολλων καί
          *kai os phonan udaton pollon kai*
          and as a sound waters of many and

          ὡς ψωνὴν βροντων ἰσχυρων
          *os phonan bronton ischuron*
          as a sound thunders of strong loud

          λεγόντων
          *legonton*
          saying)

19:17      καί ἔκραζεν ἐν    ψωνῇ μεγάλῃ
          *kai ekrazen en phona megala*
          (and he cried out in voice a great loud

          λέγων
          *legon*
          saying)

21:3       καί ἤκουσα ψωνῆς μεγάλῆς   ἐκ τοῦ
          *kai akousa phonas megalas ek tou*
          (and I heard voice a great loud out of

          ορόνου λεγούσας
          *oronou legousas*
          throne saying)

# Appendix H

## Contemporary Definitions for Worship

*Defining Christian worship in a single sentence is difficult to do at best, but many authors have attempted doing this through the years. Below are some of the more significant definitions for worship written primarily in the twentieth century. Some authors have not defined worship briefly; in some instances, extended definitions have been summarized, hopefully without losing substance.*

Worship, in all its grades and kinds, is the response of the creature to the Eternal: nor need we limit this definition to the human sphere. There is a sense in which we may think of the whole life of the Universe, seen and unseen, conscious and unconscious, as an act of worship, glorifying its Origin, Sustainer, and End.

Evelyn Underhill, *Worship* (New York: Harper and Brothers, 1936), 3.

Worship is essentially, as well as etymologically, the recognition of God's worth. It has not direct reference to the edification of the worshipers. It is an offering to God, acceptable to Him and incumbent on man.

Nathaniel Micklem, editor, *Christian Worship* (London: Oxford University Press, 1936), 19.

Worship must be in one sense a purposeless act, if it is to be true worship. An action has a purpose if it is done for the sake of something else, but worship is for its own sake, or for the sake of God. That is the same thing, because any activity is doing the will of God when it is truly itself. So there is a sense in which Christian worship ...has a meaning but no purpose; purpose means acting for a further result. Worship is the gathering up of all activities before God. In that

187

sense it is purposeless. If we try to give it a moral or social purpose, we are destroying its nature... In worship we have this mode of valuing a thing for its own sake.

> V. A. Demant, "The Social Implications of Worship," in *Worship: Its Social Significance*, edited P. T. R. Kirk (London: The Centenary Press, 1939), 107-108.

To worship is:
    To quicken the conscience by the holiness of God;
    To feed the mind with the truth of God;
    To purge the imagination by the beauty of God;
    To open the heart to the love of God;
    To devote the will to the purpose of God.

> William Temple, *The Hope of a New World* (New York, NY: Macmillan Co., 1942), 30.

Worship is man's response to the nature and action of God.

> J. Alan Kay, *The Nature of Christian Worship* (London: Epworth Press, 1953), 7.

In Christianity, the Spirit is the future which in virtue of the past actualizes itself in the present. This time-character of the Holy Spirit, connecting him with the history of salvation, manifests itself in the very essence of the Christian service, where it is no myth that is represented, but the historical facts of past time and the facts of the last days still in the future.

> Oscar Cullman, *Early Christian Worship* (Philadelphia, PA: Westminster Press, 1953), 36.

Worship is dramatic action. The principal actors in the drama of corporate worship are the people of the congregation who are aided and equipped for their role by the leaders of worship--the prompters from the wings. The drama, often scripted, has a structure and sequence based upon the nature of God's dialogical encounter with his people.

> Soren Kierkegaard, *Purity of Heart*, trans. Douglas V. Steere (New York, NY: Harper and Brothers, Torchbooks, 1956), 177-184.

It is only possible to enter into fellowship with God on the basis of God's initiative, that is, through revelation. Worship is only possible again since God has made himself known in Jesus Christ. The way to true worship is only brought about through a radical transformation and that God alone makes possible in Jesus Christ.

Gerhard Delling, *Worship in the New Testament* (Philadelphia, PA: Westminster Press, 1962), 1.

The fellowship of Christian worship is not based upon the passing unities of race or community, but upon God's purpose to "sum up all things in Jesus Christ." It is the fellowship of humanity redeemed in Christ and awaiting the fulfillment of that redemption, and therefore constantly submitted to the judgment and renewal of divine revelation in the present.

T. S. Garrett, *Christian Worship* (New York, NY: Oxford University Press, 1963), 10.

Worship is a noble word. The term comes into our modern speech from the Anglo-Saxon "weorthscipe." This later developed into "worthship," and then into "worship." It means, "to attribute worth" to an object. ...To worship God is to ascribe to Him supreme worth, for He alone is worthy.

Ralph P. Martin, *Worship in the Early Church* (Grand Rapids, MI: William B. Eerdmans Publishing Company, 1964), 10.

Worship is the acknowledgment of God's supreme excellence and the expression of man's submission to His absolute dominion resulting therefrom.

Howard French, editor, *Theology of the Liturgy*, Bellarmine College Theological Series (South Bend, IN: Fides Publishers, Inc., 1964), 4:12.

Worship is an end in itself; it is not a means to something else. Karl Barth has appropriately declared that the "church's worship is the *Opus Dei*, the work of God, which is carried out for its own sake." . . .We worship God purely for the sake of worshipping God.

Franklin M. Segler, *Christian Worship: Its Theology and Practice* (Nashville, TN: Broadman Press, 1967), 4.

I assume from the outset that nothing should be done or sung or said in church which does not aim directly or indirectly either at glorifying God or edifying the people or both... Whenever we edify, we glorify, but when we glorify we do not always edify.

C. S. Lewis, *Christian Reflections* (Grand Rapids, MI: William B. Eerdmans Publishing Company, 1967), 94.

Worship is the propitious moment of encounter between God and his people. Worship is the peculiar or special occasion of the presence of the Lord in his church.

Richard Pacquier, *Dynamics of Worship*, trans. Donald MacLeod (Philadelphia, PA: Fortress Press, 1967), 18.

Worship is drama. ...Ideally, then, worship needs to harmonize the elements of remoteness and nearness, the ideas of the family and of the symbolic people of God;... But what is always true is that to lose sight of the dramatic factor in worship is to lose altogether the key to making worship practical as well as beautiful.

Erik Routley, *Words, Music and the Church* (Nashville, TN: Abingdon, 1968), 129, 136.

...Christian worship is God's revelation of Himself in Jesus Christ and man's response;...

Paul Waitman Hoon, *The Integrity of Worship* (Nashville, TN: Abingdon, 1971), 77.

...the purpose of the church and worship is to relate men to Christ and to relate men in Christ to one another.

Paul W. Wohlgemuth, *Rethinking Church Music* (Chicago, IL: Moody Press, 1973), 66.

The Christian community assembles for worship on the basis of God's eschatological saving act in Christ which demonstrates its present power in the operation of the Holy Spirit.

Ferdinand Hahn, *The Worship of the Early Church* (Philadelphia, PA: Fortress Press, 1973), 105.

Worship is a creative encounter of man with God, a living and vital relationship which depends upon the active and unceasing quest of man in response to the call of God.

Austin C. Lovelace and William C. Rice, *Music and Worship in the Church* (Nashville, TN: Abingdon, 1976), 18.

Because it is God who always takes the initiative, Christian worship is best discussed in the terms of response. In worship man is responding to God and this is true of the whole of the liturgy, whether it be praise, thanksgiving, supplication, or repentance, whether it be Eucharist or baptism, or liturgical prayer or the celebration of the Church's year. If this is so, worship must be seen in the context of saving history, which is the record of the divine initiative.

J. D. Crichton, "A Theology of Worship," in *The Study of Liturgy* by Cheslyn Jones, editor, et al. (New York, NY: Oxford University Press, 1978), 7.

Christian worship is our affirmative response to the self-revelation of the Triune God.

Donald P. Hustad, *Jubilate II! Church Music in Worship and Renewal* (Carol Stream, IL: Hope Publishing Co., 1993), 64.

Worship is the dramatic celebration of God in his supreme worth in such a manner that his "worthiness" becomes the norm and inspiration of human beings.

Ralph P. Martin, *The Worship of God* (Grand Rapids, MI: William B. Eerdmans Publishing Company, 1982), 4.

Worship is an active response to God whereby we declare His worth. Worship is not passive, but is participative. Worship is not simply a mood; it is a response. Worship is not just a feeling; it is a declaration.

Ronald Allen and Gordon Borror, *Worship: Rediscovering the Missing Jewel* (Portland, OR: Multnomah Press, 1982), 16.

Worship is the celebrative response to what God has done, is doing, and promises to do.

John E. Burkhart, *Worship* (Philadelphia, PA: Westminster Press, 1982), 17.

...worship is a combination of head, hand, heart, and imagination [which] is to say its practice should involve more than hearing, speaking and seeing. God is concerned with the whole person, and it is appropriate to respond with one's whole being...

Raymond Bailey, "From Theory to Practice," *Review and Expositor*, 80(1983), 40.

Corporate worship is effective only when each worshiper feels his responsibility for preparation and involvement, and all the worshipers focus on their honor of and submission to the Living God.

Robert W. Bailey, "A Biblical Theology of Worship," *Music in the Worship Experience* (Nashville, TN: Convention Press, 1984), 15.

Worship in the New Testament was an act of celebration; therefore, the music of the early church was the music of celebration.

J. Wendell Mapson, Jr., *The Ministry of Music in the Black Church* (Valley Forge, PA: Judson Press, 1984), 3.

Worship is something Christians do communally to praise God.
Don Saliers, "The Nature of Worship: Community Lived in Praise of God," *Duty & Delight: Routley Remembered*, ed. by Robin A. Leaver and James H. Litton (Carol Stream, IL: Hope Publishing Co., 1985), 41.

Worship is the believer's response of all that he is—mind, emotion, will, and body—to all that God is and says and does. This response has its mystical side in subjective experience, and its practical side in objective obedience to God's revealed truth. It is a loving response that is balanced by the fear of the Lord, and it is a deepening response as the believer comes to know God better.
Warren W. Wiersbe, *Real Worship: It Will Transform You* (Nashville, TN: Oliver-Nelson Books, 1986), 27.

..., a service of worship is a two-way conversation between God and his people with a given pattern and sequence...
Harry Eskew and Hugh T. McElrath, *Sing With Understanding* (Nashville, TN: Broadman Press, 1986), 221.

Worship is the lasting metaphor for the true and perfect, and hence transformed, relationship between creature and Creator.
David R. Newman, *Worship: As Praise and Empowerment* (New York, NY: The Pilgrim Press, 1988), 34.

Christian worship is a community's response via the Holy Spirit to God's revelation of Himself in Jesus Christ.
Thomas Allen Seel.

# Bibliography

*Worship*

Abba, R. *Principles of Christian Worship*. New York, NY: Oxford University Press, 1957

Allmen, Jean J. von. *Worship: Its Theology and Practice*. New York, NY: Oxford University Press, 1965.

Baumstark, A. *Liturgie Comparee*. Trans. F. L. Cross. Westminster, MD: Newman Press, 1958.

Burkhart, John E. *Worship: A Searching Examination of the Liturgical Experience*. Philadelphia, PA: Westminster Press, 1982.

Cullman, Oscar. *Early Christian Worship*. Philadelphia, PA: Westminster Press, 1953.

Davies, J. G., ed. *The Westminster Dictionary of Liturgy and Worship*. Philadelphia, PA: Westminster Press, 1979.

Delling, Gerhard. *Worship in the New Testament*. Trans. Percy Scott. Philadelphia, PA: Westminster Press, 1962.

Garrett, T.S. *Christian Worship*. London: Oxford University Press, 1961.

Hahn, Ferdinand. *The Worship of the Early Church*. Trans. John Reumann. Philadelphia, PA: Fortress Press, 1973.

Hoon, Paul W. *The Integrity of Worship*. Nashville, TN: Abingdon Press, 1971.

Idelsohn, A. Z. *Jewish Liturgy and Its Development*. New York, NY: Holt, Rinehart, and Winston, 1967.

Jones, Cheslyn, et al. *The Study of Liturgy*. Second Edition. New York, NY: Oxford University Press, 1992.

Martin, Ralph P. *The Worship of God*. Grand Rapids, MI: William B. Eerdmans Publishing Company, 1982.

_____. *Worship in the Early Church*. Grand Rapids, MI: William B. Eerdmans Publishing Company, 1964.

Micklem, Nathaniel, ed. *Christian Worship: Studies in its History and Meaning*. London: Oxford University Press, 1954.

Moule, C. F. D. *Worship in the New Testament*. Richmond, VA: John Knox Press, 1961.

Segler, Franklin M. *Christian Worship: Its Theology and Practice*. Nashville, TN: Broadman Press, 1967.

Temple, William. *The Hope of a New World*. New York, NY: The Macmillan Co., 1942.

Underhill, Evelyn. *Worship*. New York, NY: Harper and Row, 1936.

Wainwright, Geoffrey. *Doxology: The Praise of God in Worship, Doctrine and Life*. New York, NY: Oxford University Press, 1980.

Webber, Robert E. *Worship: Old and New*. Grand Rapids, MI: Zondervan Publishing House, 1982.

White, James F. *Introduction to Christian Worship*. Nashville, TN: Abingdon Press, 1980.

*Music, Theology of Music, and Philosophy of Music*
Altenburg, Johann Ernst. *Essay on an Introduction to the Heroic and Musical Trumpeters' and Kettledrummers' Art*. Trans. Edward H. Tarr. Nashville, TN: The Brass Press, 1974.

Arnold, Denis, editor. *The New Oxford Companion to Music*. New York, NY: Oxford University Press, 1984.

Baines, Anthony. *Brass Instruments: Their History and Development*. London: Faber and Faber, 1976.

Barbour, J. Murray. *Trumpets, Horn and Music*. East Lansing, MI: Michigan State University Press, 1964.

Barnhart, C.L., ed. *The American College Dictionary*. New York, NY: Random House, 1964.

Bate, Philip. *The Trumpet and Trombone*. New York, NY: W. W. Norton, 1978.

Berglund, Robert D. *A Philosophy of Church Music*. Chicago, IL: Moody Press, 1985.

Bukofzer, Manfred F. *Studies in Medieval and Renaissance Music*. New York, NY: W. W. Norton, 1950.

Coleman, Robert E. *Songs of Heaven*. Old Tappan, NJ: Fleming H. Revell Company, 1975.

Epperson, Gordon. *The Musical Symbol: A Study of the Philosophic Theory of Music*. Ames, IA: Iowa State University Press, 1967.

Eskew, Harry and Hugh T. McElrath. *Sing With Understanding*. Nashville, TN: Broadman Press, 1980.

Gove, Philip Babcock, ed. *Webster's Third New International Dictionary.* Springfield, MA: G. and C. Merriam Company, 1976.

Grout, Donald Jay and Claude V. Palisca, Jr. *A History of Western Music.* New York, NY: W. W. Norton, 1988.

Hall, Manly P. *The Therapeutic Value of Music.* Los Angeles, CA: The Philosophical Research Society, Inc., 1955.

Hawkins, John. *A General History of the Science and Practice of Music.* London: Novello, Ewer, and Co., 1875.

Hooper, William Lloyd. *Church Music in Translation.* Nashville, TN: Broad Press, 1963.

Hustad, Donald P. *Jubilate II! Church Music in Worship and Renewal.* Carol Stream, IL: Hope Publishing Co., 1993.

Idelsohn, Abraham Z. *Thesaurus of Hebrew Oriental Melodies.* Ktav, Russia: Ktav Publishing House, Inc., 1973.

Joerns, Klaus-Peter. *Das Hymnische Evangelium: Untersuchungen zu Aufbau, Funktion und Herkunft der hymnischen Stücke in der Johannesoffenbarung.* Goettingen, Germany: G. Mohn, 1971.

Johansson, Calvin M. *Music and Ministry.* Peabody, MA: Hendrickson Publishers, Inc., 1986.

Julian, John, et al. *A Dictionary of Hymnology.* Revised edition. London: Murray, 1908.

Kierkegaard, Soren. *Purity of Heart Is to Will One Thing.* New York, NY: Harper Brothers, 1938.

Lang, Paul Henry. *Music in Western Civilization.* New York, NY: W. W. Norton, 1941.

Leaver, Robin A. and James H. Litton, eds. *Duty and Delight: Routley Remembered.* Carol Stream, IL: Hope Publishing Company, 1985.

Miller, Hugh Milton. *An Outline of the History of Music.* New York, NY: Barnes and Noble, Inc., 1947.

_____. *History of Music.* New York, NY: Barnes and Noble, Inc., 1960.

Pass, David B. *Music and the Church.* Nashville, TN: Broadman Press, 1989.

Phelps, Roger P. *Guide to Research in Music Education,* Third Edition. Metuchen, NJ: The Scarecrow Press, Inc., 1986.

Routley, Erik. *The Divine Formula.* Princeton, NJ: Prestige Publications, 1986.

_____. *The Music of Christian Hymns*. Chicago, IL: G.I.A. Publications, Inc., 1981.

Sachs, Curt. *A History of Musical Instruments*. New York, NY: W. W. Norton, 1940.

_____, ed. *The New Grove Dictionary of Musical Instruments*. London: Macmillan Press, Ltd., 1984.

_____. *The Wellsprings of Music*. Paris: The Hague, 1962.

Sadie, Stanley, ed. *The New Grove Dictionary of Music and Musicians*. London: Macmillan Publishers, Ltd., 1980.

Smithers, Don L. *The Music and History of the Baroque Trumpet*. Carbondale, IL: Southern Illinois University Press, 1988.

Strunk, Oliver, ed. *Source Readings in Music History*. New York, NY: W. W. Norton, 1975.

Ulrich, Homer and Paul A. Pisk. *A History of Music and Musical Style*. New York, NY: Harcourt, Brace and World, Inc., 1963.

Warren, Dwight Allen. *Philosophy of Music History*. New York, NY: American Book Co., 1939.

Werner, Eric. *The Sacred Bridge: The Interdependence of Liturgy and Music in Synagogue and Church During the First Millennium*. London: Dennis Dobson, 1959.

*Jewish Music*

Brueggermann, Walter. *The Message of the Psalms: A Theological Commentary*. Minneapolis, MN: Augsburg Old Testament Studies, 1984.

_____. *Abiding Astonishment: Psalms, Modernity & the Making of History*. Westminster, VA: John Knox Press, 1991.

Charlesworth, James Hamilton, ed. *The Old Testament Pseudepigrapha and the New Testament*. Garden City, NY: Doubleday and Company, Inc., 1983.

_____. *The Pseudepigrapha and Modern Research*. Missoula, MO: Scholars Press for Society of Biblical Literature, 1976.

Division of Christian Higher Education of the National Council of the Churches of Christ in the United States of America, ed. *The Holy Bible,* Revised Standard Version. Richmond, VA: John Knox Press, 1952.

Epstein, I., trans. *The Hebrew-English Edition of the Babylonian Talmud*. London: Scovino Press, 1960.

Ha-Babli, Nathan. *Medieval Jewish Chroniclers.* Oxford: Oxford University Press, 1887.

Hengel, Martin. *Judaism and Hellenism: Studies in their Encounter in Palestine During the Early Hellenistic Period.* Trans. J. Bowden. Philadelphia, PA: SCM Press, 1974.

Holde, Arthur. *Jews in Music.* New York, NY: Philosophical Library, 1959.

Holladay, Carl R. *Fragments from Hellenistic Jewish Authors.* Chico, CA: Scholars Press, 1983.

Idelsohn, A. Z. *Jewish Liturgy and Its Development.* New York, NY. Holt, Rinehart and Winston, 1967.

Josephus, Flavius. *The Works of Flavius Josephus.* Trans. William Whiston. Nashville, TN: Broadman Press, 1974.

Lietner, Franz. *Der gottesdienstliche Volkgesang im jüdischen und christlichen Alterum.* Trans. Alfred Sendrey. Freiburg: i. B., 1906.

McCann, Clinton J. *A Theological Introduction to the Book of Psalms: The Psalms as Torah.* Nashville, TN: Abingdon Press, 1993.

Miller, Patrick D., Jr. *Interpreting the Psalms.* Minneapolis, MN: Augsburg Press, 1986.

Mowinckel, Sigmund. *The Psalms in Israel's Worship.* Trans. D. R. Ap-Thomas. Nashville, TN: Abingdon Press, 1979.

Riehm, Eduard Carl August. *Handwoerterbuch das biblischen Altertums.* Trans. Alfred Sendrey. Bielefeld and Leipzig, 1894.

Rothmueller, Aron Marko. *The Music of the Jews.* New York, NY: The Beechhurst Press, 1954.

Sendrey, Alfred. *Music in Ancient Israel.* New York, NY: Philosophical Library, 1969.

Smend, Julius. *Vorträge und Augsätze zur Liturgik hymnologie und kirchenmusik.* Trans. Sigmund Mowinckel. Guetersloh, Germany: C. Bertelsmann, 1925.

Westermann, Claus. *The Living Psalms.* Trans. J. R. Porter. Grand Rapids, MI: William B. Eerdmans Publishing Company, 1989.

_____. *The Psalms: Structure, Content and Message.* Trans. Ralph D. Gehrke. Minneapolis, MN: Augsburg Fortress, 1980.

*Early Pagan, Greek and Roman Music and Drama*
Anderson, Warren D. *Ethos and Education in Greek Music.* Cambridge, MA: Harvard University Press, 1966.

Aylen, Leo. *The Greek Theatre*. London: Associated University Press, 1985.

Barker, Andrew. *Greek Musical Writings*. Cambridge, MA: Cambridge University Press, 1987.

Blevins, James L. *Revelation as Drama*. Nashville, TN: Broadman Press, 1984.

Bowman, John Wick. *The First Christian Drama*. Philadelphia, PA: Westminster Press, 1955.

Brockett, Oscar G. *History of the Theatre*. Boston, MA: Allyn and Bacon, 1968.

Buecher, Karl. *Arbeit und Rhythmus*. Leipzig, 1909.

Durant, William James. *The History of Civilization*. New York, NY: Simon and Schuster, 1954.

Ferguson, Donald N. *A History of Musical Thought*. New York, NY: Appleton Century Crafts, Inc., 1948.

Galpin, Francis William. *The Music of the Sumerians and Their Immediate Successors the Babylonians and Assyrians*. Cambridge: Cambridge University Press, 1967.

Gardiner, Cynthia P. *The Sophoclean Chorus: A Study of Character and Function*. Iowa City, IA: University of Iowa Press, 1987.

Hartnoll, Phyllis, ed. *The Oxford Companion to the Theatre*. London: Oxford University Press, 1972.

Jowett, B., trans. *The Dialogues of Plato*. Oxford: Clarendon Press, 1953.

Lippman, Edward A. *Musical Thought in Ancient Greece*. New York, NY: Columbia University Press, 1964.

Lombroso, Cesare. *Klinische Beiträge zur Psychiatrie*. Leipzig, 1869.

Mathiesen, Thomas J., trans. *Aristides Quintilianus: On Music in Three Books*. New Haven, CT: Yale University Press, 1983.

Quasten, Johannes. *Music and Worship in Pagan and Christian Antiquity*. Trans. Boniface Ramsey. Washington, DC: National Association of Pastoral Musicians, 1973.

Sachs, Curt. *The Rise of Music in the Ancient World: East and West*. New York, NY: W. W. Norton, 1943.

Sendrey, Alfred. *Music and Society and Religious Life of Antiquity*. Cranbury, NJ: Associated University Presses, Inc., 1974.

Stuart, Donald Clive. *The Development of Dramatic Art*. New York, NY: Dover Publications, Inc., 1960.

Wellesz, Egon, ed. *Ancient and Oriental Music*. London: Oxford University Press, 1957.

## Church Music and Drama

Adey, Lionel. *Hymns and the Christian "Myth."* Vancouver: University of British Columbia Press, 1986.

_____. *Class and Idol in the English Hymn*. Vancouver: University of British Columbia Press, 1986.

Appleby, David P. *History of Church Music*. Chicago, IL: Moody Press, 1965.

Bales, James D. *Instrumental Music and New Testament Worship*. Searcy, AR: James D. Bales, 1973.

Benson, Louis F. *The Hymnody of the Christian Church*. New York, NY: George H. Doran Co., 1927.

Bowman, John Wick. *The First Christian Drama*. Philadelphia, PA: Westminster Press, 1955.

Brockett, Oscar G. *History of the Theatre*. Boston, MA: Allyn and Bacon, Inc., 1968.

Church, F. Forrester and Terrance J. Mulry. *Earliest Christian Hymns*. New York, NY: Macmillan Publishing Company, 1988.

Deane, William John. *Pseudepigrapha: An Account of Certain Aprocryphal Sacred Writings of the Jews and Early Christians*. Edinburgh: T. and T. Clarke, 1981.

Douglas, Charles Winfred. *Church Music in History and Practice*. Revised edition. New York, NY: Charles Scribner's Sons, 1962.

Gardiner, Cynthia P. *The Sophoclean Chorus: A Study of Character and Function*. Iowa City, IA: University of Iowa Press, 1987.

Hayburn, Robert. *Papal Legislation on Sacred Music*. Collegeville, MN: The Liturgical Press, 1979.

Kleinig, John W. *The Lord's Song: The Basis, Function and Significance of Choral Music in Chronicles*. Sheffield: JSOT Press, 1993.

Marshall, Alfred, ed. *The Revised Standard Version Interlinear Greek-English New Testament*. Grand Rapids, MI: Zondervan Press, 1958.

McKinnon, James. *Music in Early Christian Literature*. Cambridge: Cambridge University Press, 1987.

Messenger, Ruth. *Christian Hymns of the First Three Centuries*. New York, NY: The Hymn Society of America, Paper IX, 1942.

Montefiore, Hugh. *Josephus and the New Testament*. London: A. R. Mowbray, 1962.

Routley, Erik. *Church Music and Theology*. Philadelphia, PA: Muhlenberg Press, 1959.

_____. *Christian Hymns Observed*. Princeton, NJ: Prestige Publications, Inc., 1982.

_____. *The Music of Christian Hymnody*. London: Independent Press Ltd., 1957.

Rowdon, Harold Hamlyn. *Christ the Lord: Studies in Christology Presented to Donald Guthrie*. Downers Grove, IL: Intervarsity Press, 1982.

Sanders, Jack T. "The New Testament Christological Hymns." *Society for New Testament Studies*, Series 15. Cambridge, MA: Cambridge University Press, 1971.

Smith, William Shepherd. *Musical Aspects of the New Testament*. Amsterdam: Vrije Universiteit te Amsterdam, 1962.

Whiston, William, trans. *The Complete Works of Flavius Josephus*. Grand Rapids, MI: Kregel Publications, 1981.

Wiseman, Luke, ed. *The Methodist Hymn-Book*. London: The Methodist Publishing House, 1954.

Zerwick, Max and Mary Grosvener. *A Grammatical Analysis of the Greek New Testament*. Rome: Biblical Institute Press, 1981.


### Theology

Anderson, Ray, ed. *Theological Foundations for Ministry*. Edinburgh: T. & T. Clark, Limited, 1979.

Berkouwer, G. C. *Man: The Image of God*. Grand Rapids, MI: William B. Eerdmans Publishing Company, 1962.

Gray, Herbert A. *Religion in Life*. London: Student Christian Movement Press, 1947.

Hopko, Thomas. *All the Fulness of God*. Crestwood, NY: St. Vladimir's Seminary Press, 1982.

Leeuw, Gerhard van der. *Sacred and Profane Beauty*. Trans. David E. Green. Nashville, TN: Abingdon Press, 1963.

MacQuarrie, John. *God-Talk*. New York, NY: Harper and Row, 1967.

Nygren, Anders. *Essence of Christianity*. London: The Epworth Press, 1960.

_____. *Meaning and Method*. Trans. Philip S. Watson. Philadelphia, PA: Fortress Press, 1972.

Nyssa, Saint Gregory of. *Commentary on the Song of Songs*. Trans. Casimir McCambley. Brookline, MA: Hellenic College Press, 1987.

Pike, Alfred. *A Theology of Music*. Toledo, OH: The Gregorian Institute of America, 1953.

Rad, Gerhard von. *Old Testament Theology: The Theology of Israel's Prophetic Tradition*. Trans. D. M. G. Stalker. Edinburgh: Oliver & Boyd, 1965.

Smart, Ninian. *The Concept of Worship*. London: Macmillan Press, Limited, 1972.

_____. *The Philosophy of Religion*. New York, NY: Oxford University Press, 1979.

_____. *The Religious Experience of Mankind*. New York, NY: Scribner, 1969.

Tracy, David. *The Analogical Imagination*. New York, NY: Crossroad Publishing Company, 1981.

Zerbe, Alvin Sylvester. *The Karl Barth Theology or The New Transcendentalism*. Cleveland, OH: Central Publishing House, 1930.

### Biblical Reference

Aland, Kurt, et al., eds. *The Greek New Testament*. Stuttgart: United Bible Societies, 1983.

Blevins, James L. *Revelation*. Atlanta, GA: John Knox Press, 1984.

Charles, R. H. *Studies in the Apocalypse*. Edinburgh: T. & T. Clark, 1915.

Conybeare, Fred C. *The Armenian Version of the Revelation, Apocalypse of John*. Amsterdam: Philo Press, 1986.

Culpepper, R. Alan. *The Anatomy of the Fourth Gospel: A Study in Literary Design*. Philadelphia, PA: Fortress Press, 1986.

Earle, Ralph. *Word Meanings in the New Testament*. Grand Rapids, MI: Baker Book House, 1982.

Epstein, I., trans. *The Hebrew-English Edition of the Babylonian Talmud*. London: Scovino Press, 1960.

Fiorenza, Elisabeth S. *Invitation to the Book of Revelation*. Garden City, NJ: Image Books, 1981.

Guthrie, Donald. *New Testament Introduction*. Downers Grove, IL: Intervarsity Press, 1970.

_____. *The Relevance of John's Apocalyse*. Grand Rapids, MI: William B. Eerdman's Publishing Company, 1987.

Jenkins, Ferrel. *The Old Testament in the Book of Revelation*. Marion, IN: Cogdill Foundation Publications, 1972.

Kierkegaard, Soren. *Purity of Heart Is to Will One Thing*. New York, NY: Harper Brothers, 1938.

Marshall, Alfred. *The Inter-Linear Greek-English New Testament*. London: Samuel Bagster and Sons, Ltd., 1958.

May, Herbert G. and Bruce M. Metzger, eds. *The New Oxford Annotated Bible with the Apocrypha*. New York, NY: Oxford University Press, 1977.

Mounce, Robert H. *The Book of Revelation*. Grand Rapids, MI: William B. Eerdmans Publishing Company, 1977.

Rowley, H. H. *The Relevance Of Apocalyptic: A Study of Jewish and Christian Apocalypses from Daniel to the Revelation*. Greenwood, SC: Attic Press, 1980.

Seiss, J. A. *The Apocalypse*. New York, NY: Charles C. Cook, 1909.

Shepherd, Massey H. "The Paschal Liturgy and the Apocalypse." *Ecumenical Studies in Worship*. Richmond, VA: John Knox Press, 1960.

Strong, James. *The Exhaustive Concordance of the Bible*. New York, NY: Abingdon Press, 1890.

Summers, Ray. *Worthy is the Lamb: An Interpretation of Revelation*. Nashville, TN: Broadman Press, 1951.

*Biblical Commentaries*

Arndt, William F. and F. Wilbur Gingrich. *A Greek-English Lexicon of the New Testament and Other Early Christian Literature*. Ed. Walter Bauer. Fifth Edition. Chicago, IL: University of Chicago Press, 1958.

Beasley-Murray, George R. "The Book of Revelation." *New Century Bible Commentary*. Grand Rapids, MI: William B. Eerdmans, 1981.

Beckwith, Isbon T. *The Apocalypse of John.* Grand Rapids, MI: Baker Book House, 1979.

Buttrick, George A. *The Interpreter's Dictionary of the Bible.* Nashville, TN: Abingdon Press, 1962.

Charles, R. H. *A Critical and Exegetical Commentary on the Revelation of St. John.* Edinburgh: T. & T. Clark, 1920.

Cross, F. L., ed. *The Oxford Dictionary of the Christian Church.* London: Oxford University Press, 1983.

Ford, John Massyngberde, ed. *The Anchor Bible: Revelation.* Garden City, NY: Doubleday and Company, Inc., 1975.

Friedrich, Gerhard, ed. *Theological Dictionary of the New Testament.* Grand Rapids, MI: William B. Eerdmans Publishing Company, 1971.

Karleen, Paul S. *The Handbook to Bible Study.* New York, NY: Oxford University Press, 1987.

Kiddle, Martin. *The Revelation of St. John.*, from the *Moffett New Testament Commentary* series. New York, NY: Harper and Brothers Publishers, 1940.

Kümmel, Werner Georg. *The New Testament: The History of the Investigation of Its Problems.* Nashville, TN: Abingdon Press, 1972.

Liddell, Henry George and Robert Scott. *A Greek-English Lexicon.* Sir Henry Stuart Jones, ed. Oxford: Clarendon Press, 1948.

Mcagher, Paul Kevin, ed. *Encyclopedic Dictionary of Religion.* Washington, DC: Corpus Publications, 1979.

Moulton, James Hope and George Milligan. *The Vocabulary of the Greek New Testament.* Grand Rapids, MI: William B. Eerdmans Publishing Company, 1982.

Robertson, A. T. *A Grammar of the Greek New Testament in the Light of Historical Research.* New York, NY: Hodder and Stoughton, 1914.

Swete, Henry Barclay. *The Apocalypse of St. John.* London: Macmillan and Company, 1909.

Trench, R. C. *Synonyms of the New Testament.* Grand Rapids, MI: William B. Eerdmans, 1958.

Unger, Merrill and W. White, Jr., eds. *Nelson's Expository Dictionary of the Old Testament.* Nashville, TN: Thomas Nelson Publishers, 1984.

Vines, W. F. *Vine's Expository Dictionary of Old and New Testament Words*. Ed. F. F. Bruce. Old Tappan, NJ: Fleming H. Revell, 1981.

*Periodicals and Journals on Music, Worship, and Drama*

Bailey, Raymond. "From Theory to Practice in Worship." *Review and Expositor*, 80(1983):1:33-52.

Bauckham, R. "The Worship of Jesus in Apocalyptic Christianity." *New Testament Studies*, 27(1981):322-341.

Blevins, James L. "The Genre of Revelation." *Review and Expositor*, 77(1980):393-408.

Charlesworth, James. "A Prolegomena to a New Study of the Jewish Background of the Hymns and Prayers in the New Testament," *Journal of Jewish Studies*, 33(1982):1-2:265-285.

Dölger, Franz Joseph, "Zu den Zeremonien der Messliturgie, II: der Alterkuss," *Antiqua Christiana*, (1930):26-35.

Hughes, Edwin Holt. "Music and Theology," *Worship and Music*, (1927):32-44.

LeClercq, Jean. "Theology and Prayer," *Encounter,* 24(1963):349-364.

McKinnon, James. "On the Question of Psalmody in the Ancient Synagogue," Iain Fenlon, ed., *Early Music History*, 6(1986):159-191.

_____. "The Exclusion of Musical Instruments from the Ancient Synagogue," *Proceedings of the Royal Musical Association*, (1979-1980):81-96.

Mendenhall, George E. "Biblical Faith and Cultic Function," *The Lutheran Quarterly,* 5(1953):235-258.

Mowry, Lucetta. "Revelation 4-5 and Early Christian Liturgical Usage," *Journal of Biblical Literature,* 71(1952):75-84.

O'Rourke, John J. "The Hymns of the Apocalypse," *The Catholic Biblical Quarterly*, 30(1968):49-72.

Sachs, Curt. "The Mystery of the Babylonian Notation," *Musical Quarterly*, 27(1941):62-69.

Smith, J. A. "First-Century Christian Singing and Its Relationship to Contemporary Jewish Religious Song," *Music and Letters*, 75(1994):1-15.

_____. "The Ancient Synagogue, the Early Church and Singing," *Music and Letters*, 65(1985):1-16.

Spencer, Herbert. "The Origin and Function of Music," *Essays,* (1904):18-25.

Staehlin, Wilhelm. "The Church Hymn and Theology," *Response: In Worship—Music—The Arts,* 1(1959):22-30.

Wellesz, Egon. "The Doxology in Synagogue and Church," *Hebrew Union College Annual,* 19(1946):111-132.

Wilkey, Jay W. "Music as Religious Expression in Contemporary Society," *Review and Expositor,* 67(1979):507-517.

*Dissertations on Music, Worship, and Drama*

Culpepper, R. Alan. *The Johannine School: An Evaluation of the Johannine-School Hypothesis Based on an Investigation of the Nature of Ancient Schools.* Ann Arbor, MI: University Microfilms International, 1985.

Gwaltney, Robert Eugene. "The Concept of the Throne in Revelation." Th.M. thesis. Louisville, KY: The Southern Baptist Theological Seminary, 1986.

Harris, Michael Anthony. "The Literary Function of Hymns in the Apocalypse of John." Ph.D. dissertation. Louisville, KY:The Southern Baptist Theological Seminary, 1988.

Hatfield, Daniel Earl. "The Function of the Seven Beatitudes in Revelation." Ph.D. dissertation. Louisville, KY: The Southern Baptist Theological Seminary, 1987.

Hull, William Edward. "The Background of the New Temple Concept in Early Christianity." Th.D. dissertation. Louisville, KY: The Southern Baptist Theological Seminary, 1959.

Johansson, Calvin M. "Some Theological Considerations Foundational to a Philosophy of Church Music." D.M.A. dissertation. Fort Worth, TX: Southwestern Baptist Theological Seminary, 1974.

Keathley, Raymond Haskins. "The Concept of the Temple in Luke-Acts." Th.D. dissertation. Louisville, KY: The Southern Baptist Theological Seminary, 1971.

Pippin, Tina. "Political Reality and the Liberating Vision: The Context of the Book of Revelation." Ph.D. dissertation. Louisville, KY: The Southern Baptist Theological Seminary, 1987.

Poole, Thomas. "Towards a Theology of Music." D.M.A. dissertation. Louisville, KY: The Southern Baptist Theological Seminary, 1988.

Seel, Thomas A.  "Toward a Theology of Music for
    Worship Derived from the Book of Revelation." D.M.A.
    dissertation. Louisville, KY: The Southern Baptist Theological
    Seminary, 1990.
Whirley, Carl F.  "The Significance of the Temple Cultus in the
    Background of the Gospel of John." Th.D. dissertation.
    Louisville, KY:  The Southern Baptist Theological Seminary,
    1957.
Wright, LeRoy Evert. "The Place of Music in Worship." Ph.D.
    dissertation. Evanston, IL: Northwestern University, 1949.

# Index

207